P9-DIA-259

. . . I liked this book.
. . . . . You will too!

W. Clement Stone

020

# POWER-STEERING
## WITH WORDS

*By the Same Author*

SPEAK UP!

ARE YOU TELLING THEM?

EVERYDAY SPEECH

THE HUMANITY OF WORDS

COMMUNICATION, A FIELD THEORY

*Bess Sondel*

# POWER-STEERING
# WITH
## WORDS

*Chicago 1964*
FOLLETT PUBLISHING COMPANY

ABIGAIL E. WEEKS MEMORIAL LIBRARY
UNION COLLEGE
BARBOURVILLE, KENTUCKY

808
S698p

Copyright © 1964 by Bess Sondel. All rights reserved.
No portion of this book may be reproduced in any form
without written permission of the publisher.

Library of Congress Catalog Card Number: 64-22269
Manufactured in the United States of America
2nd Printing

DESIGNED BY PATRICK J. BIRCH


COMBINED REGISTRY EDITION

Combined Registry Company
Publishers of Personal Development Materials
5050 Broadway
Chicago, Illinois   60640

*to* **PAMELA**

# Acknowledgments

I should like to express my appreciation to the Alfred Korzybski Estate for permission to quote from *Science and Sanity: An Introduction to Non-aristotelian Systems and General Semantics,* copyright 1933, 1958, by Alfred Korzybski; to the Institute of General Semantics and *General Semantics Bulletin* for permission to quote from "The Need for Generalization in Biological Research: The Role of the Mathematical Theory of Ensembles," copyright 1963, by Henri Laborit; to the Josiah Macy, Jr., Foundation for permission to quote from "Communication Between Men: Meaning and Language," copyright 1952, by I. A. Richards, in *Cybernetics, Transactions of the Eighth Conference;* to John Wiley & Sons, Inc., for permission to quote from

ACKNOWLEDGMENTS

*Theories of Perception and the Concept of Structure,* copyright 1955, by Floyd H. Allport; to Cambridge University Press for permission to quote from *What Is Life?*, copyright 1944, by Erwin Schrodinger; to Harper & Row, Publishers, Incorporated, for permission to quote from *Personality, A Biosocial Approach to Origins and Structure,* copyright 1947, by Gardner Murphy; to Harcourt, Brace & World, Inc., for permission to quote from *The Meaning of Meaning,* copyright 1938, by C. K. Ogden and I. A. Richards; to W. W. Norton & Company, Inc., for permission to quote from *The Living Brain,* copyright 1953, by W. Grey Walter; and to Stanford University Press, for permission to quote from "The Policy Sciences," by Harold D. Lasswell, in *The Policy Sciences,* copyright 1951, Daniel Lerner and Harold D. Lasswell, editors.

My indebtedness to the authors quoted goes far beyond the quotations. I have felt keenly the catalytic force of these scholars in the genesis and projection of my ideas. I have had the privilege of a long and close and illuminating association, first, with the founder and great exponent of General Semantics, Alfred Korzybski. After his death, and particularly at the time of publication of *The Humanity of Words,* my friend M. Kendig, formerly Secretary and Educational Director and now Director of the Institute of General Semantics, acted as editor of the section on Alfred Korzybski. And I think especially of my association with Charles Morris, whom I knew first when I sat in his classroom in the University of Chicago. I still look to him for definitive support.

Over the years there have been conversations with friends; I shall mention only a few of those whose ideas are reflected in this book.

For the section entitled "Man and/or Machine," I would be remiss if I did not mention the name of Mr. Frank H. McCracken, Vice President of the Data Processing Division

# ACKNOWLEDGMENTS

of International Business Machines and Manager of the Midwestern Region. Mr. McCracken's genius in this area has nourished my interests and enlightened me. It was he who fostered the pilot study I made on Abstracting in the Education Department of IBM from which I learned much.

In the exact sciences, Dr. Abraham Mannes Max, researcher, Radio Corporation of America, has been my "conscience." He has read my copy, and, I might add, over and over again, and has advised me in areas far beyond my competency.

Dr. Otto Wirth, Dean of Arts and Sciences in Roosevelt University, has been a patient and willing listener. We have discussed every topic on which I have questions—and always to my great benefit.

And, finally, the writings and the words of Dr. Dwight J. Ingle, Head of the Department of Physiology, The University of Chicago, have made me realize ever more fully that knowledge and values must meet on the common ground of the science of Man.

Permit me, too, to express my sorrow in the loss of my husband, Dr. Herman Martin Sondel, who, for the first time, did not see me through the writing of a book, and to express my joy in the others, our Shann and her Joe, their Jillian, Pamela, and Wendy, who listened attentively and critically, but inquiringly and provocatively and delightfully.

My last word must be for my editor, Mr. Louis Zara, whose understanding has made something better of this book than I could have made alone.

BESS SONDEL

*May, 1964*

# Table of Contents

TABLE OF CONTENTS

# TABLE OF CONTENTS

**POWER-STEERING**
WITH   **WORDS**

*Introduction*

# The Greatest Power
# at the Service of Man Is Words

## THE USE OF WORDS
### IS A *PERSONAL TRANSACTION*

Every word I write is from me to you. Personal. A transaction between you and me. I give you something—my ideas, my thoughts, my feelings—and you give me something—your attention.

Your responses to my words are uniquely your own. The pattern of your past experience, your interests, your goals, will monitor your responses to the stimuli that confront you on these pages. You will be a selective reader. And our ideas will mesh in such a way as to create something that is yours and yours alone.

3

No one else in the world will respond to my words exactly as you do. And how someone else reacts is really no concern of yours—for your purposes. How he reacts concerns only him—for his purposes. I write for you.

*But how can this be?* you will ask yourself—and me.

It is possible insofar as we make it possible.

As for me, I have only to think of my classes at University College of the University of Chicago. With each new class I would see before me an exciting array of faces. Men and women, old and young. Here a serious Chinese student—how young or old I can never be sure—working for his doctorate in International Law. Next to him a fresh young art student, wide-eyed and sure. Here a tired M.D. Here a little man who, though responsible for the building of great bridges, is hardly articulate. Here a young South American who tells me he wants to learn to speak as a North American. Next to him a social worker. Then a nurse, a musician, a labor leader, a housewife, a stenographer, an economist, a chemist, a clubwoman, an engineer. Lawyers. Salesmen. Bosses. Employees. All races. All creeds. Each one born into an environment of values just as surely as he was born into an environment of weather.

Each one driven by his own needs, his own hopes, his own ambitions. *Each one different*. Each one seeking greater strength, greater competence, better to control his own moving world.

And so as I write, I can think of *you*. A single human being. *An original. One of a kind. No duplicates*. The transaction between us is personal. Conceivably, millions may read this book, but your eyes are on this page.

I write for you.

The words uttered by one voice can ignite a conflagration. The irrational ravings of a Hitler can stir human beings to unsane if not insane behavior. This we know.

But this, too, we know: the words of one who stood upon a mount spoke to generations as yet unborn; the words of a Mendel, a solitary monk, became, years later, a pattern for modern genetics.

Words are Manpower, Unlimited. But words are not darts that deflect upon stone. They penetrate into the living life of human beings—human beings immersed in Man's world.

**The fate of words is dependent as much upon the target and its history, past and present, as upon the speaker or writer.**

Words are a transaction and cannot be separated from all the elements of that transaction. Words live or die in an environment of social and physical forces. This is at once their power to create—and to destroy.

What I say to you now, then, is that I must find the deepest kernel of your self if I would help you to use words as the greatest living power by which to develop that potential which is uniquely your own. If I would stir you, I must reach you.

The greatest power at the service of man is words. But do not misinterpret the title of this book. It is not a "manipulatory" power of which I speak. If you want to make puppets of others, you are not my reader.

The power of which I speak is *within you*. The use of words is your means by which to become what you hope to be. The primary purpose of this book is to help you become a self-steering person, a human being in transition from your present self-image to your ideal self-image. Only through words thought and said can we surpass our selves.

This power of which I speak is not one which will transform you into something intrinsically different. It is, rather, the power by which you make *real* that which is now an emergent potential within you. This is what is meant by the word "self-realization." And self-realization is the primary objective of Power-Steering with Words.

Our goals are not circumscribed by our personal interests alone. Our hopes, our dreams, our plans, include others, some whom we know and love and some whom we do not know—and yet love. Goal-seeking behavior invites others to the accomplishment of human goals. We live in a world—man's world—everyman's world. And man's world today is the immediate concern of everyone who lives. Through words thought and said, each one may become a dynamic force in this ongoing enterprise we call life. We may, if we will, "steer" others in the common cause of mankind.

The great power of words comes, first, from the living force of words. This means that even if we knew all the words that were ever invented and knew all the wondrous ways in which to put them together, these words would be as ghosts unless a human being accompanied them.

I know. You think of the power of words as something you can switch on or off, like a light bulb. And you want to turn that power on right now. You want to start right now to use words to reach a goal that will satisfy your pressing need. This you could do if words, spoken or written, could go their private way without you. But they cannot.

Semantics, it is true, is the "science" of words. Words crystallize human behavior. Words intervene in almost everything we do.[1] Because this is so, semantics is subordinate to the broader subject of human behavior. Human behavior is a social "science," though rapidly becoming a bona fide biological science. Semantics draws upon this science—however tentatively, however haltingly. The adventure is admittedly exploratory; it is an invitation to further inquiry and, hopefully, to more knowing.

**The power of words is not something you can switch on or off. That power is you—your whole self. Wherever your words go, there you go.**

The use of words is a personal transaction. No two persons in the whole world will see or hear the same words in exactly the same way. Wasn't it Einstein who said, "The light that enters your mind is never the light that enters mine"?

## THE USE OF WORDS
## IS A *UNIQUE* TRANSACTION

Of course, we're all human. In many ways, I am like everyone else. And so with you. But it's the differences that make me *me* and you *you*. Nor is any life situation exactly like any other life situation. There is the absolute uniqueness of each individual as well as the absolute uniqueness of each physical situation. Add to this the fact no two persons, things, events, etc., are exactly the same at two different moments in time. We live in a process world in which *change* is constant.

It is difficult for the user of words to grasp the idea of the absolute uniqueness of every one, of every thing. For words, themselves, are the culprits. Words, by their very nature, describe only the samenesses of persons, things, events, etc. They do not, they cannot, go beyond samenesses to include differences. The differences must always be left out.

Is there a boy in the world who is exactly like any other boy? No. But the word "boy" does not give even a hint of the differences between one boy and another. A boy is a boy. When I say I have a *Chevy*, how can you know that mine is an old crate and not a shining showy Sting Ray? You cannot. A Chevrolet is a Chevrolet. When Gertrude Stein wrote "A rose is a rose is a rose" she wasn't crazy. She was undoubtedly pointing to the fact that nothing we can say about a rose can get to its absolute uniqueness.

**Every word in any language is a class word.**

This means that a word picks up the similarities of the class of objects it stands for and leaves out all the differences. The word "child" makes a place for every child in the world, regardless of individual differences. The word "run" makes a place for every running, no matter where, when, or how. This is what we mean when we say that every word is an abstraction. We mean that a word abstracts (takes away from the thing represented) only such characteristics as are *common* to the class to which it belongs and leaves out all the differences.[2]

**A word encapsulates only samenesses.**

This is probably what Alfred Korzybski means when he says every word is, in this sense, *under*defined. The word can never include the differences left out of the class of objects it represents. My dictionary, for instance, defines a house as "a building for human beings to live in." We buy a house and move in. No dictionary in the world would include the mice in that house or, though we had inspected the building carefully, reveal those characteristics of the house that we cannot *see*.

To get closer to uniqueness we are obliged to use more and more words. But this isn't the answer either, *because every word is a class word that leaves out all the differences.* We can never get to all those differences!

When people demand, "Define your terms!" hoping somehow to get to the differences left out, again there is frustration. Definition of terms is not the answer, because the only recourse we have is the use of other words—all class words, all abstractions. But we try. Soon we run out of words and are right back where we started. We learn the hard way that language is a *closed system*, that we can define any given word in the system only by using other words in the system.

Define an apple.

*An apple is a fruit*, you say.

But what is a fruit?

*It's a natural food*, you answer quickly enough.

Natural food? What do you mean?

*I mean it grows. It's a plant product.*

Plant? What's a plant product?

*Like a vegetable,* you yell, *or . . . or . . .* (and now you're red in the face) *like a fruit!*

We can't help it. It is impossible to get to the uniqueness of anything by words alone.

**It is only when we live on the silent level of immediate experience that we can live life in its completeness.**

The dictionary will not help us capture uniqueness; it will give us the runaround.

9

Take the word "courage," for example. Just what does it "mean"? The dictionary will take us on a tour from courage to bravery to fearlessness to pluck to daring to valiancy to audacity—and back again to courage. How else? We are in a word cycle and cannot extricate ourselves. We find ourselves in a fix where we must define the words that have been used to define the word "courage" by using the very word "courage" to define *them*! If I sound as if I am on a merry-go-round, I am. There is no escape. Ultimately, we must come to "meanings" that we take on faith, that must be assumed as known by immediate experience.

In *Science and Sanity*,[3] Alfred Korzybski gives us a device that will keep before us, always, the fact of absolute uniqueness.

*Index everything!* he says.

$Chevrolet_1$ *is not* $Chevrolet_2$.

Old crate $Chevrolet_1$ *is not* old crate $Chevrolet_2$.

Old crate $Chevrolet_1^{1948}$ *is not* old crate $Chevrolet_2^{1948}$.

Green old crate Chevy . . . etc.

Notice, now, that the index calls attention to the uniqueness of whatever it is that is being described, to the omission of the *differences*—whereas the word itself calls attention to the *similarities* of the class of objects it represents.

When we talk about things, we are likely to be interested in samenesses. $Chevrolet_1$ just off the production line is just as good as $Chevrolet_2$ just off the production line; $Chevrolet_1$ may be a lemon and $Chevrolet_2$ a dreamboat. Anyway, we put down our money without an argument.

In a question period after a public lecture, a man confronted me with this:

"I contend that Desk #104 brown $mahogany_1$ is exactly like Desk #104 brown $mahogany_2$."

"With or without termites?" I asked, which seemed to settle the matter.

Anyone will agree that there are times when the differences
left out are not significant, but when we talk about human
beings the situation is quite different. It is imperative to remember that every member of a class is unique:

White collar worker$_1$ *is not* white collar worker$_2$.

Prisoner$_1$ *is not* prisoner$_2$.

Protestant$_1$ *is not* Protestant$_2$.

Negro$_1$ *is not* Negro$_2$.

Russian$_1$ *is not* Russian$_2$.

Etc., etc., etc.

Because we can never tell all about anything, because we
can never get to absolute uniqueness, Korzybski cautions that
after every description, after every definition, it is important
to think, if not actually to say, *et cetera,* to remind us of the
differences that have been left out.

When you would tell a friend of a deep and stirring experience, you struggle to find the precise words that will express
uniqueness, that will tell just what happened, just how it happened, and just how you felt. You are never quite satisfied.
How can you be? Every word you choose to use is restricted
to samenesses. *And yet what happened to you was so different!*

**The first lesson semantics teaches is that understanding be-
tween human beings is always approximate, never complete.**

Let Shann Krueger say it in a nutshell:

*Approximation*[4]

The Beatnik says
"like love—like living, man."

11

> That glee-eyed cat's no fool;
> he knows that
> *Love*
> and *Living*
> are hard to come by.
>
> Most of us
> settle for like love—like living.

When the beatnik *talks* about love and about living, he knows that he is one step removed from whatever it is that he is trying to describe. When we use words, there is no other way. Words can never rise above "*like* love—*like* living." But *experience* love—mutely, all-consumingly—and live!

**To assume completeness of understanding is to jump into the deepest semantic pit. Assume, instead, a degree of understanding and become a striving, perceptive, sophisticated communicator.**

Every now and then I hear someone say, "I wish you had been there. It was utterly indescribable." And so it was. . . .

F. S. C. Northrop, Sterling Professor of Law and Philosophy in Yale University, calls the living *now* the only area of pure fact. I cannot resist giving his exact words:

The only way to get pure facts, independent of all concepts and theory, is merely to look at them and forthwith to remain perpetually dumb, never uttering a word or describing what one sees, after the manner of a calf looking at the moon.[5]

See a sunset! The immediate, silent experience is pure fact; but when we try to tell about it, this is theorizing. How can it help but be? Every word we choose to use is an abstraction, a class word. And to classify is to theorize.

The living *now* is the moment of relish. Eat a steak and you may be a gourmet with every indescribable bite; talk about it and you may be only a theoretical bore.

## *UNIQUENESS* AS *POWER*

Acceptance of the fact that the use of words is a unique transaction has liberating—and automatic!—effects on the user of words if he will let it get under his skin and work for him. He will find that the acceptance of uniqueness, both of the self and of the situation as a whole, will augment and release power in ways never before suspected or experienced, with the result that self-confidence will flow in his life-stream toward cherished goals.

In a face-to-face speaking situation, this freedom is immediately apparent. Because this is something *intra*personal, I can tell you only what it does for me (and what I have seen it do for others). You will have to experience it yourself to know what I mean.

First, because immediate experience is something that is *nonverbal,* I give silence its due. I am content with friendship on the wondrous silent level. I feel no compulsion to break silence. . . .

Words, it is true, describe life as it is or as we wish it to be, but every verbal description is a creative effort *once removed* from the event described. So, even as I have difficulty in finding words, I will sympathize with an inarticulate friend. And even as I would have him try to understand me, I will do my best to understand him, knowing always that in our communion we go, at least in part, our separate ways.

Even as I accept my own uniqueness, I respect the uniqueness of others. I do not set up universal standards. Each of us is a unique personality with the one obligation to be honestly expressive of that personality.

This acceptance of uniqueness of self gives me a freedom that affects everything I say and do. I have a validity, an integrity, all my own. Every time I speak, I know that I am myself, that I am different from every other person in the whole world. I know that what I say has uniqueness *for me*. My words have meaning *for me*. Knowing what I am trying to say, and why, I choose my words carefully, with an awareness of their peculiar significance to my purposes. With an awareness, too, of their relevance to the interests of my listeners.

My words are right *for me* at this particular moment in my life. Yesterday, under other circumstances, they might not have been right. Tomorrow, they may be altogether unsuitable. But today—*now*—with these listeners, they are right for me. As right as I can make them.

This realization of the uniqueness of my self and of the uniqueness of the moment automatically purges me of that vitiating and destructive something which has been labeled "self-consciousness." I am, instead, *conscious of self, conscious of the uniqueness of my self.*

Self-consciousness is a fear that thrives on the feeling that we are not conforming to our "betters." But conformity is actually not possible! And even if it were possible, would it be desirable? The outstanding person does not fit into a groove. His ideas are different. And his way of expressing them is uniquely his own. Others notice him and listen attentively.

My respect for my very uniqueness constitutes the measure of my self-respect.

14

**Conformity is not our goal. The goal is continuous development, rather, of our own potentialities, whatever they may be.**

This consciousness of the uniqueness of self liberates me for the free use of my resources. I know that I must be myself. There is no way out. I might as well like it and make something of it. At every moment of my life, I can strive to be myself at my best, at my constantly better best. That is the goal.

Again, self-consciousness is a paralyzing fear that derives from the feeling that someone who is listening would say it differently, would say it better.

There are no absolutes in speech. No absolute "right." No absolute "wrong." What is right for you may not be right for me. What is right for me today may not be right for me tomorrow. But if I succeed in making you understand me, if I succeed in *effecting* my purpose, then my words have been "effective." What I have said and how I have said it are "good." "Right" *for me*. And the judge of my efforts must be the judge of that unique instant in time.

Someone else might have done it differently? Of course! *Everyone else would have done it differently*. But not necessarily better.

Have you ever tried to delegate someone else to plead *your* cause? To explain *your* idea? To present *your* plan? Try it someday. You will find that it is *your* job. Your whole life has led to this moment. You must do it. You alone. No one else can do it better—*for you*.

This freedom from self-consciousness, born of this liberating attitude, extends to everything I say and do. I give my

15

impulses the same respect that I give my self in the light of past performance.

An impulse is a forward-surge that grows out of the past as it meshes with the immediate purposive *now*. An impulse is an invitation to life; an impulse is the pivotal point that ushers in new experience. And so I proceed confidently but carefully from impulses to their organization into activities, to maturation in the test of words and deeds.

I recognize in my raw impulses the very source of my human activity, and I nurture them. I try not to let them die stillborn if I can help it. I could kill them off, but that would be premeditated murder. No less.

An impulse makes me an animated human being. It puts adventure into my life. And gaiety, too. For to stifle an impulse is the most deadly of all experiences, and the most depressing. We become aware of a sense of loss that is deep and rankling. Who does not look back, even now, and mourn *If only I had said that!*

I know. Sometimes we look back and say *If only I had not said that!*

"Do you trust your impulses?" I asked Wendy when she was a high school freshman.

"Yes, Gram," she answered confidently.

"Why?" I wanted to know.

"Because they turn out well," she answered.

Do we have any other criterion? We may trust our impulses only so far as we trust our selves; to put a stopper on them is often to repress life itself.

If uniqueness of every one and every situation is the rule, when I speak and you listen, I must look outward at you and *see*. You enter, then, as an active force into my very personality. You bring out in me certain characteristics that are suitable to the occasion. Suitable to *you*.

Will you want to penetrate to my ideas?

Will you want to probe into my purpose?

Will you be interested? Or indifferent? Will you accept? Or reject?

There is only one way for me to know. I must look and see and listen. I must attempt to perceive the consequences of my own words. If my words are returned to me as an echo, their purpose and value are vitiated. If your reactions are not what I desire, something is wrong. Probably with me. I must use other means, other words, other tactics, to accomplish my purpose.

When we look outward and see, we are less unsure, for our confidence is found only in the ears and the eyes of listeners. When we look inward, we isolate ourselves from our possible collaborators. We deprive ourselves of the opportunity to meet and to like others and, reciprocally, to be liked.

**Acceptance of uniqueness promises individual freedom that can be converted into personal power that becomes expressive in our words.**

## THE USE OF WORDS IS A *RISK–TAKING* ADVENTURE

If uniqueness of every person and every event is the rule, how can we predict the future with any degree of certainty when human beings are involved? All we can do is make an educated guess about what is likely to happen. We use what information is available, but information about human beings is never complete.

When I speak to you, how in the world can I predict what

17

you will say, how you will respond? I cannot. When we use words, life is chancy beyond compare. But the alternative, absolute prediction, would mean that a speaker would know *in advance* how his listeners would respond. This, fortunately, is asking too much, even of the Great God Science. We are spared this dismal boredom. We are spared this automation. Happily, human behavior cannot be reduced to simple, dependable, invariable laws. Life is still adventure into the unknown and the unknowable.

So let's face it.

Uniqueness of every person, every thing, and every human event does imply a high degree of unpredictability; and a situation that is even slightly unpredictable is, necessarily, risky. Power-Steering with Words, you will find, will reduce, if not actually control, change and chance in the communication process.

We must begin with the premise that we live on the razor's edge of time between the past and the future. We live in the *now* of a *process* world.

It is hard to believe that the chair I am sitting on right now is atomic process. It looks so substantial, so solid, so "permanent." But this reliance on sufficient endurance does not explain process away, nor does it negate process in any sense. I cannot see my hair grow, but I need a haircut every three weeks. I cannot see the planets move, yet Venus, a while ago a morning star, is now an evening star.

Universal process may easily be forgotten in a world in which complex spatial patterns may be considered apart from the time dimension of the process world. But we know that time and space are complementary to each other. When we think about human behavior, our interest is centered on changes in time; that is, on process. We think secondarily of spatial arrangements, or even ignore them altogether.

**Power-Steering with Words is a semantic procedure by which we can exert a measure of control over any situation that involves the use of words.**

## *ORDER* AND *RANDOMNESS* IN NATURE

The task of science is to discover order in a universe that holds an element of randomness, of disorder. There is both order and randomness in nature—human nature included.

In many physical events it is possible to predict the future with a high degree of probability. Our knowledge of recurrent patterns in nature makes prediction possible. Astronomers can predict an eclipse with hardly a margin of error.

We know that there is order in the universe, but we know, too, that there is that which cannot be predicated on the basis of a known cause. Even physical nature has its surprises.[6]

Statisticians can assemble, classify, and tabulate significant information, and make many useful so-called predictions about future social behavior. But statistical prediction is far from prediction in an *individual* case.[7]

We know that there is order inside our skins. The human being is not a bag of odds and ends.[8]

We know that there is order *between* the individual and his world. We are not isolated bits of flotsam drifting aimlessly at the mercy of external physical and social forces.[9] But, we are told, there is no general scientific theory that can tell us what an individual human being will say or do—or even why.[10]

**There is order in all of nature—man included. But there**

**is also randomness. The use of words is a unique transaction that is full of surprises.**

## WE EXPECT THE *UNEXPECTED*—AND *STEER* TACTICALLY

As purposive human beings, it is necessary for us to anticipate what the future holds. As seekers after goals, we direct our lives by our expectations.[11] Only our knowledge of recurrent patterns in nature can help us. So, when we plan for the future, we use foresight.

Foresight is thinking ahead, and this involves what is probably our most important use of words. When we are concerned with goals that require operations by human beings, thinking ahead is always a calculated risk—never certain. The semantic controls of Power-Steering with Words are required to cope with the hazards of change and chance.

We set up possible strategies ("verbal patterns," we shall be calling such strategic plans) by which to move from the present state of affairs to a more desirable state, to a goal-state.

We look at these possible strategies critically. We compare these verbal patterns that anticipate possible actual patterns and decide which plan seems to be the most likely to succeed. We choose the most probable, the least risky, and the least costly in time, in effort, and in sacrifice of other possibilities. This is common sense. But what is required, in addition, is a dash of "uncommon" sense. What is required is Power-Steering with Words.

Every time we use words, we want something, whether we are conscious of it or not. Words intervene in almost everything we do. We may ask only for a sign of friendship, of love, of trust, of understanding. But the purpose is always there.

Every time we speak, *we are asking for change of some sort!* We are in search of satisfactions as varied as life itself. We send out words as feelers, as probers. We pay attention to the consequences of our words and redirect our efforts, if necessary, to become *makers* of change.

Every business and professional man or woman is sensitive to change and chance. And must be.

A junior executive, alert to process, asked me during a seminar, "Isn't writing a letter a risky business? Whatever we write may be hot when we mail it but stone cold by the time it gets to the other end. How can I get around this?"

My answer was simple: "Date your letters."

We put process and change into our written transactions by the simple expedient of dating them. An undated report is worthless to a medical man, to a broker, to the Internal Revenue Service. Yet in our everyday experience we are inclined to stop the clock. We all know the person who has a repertoire of stock phrases that roll off his tongue regardless of their suitability to the moment.

Korzybski says flatly in *Science and Sanity: Date everything!*[12]

John Smith[1960] *is not* John Smith[1963].

Russia[1962] *is not* Russia[1963].

Science[19th century] *is not* Science[20th century].

"Fact"[yesterday] *may not be* "Fact"[today].

Etc., etc., etc.

We cannot, of course, date our every statement, but we can, as Korzybski suggests, get the notion of process and change under our skins and let it work for us on the unconscious as well as the conscious level.

21

When we shut out process and change, we become *closed* selves. This means that our channels of intake from the outside world are restricted to samenesses. Automatically, we shut out the new, the different. Change is suspect—to be regarded with suspicion. As a result, our inner coordination of routine and habitual experience becomes solidified, impervious to reorganization of the self on the basis of new experience. This affects our whole lives. We make ineffectual responses to changes in the environment and we limit the range and the diversity of goals which we might otherwise pursue. Did it ever occur to you that a great opportunity may lurk in the unexpected change that confronts you?

As a speaker, the closed self is a bore, and unreliable. For him, an opinion is something to swear by and to live by, come hell or high water. He forgets (if he ever knew) that an opinion is an opinion because all the "consequentially" relevant facts (facts that have important consequences with respect to the opinion involved) are not in. And perhaps cannot be in. Who knows all about a single human being—to say nothing of so-called classes of human beings! *An opinion is always a leap beyond the known facts*. Important, of course! Some of the most important areas of knowledge—and I mean *knowledge*—can never rise above opinion. So an opinion is open-end, and must be dated and looked at critically as new information becomes available.

*How do you know an opinion when you hear it? When you say it?*

If you are *appraising* a human being or discussing a complex social problem, you are in the area of opinion. So you will listen and read and learn and update your opinions as carefully and conscientiously as you can. You will make a conscious effort to be an *open* self and not a *closed* self.

Inevitably the closed self is anxious and insecure in the grip of change.[13] He is left behind in the world. Resistant, of course, and even hostile. But pitiable.

**Let's put it boldly. The use of words is a risk-taking adventure. Life is full of surprises. If it were not, we should not be obliged to steer our resources, our words, our power.**

Anything we can predict, we know in advance of its happening. It follows that the only new information we can get in a life situation is what we cannot predict! Even the unexpected obstacle—misunderstanding, opposition, competition, indifference, rejection, hostility—is new information that has value for us as a clue to remedial changes in tactics, if not in actual strategy.

When we plan ahead, we frame strategy. But strategy is not enough. Tactical change is of such significance to the user of words that the semantic device *feedback* (defined as "corrective tactical change") becomes indispensable to goal-seeking behavior. Feedback is the steering operation in Power-Steering with Words, as will be shown.

## RESISTANCE TO CHANGE IS LIKE SWIMMING UPSTREAM

Resistance to change is the most natural thing in the world.

We are creatures of habit. If we were not, we should have to figure out how to rig a sail, how to set a table, how to fix a fuse every time anew. Our habits supply us with a mighty task force inside our skins. We can do many intricate things without a conscious thought. A typist can swing around and talk with a passing co-worker as her fingers fly. I, too, have a strange motor memory. If I want to remember something, I write it. It is then indelibly recorded in my memory.

23

As a youngster, I played the piano by what typists call the touch system. But if those mechanical fingers were brought to an unexpected stop, I was lost. I had to start all over from the beginning.

Think of the speaker who has memorized his speech. Think of the lawyer who has memorized his brief. Think of the salesman who has memorized his pitch. Think of the teacher who has memorized the lesson. Think of the employee who has memorized his complaint. One interruption and the speaker forgets where he came in. Brought to an unexpected stop, he is lost. He cannot, as a child might, start all over again. He is in the position of the surgeon who makes an incision in the wrong patient. If there is anything he cannot do, it is to uncut. He can't go backwards. Nor can we. The moment is gone.

Habits are basic efficiencies. Our conditioned responses are learned patterns of behavior. They are short cuts that eliminate the need for thinking. This is fine when such behavior is suitable. But it is not suitable to the use of words in goal-seeking behavior. Our listeners are human beings. Alive. And each one unique. It is impossible to know in advance precisely how each will respond. Constant vigilance and adaptation are required. In a conversation, in a conference, in a discussion, in an interview—in any face-to-face situation—we are brought up against something that, in the nature of the case, we just cannot predict.

We can float downstream, but aren't we on our way up?

## UPSTREAM[1964]

In a complex life situation, planned strategy is, of course, the primary requisite. But there is need also for tactical change, adjustment to the unpredictable, in the interest of a

24

predetermined goal. Stability without flexibility is glorified stupidity in the space age.

Recall the interesting phrase "trained incapacity" of the economist Veblen. Kenneth Burke comments on this phrase with respect to goal-seeking behavior. The training of a man, Burke says, can cause him to misjudge a present situation. His training, in this sense, incapacitates him in respect to the situation.[14] This pair of seemingly incongruous terms has peculiar validity today. Change is so rapid and so awesome that few of us do not suffer "trained incapacity" of one sort or another.

Flexibility without planned strategy is equally disastrous.

Strategy derives from knowledge of recurrent patterns in nature. Adjustment to the new, to the different, to the unpredictable, should not spring from chaos. We must presuppose cosmos (order) as a law of nature.

Nothing less than the full human potential, strategy and tactics, is adequate to goal-directed behavior. We need power to turn us on, but once on, we must steer our resources while watching for obstacles, for detours, for short cuts, ever ready to accommodate power to needs.

Power-Steering with Words is just this combination of planned strategy and corrective tactics, just this combination of force and control, just this combination of order and creative freedom.

**Words are the greatest power at the service of man. The power is there for us to use—to mobilize and to direct toward human goals.**

ABIGAIL E. WEEKS MEMORIAL LIBRARY
UNION COLLEGE
BARBOURVILLE, KENTUCKY

# Part One

# Manpower, Unlimited

*Chapter I*

# From Oratory to PS/W*

## THE DAY OF THE DULCET VOICE

I am wondering, as I write, if the days of oratory have gone forever.

Not long ago, a young Japanese student working for his doctorate in political science came to one of my classes. He listened to an opening statement of the aims of the course and of the general nature of our approach to the accomplishment of those aims. After the seminar he came to me and said, "But I wish to learn speechmaking."

"Are you planning to go back to Japan?" I asked. My mind was darting ahead to his future plans.

---

* Power-Steering with Words

"Yes," was his grave reply. "I shall have to speak in assemblies, large assemblies, as well as to smaller groups and to individuals."

"And you wish to learn to write thoughtful speeches and declaim them powerfully."

He nodded. "You understand precisely."

I was sympathetic with his needs but believed that his ultimate goal must be approached by indirection.

I think of oratory, first, as a literary work, and second, as a dramatic performance. Such artistry would combine the talents of a writer and an actor.

As a written work, the speech can be polished until, without error or flaw, it becomes a document of elegance. In the days of William Jennings Bryan, such works were not read. They were memorized and declaimed. Again, the performance was practiced until, in delivery, it became something of a dramatic art.

We reject such oratory today mainly because its methods are not adequate to our needs.

The memorized speech fails to take into account the most important factor in our lives—change. The memorized speech speaks for yesterday, if not last week or last month. Or even last year! It cannot speak for the *now*, for the uniqueness of the immediate, cyclic, dynamic present in which every aspect of the situation as a whole affects every other aspect of that situation as a whole.

## PUBLIC SPEAKING—THE NEWER VOGUE IN *DECLAMATION*

Over two decades ago, a perceptive Dean of Faculty recognized the inappropriateness of the label "public speaking" to describe a skill that everyone admires and hopes to attain. But the catalog of the university still listed a course in Public Speaking.

The Dean asked me if I would care to teach the course. The term "public speaking" set up adumbrations of "elocution" in my mind. When I told him I knew nothing about public speaking, he smiled and said, "And that, my friend, is your chief qualification for the job." I accepted.

The first thing we did was to change the title and the description of the course. At first we called the course, "Better Speaking." The fact was that we did not know exactly where we were going. We were learning. It took some five years before the course was called "Communication," and after a decade or more it was offered, frankly, as "Semantics."

Today, because we recognize that semantics is a subject that belongs with the social sciences, we make an effort to keep pace with present-day supportive knowledge in the biological sciences. The subject is projectile. As projectile as life itself.

Because of its association with "fine oratory," Public Speaking was taught, frequently, as song. *How* the words came out was important. Voice development and control were therefore the objectives. "Diaphragmatic breathing" was recommended, according to the books. Gesture, too, was studied. Words—vocabulary and grammar—were regarded as ends in themselves.

The speaker's repertoire was *words*, and his delivery was evaluated by the fluency and the artistry with which words rolled off his tongue.

Let's look at these objectives and at the methods used to accomplish them.

31

Face the fact, first, that the sound of your voice does make a difference.

Some voices are dead. We do not notice a dead voice if it is our own, but our ears are quick to catch it in someone else. Monotony of voice is a common fault. Too many voices can be charted in a wavy line marked off by evenly measured stops. Something like this:

No changes in timing. No sharp ups and downs. No changes in volume. Neither hot nor cold, but tepid.

Notice that the sentences are about even in length. When all the stops are periods, the regular rise and fall of the voice is as stimulating as a lullaby.

Timing should be directly correlated with meaning. The timing of words, of phrases, of sentences, and the long pauses between transitions in thought, make understanding possible, very much as punctuation is the guide to meaning on the printed page.

When thought-feeling and timing are coordinated, the results are natural and "right" for the speaker. This is true also of changes in pitch and of changes in volume.

In its earlier days, Public Speaking gave little attention to the correlation of thought-feeling and vocal expressiveness. Instead, emphasis was placed primarily on the coordination of vocal expression and gesture. That both are directly referable to thought-feeling was probably considered to be too remote to be given attention. Standardized gestures were used to express stereotyped emotions. Fear, sorrow, joy, hate, command, approval, reprobation, etc.

Students of mine even now complain that they cannot move their hands or their feet on a platform. All I can tell them, and you, is this: *When thought-feeling pushes you, let yourself go. Move. Otherwise, stay put. A gesture that is "made" is caricature.*

*But I don't know what to do with my hands* is the invariable response.

*Forget your hands. When you get into trouble and can't find the right words, you will discover that your hands will, somehow, come up and take over.*

Why do you suppose foreigners make such excellent use of their hands in conversation? The whole body becomes expressive, as a unit.

We cannot learn to make gestures. All we can do is think-feel deeply enough to forget our hands. And our selves. Our hands should be given no more thought than our ears. They will take care of themselves.

Public Speaking gave particular attention to vocabulary. Words were to be elegant; phrases, sonorous; sentences, polished and declamatory. Vocabulary? Of course! But the emphasis in PS/W will be on the utility of words in goal-directed behavior. Our concern is with the communication of ideas and ideals. Words are the minimal units of the communication process. We shall be very much interested in vocabulary, but we shall be more interested in the ways in which words are *arranged*—put together—in order to transmit thought-feeling as a prelude to concerted action.

It is my opinion that psychological tests that rely strongly on vocabulary have great usefulness in giving clues to the interests, the aptitudes, the experience, and the knowledge of the individuals tested. I believe, too, that these tests have value also in the determination of the relative intelligence of individuals within a homogeneous cultural environment.

The vocabulary of a person is the key to his interests and his aptitudes. And his knowledge!

Who said this? *Laboratory tests show streptococci. Sulfanilamide is indicated.*

Or this? *Due process must be guaranteed.*

Or this? *Semantics is a social "science," and everything that can be said about it is a matter of opinion, at a date. Even this statement.*

Listen to people conversing almost anywhere. This is almost as good as an aptitude test.

But here is something that may surprise you. It surprised me. The character of a vocabulary will indicate *how* (not *what*) a person thinks.

Some persons will think primarily on the lowest level of description. They *name* persons, places, things, events, etc. *Johnny said this. Mary did that.* Others will move away from such particulars and talk about classes of persons, places, things, etc. These talk about "boys" and "girls," their favorite pastime, their problems, etc., without getting down to specific examples. Yet others will move to a high level of abstraction and talk about "juvenile delinquency," "politics," "religion," "philosophy," etc.

Dr. W. Grey Walter, author of *The Living Brain*, says there is now proof that personalities can be identified by the characteristic level of abstractions which their words take.[15] Let me quote exactly from an example given by Walter:

Supposing Peggy and Michael at breakfast receive an invitation to a party and have to decide whether they shall go to it. Michael will have a whole series of vivid pictures. He will see them going to the party, the party itself, the people they will meet. He will come to a decision that way very quickly. But Peggy, who does not use visual images in this quick and easy way, has a more abstract method of thought . . . their language, their mental accents, so to say, are incompatible.

Perhaps this explains something about human relations in everyday experience. Are we attracted to a person who habitually levels off—verbally—either way above us or way below us? *And stays there?*

There is one thing more. Some tests are probing now into the *linkages between words.* A great Midwestern university now gives an admission test that is called an Analogical Test. This test is concerned with comparison—with similarities and differences between the structure, the *pattern*—of different things, events, ideas, etc.

Discovery and exploration of analogies is an invaluable tool of science. By looking at two things with similar structure, new knowledge of both may be gained. The computers are like (*not* identical with) human beings in some respects. (Both, for instance, have "memories.") The important thing is that the analogy is good or not good depending on the degree of similarity of structure.[16] Of pattern. Here, then, the test has to do, not with isolated words, but with word-patterns. With ideas.

The importance of vocabulary in personal development can hardly be overemphasized. A word by itself is not information. A word takes its place among other words to become information.

Let's put it this way. Every word in your vocabulary is an element within a context. That context is your past experience. For you to know a word, to recognize a word, you must relate it to other words. The number of related words a person knows is some indication of the breadth of his knowledge. To say this differently, the vocabulary as a whole is a composite of the past experience of a human being.

Lists of words, dictionary style, are like bits of a jigsaw puzzle. When put together properly, words make something recognizable, understandable. But if you arrange them alphabetically or shuffle them at random, what have you got? An assortment of items that you have little or no use for. Certainly, you have a lot of words, but you don't know what to do with them. You don't know what goes where.

There are various ways to increase the vocabulary. Our way is to link a "new" word to words already known. Ultimately, all the words we know hang together like a finished jigsaw puzzle, such that our knowledge is integrated. Everything we know is related to everything else we know. And the whole, taken together, makes a unified pattern. This unified pattern is the image of our world, as we know it. The pattern is not static, as a mosaic, but dynamic as a living, evolving, self-organizing system.

We pay great attention to words because they are the minimal elements of our knowledge, of the composite idea-system that controls our choices, that monitors our behavior, and that opens our world to new knowledge.

Many books have been written on how to build a vocabulary. The method we have used with a high degree of success is so simple that I need only mention it. And there is no advantage in complicating the matter. It is as simple as it sounds. Virtually automatic.

**Read aloud in a field of interest. Read aloud in a field about which you need to know more. You will add every**

**word you knew in a context but which you had never said before to your active vocabulary.**

As you read aloud in a field of interest, you are bound to come across hundreds of words which you have known for years but which you have never before uttered. In reading aloud, you *say* these words for the first time. Everyone knows that his reading vocabulary is very much broader than his oral vocabulary. We all recognize and understand innumerable words in a printed context (or even in a spoken context) that we have never used orally.

The first step is to make use of this broad latent vocabulary. You will want to take advantage now of the words you know but have never used in talk. And why have you never used them? You have never used them because you have never *said* them. This may sound as if I am stuttering, but I know this to be a fact. We will not use a word that we have never said before if we are under a stress of any kind. We sidestep it, more often unconsciously than consciously. We are likely to avoid the hazard, slight though it may be.

I stumbled on this point years ago. In giving a public lecture, I used the word "expeditionary." Now this certainly was an old familiar, but I knew immediately, as I took the plunge, that I had never really *said* that word before. It toppled off my lips clumsily—awkwardly. It sounded strange to my ears.

The only way—*is there any other?*—to make the transition from the latent to the active vocabulary is to *say the words*. Reading aloud bridges the gap between familiarity with a word in a context and readiness to use that word orally under pressure.

If you read regularly in the same field, you will derive a maximum of value. You will meet the same "new" words and they will become firmly established in the context. And having read them aloud three or four times, they are yours—for the saying.

As you read aloud, you will also find words that are unfamiliar to you even on the printed page. Every topic has its specialized jargon. And these terms will require special attention. You will find that the author may define specialized terms by referring to other portions of the context. The process is circular and will be painlessly reinforcing.

Every author has his own vocabulary. His vocabulary, however, is not without limit. You will find that he will use the same words over and over again until the verbal pattern is complete, and there is a wholeness. Your understanding of any one specialized word will be essential to your understanding of other specialized words. The vocabulary as a whole is essential to the unity of the author's project.

For the reader, such specialized words are the pivotal points that usher in new experience. They are the very reason for his reading such a book.

If you will now read aloud as *we* go, you will soon be alerted to my specialized terms. I give special significance to the words "character," "personality," "pattern," "feedforward," "feedback," and, of course, "semantics," which will require this entire book to explain.

You will move from familiar ground to unexplored territory, in which, however, you will soon feel at home. Know my vocabulary and you will know me. And, because you will have read aloud, you will find my words in your active vocabulary.

Grammar is one of the basic semantic clues to meanings and to purposes.

As for meaning, try to read words that are put together

as nonsense syllables. Words must have order, and that order is established by grammar.

As for purpose, the sentence structure itself is an important clue to the intention of the speaker or the writer.

When the intention is to inform others, the simple (subject-predicate-period) sentence structure is proper and effective. The sentence structure may also indicate the intention to incite to a specific attitude or action response. Here the imperative sentence structure is proper and indispensable. But grammar may play an unusual role in persuasion. Only the proper use of adjectives and adverbs, of emotive nouns and slanted verbs, can express human values.

Grammar may also be used as an aid in gaining and holding attention. Differences in grammatical structure lend excitement and variety to the tone quality. The voice rises in question. The voice drops with a period. The voice projects positively and outwardly with the sharp staccato of the imperative. Long sentences. Short sentences. Is there a better way to kill monotony? To invite attention and interest? We all do this on the unconscious level now and then. With a little conscious effort it may easily become a useful habit.

We cannot dispense with an understanding of grammar. But grammar is taught, not as an end in itself, but as a means to Power-Steering with Words.

As for fluency, I ask you, simply, *What's wrong with struggle?* For me, struggle is not a negative but a positive word. Struggle means that I want something and that I need your help, your understanding, your cooperation in getting it. My words come haltingly only because I want so very much to find words that are suitable to *you* at this particular moment in our lives.

When words tumble from the mouth of a speaker, I begin

to wonder *Is he grinding an old ax?* Fluency may be suspect, for it rarely indicates life in the making.

The words of Sacco and Vanzetti had none of the so-called skills of Public Speaking to commend them. Yet the world wept for and with them on the occasion of their tragic execution. Smooth words? No. But their speech had the impact of their broken phrases, of their stammering and unpolished, their untried and faltering, words.

Public Speaking was concerned with finesse, with the studied flow of words. To hesitate was to err. For us hesitation is the forerunner of the creative surge into novelty. Memorized words intoned in the accepted oratorical fashion exhibited a "finished" product. Our words shall exhibit the forever unfinished task of *becoming* what we hope to be.

## PUBLIC SPEAKING AS *PROCLAMATION*

Proclamation is different from declamation.

Proclamation is the voice of leadership under the stress of becoming, not on the individual level, but on the broad human, national, if not world-wide, scale.

Public-speaking-as-proclamation is practiced by many persons in high public office, and rightly so. We shall call it *Public Address* to differentiate it from Public Speaking and its outmoded methods.

In Public Address, words must be a matter of record. They are therefore written. The Public Address must, in many instances, be approved by others before delivery.

In Public Address, the words of the speaker are rarely, if ever, memorized. To memorize is risky, for in memory a word may be omitted, changed, juxtaposed, or added. An idea may be ambiguously stated. The speech is therefore read, and without apology, for the reading is a sign of meticulous care—of deep concentration on a matter of concern to those who are listening.

In the archives of political history, these speeches are available for reading and rereading. They are "literature." *Purposive* literature. But literature.

Such speeches are very well written by present-day standards. They are clearly and accurately informative, and frequently persuasive. Sometimes they are incitive in intention. They are deeply expressive of thought-feeling and hoped-for action. The ideas expressed are projected toward the future.

The speaker may or may not be the author. The speech may be, and frequently is, a collaborative effort. Such a speech has the status of proclamation. The speech is dated and has relevance to that date. And the official standing of the speaker is judged by the printed record.

In a press conference or in other informal extemporaneous or impromptu speaking situations, the speaker is usually outstanding by present-day standards. In official matters of state, no one objects to the formal procedure. Public Address is a necessary, and common, practice.

Public Address is rarely a one-way process. If there is any doubt in your mind about this, consider President Kennedy's speech before the Irish Parliament on June 28, 1963. Though read, the speech seemed very like conversation with friends and kinsmen whose participation, both verbal and nonverbal, was unmistakable. So human. So personal. And yet so deeply thoughtful—so characteristic of the dignity and the responsibility of the holder of high office.

There are times when speakers in Public Address appear to millions via Telstar and television. Are their speeches necessarily one-way, addressed as they are to a nation-wide or world-wide audience?

Who can forget Roosevelt's "The only thing we have to fear is fear itself," on the occasion of his First Inaugural Address on March 4, 1933?

And who can forget Churchill's "I have nothing to offer but blood, toil, tears and sweat," on the occasion of his first statement as Prime Minister in the House of Commons in May 1940?

And who can forget the words of John Fitzgerald Kennedy on the occasion of his inaugural on January 20, 1961?

In the long history of the world, only a few generations have been granted the role of defending freedom in its hour of maximum danger. I do not shrink from this responsibility; I welcome it. . . . The energy, the faith, the devotion which we bring to this endeavor will light our country and all who serve it, and the glow from that fire can truly light the world. And so, my fellow Americans, ask not what your country can do for you; ask what you can do for your country.

These words will never die, as long as there are human beings to remember. We do not, perhaps cannot, talk back. But we *feel* back. We *think* back. We *respond*. And if our responses affect our future behavior even in the slightest degree, Public Address must be recognized as something more than one-way process. Such speeches may properly be called two-way communication.

Public Address is our best example of the utility and the limitations of two-way communication in goal-seeking behavior.

## *PUBLIC ADDRESS* AS A TWO-WAY COMMUNICATION, EVALUATED

When the words of an official must be read for reasons of security and accuracy, the occasion is usually one of common interest and immediate concern to the listeners. A great number of persons will listen. These are bona fide listeners.

They are not pretending. They are not waiting for the speaker to finish so that they can talk back. Their function—and their desire, I might add—is simply to listen, to understand, and to evaluate the significance of the spoken words to their personal lives.

These listeners cannot talk back to the speaker; but they can talk back to themselves: they can think. And they can discuss the ideas and intentions of the speaker with others. But in Public Address this is not enough.

If left to his own devices, the speaker may get "too far out in front." When he does, as Norman Cousins says,[17] he is unable to lead the great groups whose collaboration he solicits and needs. Many will listen and approve, who yet will not indicate their responses. Without some evidence of response, positive or negative, the position of the leader is weakened. His position is, of course, mightily strengthened by sweeping positive response.

There can be no doubt about the nature of the response to Kennedy's speech in Dublin. But there is frequently great doubt about the nature of the response of listeners to Public Address on matters of policy and administrative procedure. Here the responsiveness is not primarily on the emotional level, even though the intentions—the purposes—of the speaker will affect the lives of listeners in some actual and practical way.

The success of a leader is dependent upon strong and positive responsiveness. To insure that responsiveness he must do something to concretize the values about which he speaks.

To speak of concretized values is to speak of the great work of Max Kadushin, whose *The Rabbinic Mind*[18] places religious values in the actual human experience—in the home, in the nation, in the world.

To concretize a value means that we apply that value to a living situation. Thus the judge concretizes mercy when he releases an unwitting offender. Thus the speaker concretizes a value when, in talking about employment, *he provides jobs*.

Responsiveness to Public Address comes by the use of words—written or spoken. Responsiveness can be (and usually is) shown by the press, by the vocal statements of persons within the body politic, and by letters and telegrams from the people—the listeners.

The democratic way of life requires just this kind of two-way communication, Cousins insists. Leaders must lead, but the people must respond.

**The utility of two-way communication in Public Address should be recognized for the important role it plays in our lives.**

## TWO-WAY COMMUNICATION IN *BIG BUSINESS*

Big Business recognized early that the one-way process of communication was not conducive to profit making. The boss could give out a dictum—clear and specific—but nothing would happen. Nothing changed.

Orders that come down the line to workers can meet with a kind of passive resistance that undermines the purpose of management. Without outward signs of rebellion, workers can quietly sabotage any plan in which they do not choose to cooperate. Every manager is, in this sense, at the mercy of his subordinates.[19]

So Big Business embraced the two-way communication process. Hopefully, they called it "the democratic method." And this method is still favored in some unenlightened quarters, although it has become apparent that it is ineffectual, not only in the internal economy of the organization, but also in the relation of the organization to its public.

"Competition" is not a bad word; it is an action word. But the two-way communication process, if used in a competitive situation, can be more obstructive than constructive.

Competition is one of the facts of life. There is competition everywhere. Within the human being there is competition between conflicting impulses, conflicting interests. The individual is also in constant competition with the environment, both social and physical, for his "place."

In competition the two-way process is obstructive because it is likely to set opposing forces against each other—head on. (*You've had your say, now I'll have mine, by god!*) There are, indeed, *two ways* in the two-way communication process—the speaker's and the listener's—but the one is pitted against the other. How much better to consider the situation cyclic in which there is a speaking-listening-perceiving-speaking continuum, with change at both ends. Like this:

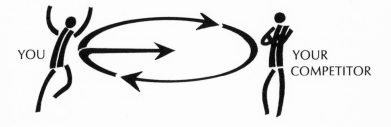

In the cyclic communication process there is honest listening to the other person's ideas and attitudes. There is constant entertainment of incoming stimuli—at both ends. There is never a continuation of an argument without an acknowledgment of those incoming stimuli:

*I see your point of view and we shouldn't forget it. But*

45

*let me call your attention to another aspect of the matter that may have bearing on this problem.*

A few years ago, I listened to a Professor of Personnel Management in the Graduate School of Business at the University of Chicago expound on the principles of two-way communication. I was a visitor in the classroom, invited because the discussion had to do with communication inside the industrial organization. I was asked to evaluate the two-way method. Because my academic function was to do just that, I went, first, to the blackboard and drew this diagram of the structure of the industrial organization:

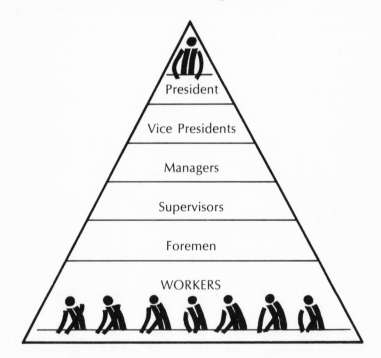

President

Vice Presidents

Managers

Supervisors

Foremen

WORKERS

Whether an organization uses the autocratic one-way communication process, the so-called democratic two-way communication process, or the cyclic speaking-listening-speaking continuum, with change at both ends, communication must be accomplished within the framework of this structure.

Usually there is one executive at the top of the structured organization and hundreds of workers at the bottom. If you are connected with an industrial organization, you can place an X to mark the spot—for yourself.

This hierarchical structure is not limited to business. You will find it in varying degrees of complexity wherever there is organization. You will find it in a family, in a private club, in a school, in a P.T.A., in a hospital, in government, in the Catholic Church, at the United Nations—everywhere.

**"Communication is the cement that makes organizations."**[20]

The leader is at the peak of the pyramid and the man in the street is at the bottom. When a businessman speaks of his work as "a rat race," he refers, usually, to the hierarchical structure of the organization in which everyone is in a kind of maze trying to move up and fearful of being pushed down. This, you may be sure, affects his output of words.

Now look at this diagram:

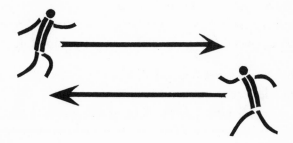

Or this:

Notice that the individuals are face to face. All of them are, hypothetically, both speakers and listeners. The flow of words goes in two directions.

In two-way communication the boss is informative and incitive. *This is what he wants, and this is what he wants them to do.* The men wait for him to finish. (They can hardly wait!) No one really listens. The men speak, but they rarely, if ever, acknowledge what has been said by a previous speaker (the boss included). They are evasive and noncommittal. The boss waits for the men to finish and treats what they have said as interruptions to his pronouncements. He concludes that it would have been better to send a written directive down the line and then crack the whip, if necessary.

Big Business has decided that the two-way "democratic" communication process has somehow gone sour. The two-way communication process does, indeed, move in two directions, but the words are likely to flow in parallel lines.

The reason is simple. No one wants to be told what to do. Workers want to feel that their efforts are a vital part of an

enterprise. They want more. They insist that a proposed
project be related to their personal goals. If their goals are
not considered in the formation of a plan, the workers will
find a way to evade involvement in the operations necessary
to the successful fulfillment of the plan.[21]

Big Business has now become interested in "human relations." This is a big broad jump in the direction of PS/W. For
if words have any power at all, it is the power generated by
a human being. And if power is steered at all, it, too, is steered
by a human being. Like this—wherever you are in the organization:

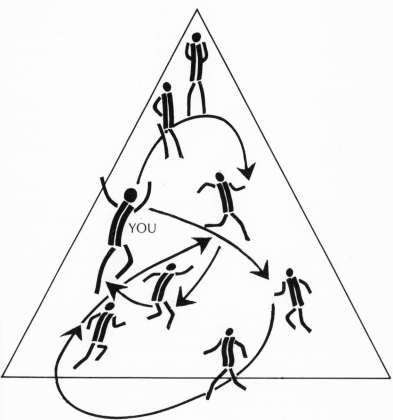

**Power-Steering with Words is the answer. And Big Business leads the way.**

## PS/W IN OUR EVERYDAY LIVES

Strangely enough, in our everyday lives we exercise our natural human gifts with a skill that is remarkable. When this skill is looked at analytically, it becomes apparent that our goal-seeking behavior generates power and steers it with strategic and tactical expertise—whether or not we have ever heard the word "semantics."

We start always with the fact that we do not speak unless we want something. The purpose may be deep-seated and unspeakable, actually on the unconscious level. But when the purpose is specific and urgent and looks to a preconceived goal, what happens?

We begin sentences hardly knowing how we shall end them, yet we end them. We hear responses that are explosive, shocking, disarming, and yet we manage, somehow, to reorganize our forces and direct them toward the goal.

When the need is strong enough—imperative—the personality is intensely alert. We use every resource at our command, not after leisurely study, but spontaneously. On the spot! For, more often than not, *this is conversation*.

We talk with people everywhere. We may call that talk "conversation" over a cocktail or at a luncheon. But even the Internal Revenue Service acknowledges that business sometimes is done under informal guise. Sometimes we give conversation more important names. We call it "interview" or even "conference." In a court of law, we may call it "argument"; in a hospital, "consultation"; over a counter, "salesmanship." And over the phone it might be anything!

50

Give conversation a formal name and you freeze! But call it conversation—which, indeed, it is—and you become an inspired, energetic, risk-taking creature who has his heart set on a cherished goal.

Like this:

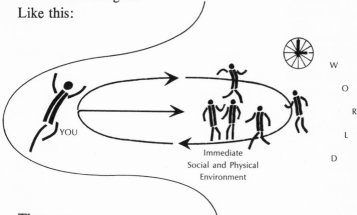

There you are.

You may be standing on a platform or sitting down at your desk behind closed doors with an associate. You may be in your shirt sleeves in the plant or at a directors' meeting. One person or hundreds may be listening. *It makes no difference.*

**When we speak with purpose, regardless of the social situation or the physical surroundings, the semantic techniques do not differ. The method remains the same.**

**All speech is public.**

**The label "Public Speaking" rates a public burial.**[1964]

If you will let this indubitable fact get under your skin and work for you, you will find that you can move from one purposive speaking situation to another with the ease with which you change shoes. In every moment of your purposive life, and especially in the freedom and ease of conversation under familiar circumstances, you can be in training for those situations that single you out and give you an opportunity for leadership.

Look at the last diagram again.

Notice now that when you use words, you are *related* to the immediate environment. You are talking to specific human beings at a particular time and a particular place. But the immediate relevant environment is part of a broader situation as a whole. A purposive situation is never encapsulated. Think of the businessman who restricts his attention to the immediate environment and closes his mind to competition—wherever it is! We live in the world. (Notice that the line which indicates connections within the immediate speaking situation is a broken line. And notice that the situation as a whole is *open—not closed.*)

Look now at Arrows 1, 2, and 3.

Arrows mean *process.* And process means change; sometimes predictable, sometimes not predictable.

Arrow 1 is your *output*—your words. This is planned strategy by which you hope to achieve your goal. This we shall call *feedforward.*

Arrow 2 is the response of your listeners. This response may be complete indifference. It may be totally unexpected. It may be verbal or nonverbal. Raised eyebrows or a shrug of the shoulders may be more expressive than words. You will look and *see;* you will listen and *hear.* You will perceive the consequences of your own words in every possible way. Vigilance is never lowered, even while you speak.

As you perceive this response, this is your *input* (and the output of your listeners.)

Now look at Arrow 3. Notice that it has deviated from planned strategy (from Arrow 1). This means that the response of your listeners (Arrow 2) which you perceive is such as to require corrective measures. You are now using *tactics* to stimulate attention, to minimize opposition, or perhaps to control and to make use of unexpected change. These corrective tactics we shall call the exercise of *feedback*.

**Feedforward is word-power; feedback is steersmanship. Together, as one cyclic process, we have Power-Steering with Words.**

Look again at the diagram.

Notice that the process is not one-way, not two-way, but cyclic—a speaking-listening-speaking continuum. This means that the power is never disconnected. The flow of energy is cyclic. You give and you receive and you give again, moving always toward your goal.

This means *dynamic* relatedness. The relationship between you and your listeners is cyclic.

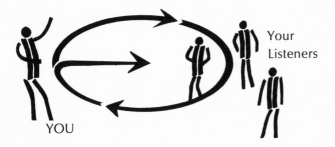

A cyclic relationship means that we have, not a disconnected series of words and actions, but a situation as a whole. And ceaseless process. Ceaseless change. Your words, your goal-seeking behavior, affect the relevant environment; but the relevant environment affects your behavior. The process is cyclic.

This dynamic situation is *unique,* and unique at every instant in time. This is a situation that has never been lived before and will never be lived again in precisely the same way. Time, the fourth dimension of life, calls for constant reassessment of and adaptation to the moving, changing, highly unpredictable scene.

You have questions? Of course!

*How shall we entertain this absolute uniqueness and yet maintain direction toward our goals?*

*How shall we control this interlocking process so that we can move in the direction of our goals?*

*How shall we maintain order—movement toward our goals—in a behavioral situation in which randomness is inevitable?*

*How shall we control and use change in the interest of our goals?*

**Nothing short of Power-Steering with Words is adequate.**

*Chapter II*

# Searchlight on Words

SEMANTICS HAS TAKEN ON *NEW DIMENSIONS*

I regard words as Manpower, Unlimited.

The greatest power at the service of man is *words*. To express our thoughts, even to our selves, would be impossible without words. Every word that was ever uttered was invented because someone had a use for it, a need for it, in order to reach out to another human being. And perhaps to say something that had never been said before.

Semantics has taken on new dimensions. Some years ago semantics might have been defined merely as the "science of signs"—the science of words. In 1942 the semanticist Charles Morris said that the study of signs must assume a

55

central place in the science of man. But I believe it is generally conceded today that, in order to know something about the science of words, it is necessary to know something about the science of man. Actually, the process is circular. Any knowledge of the one adds to our knowledge of the other.

In this book, I introduce the phrase *power-steering with words*. I have a use for it. I need it. This title has literal significance for me.

## WIENER'S *SEARCHLIGHT*

Power-steering means *control* of power. Norbert Wiener's research into the control mechanism in communication has turned a searchlight on the use of words in goal-seeking behavior.

From the title of Wiener's book, *Cybernetics, or Control and Communication in the Animal and the Machine,*[22] you know at once that he is interested in the analogy between man and the machine. The analogy is now being explored in many scientific areas, as well as under the inclusive term "bionics" (biology and electronics).[23] The interesting thing about the title is that Wiener is stressing, not the analogy as such, but the *control mechanism* in communication in both man and the machine. The control mechanism is *feedback*.

**In this context, I shall define feedback as a system of verbal controls that enables a speaker to correct the unfavorable consequences of his own words.**

In the title of Wiener's book, *Cybernetics* is equated with *Control and Communication in the Animal and the Machine*. The word "cybernetics" is derived from the Greek *kybernētikē,* which means "steersman."[24]

Obviously, the scope of cybernetics is much broader than

the scope of semantics. Cybernetics, as explicated by Wiener (and others),[25] is a technical subject that is underscored by mathematics. We are concerned here only with Operation Feedback, which has come to be the accepted method of control in human communication; and because we are goal-seeking creatures, our method of control will be underscored by steermanship—by Operation Feedback.

Cybernetics suggests that steering, Operation Feedback, is one of the most significant processes in both Man and the Machine, that the use of words is man's means by which he may supersede himself in his everyday life and become a dynamic force in the lives of others.

## THE *CYBERNETIC* APPROACH
## TO COMMUNICATION

The cybernetic approach to communication enables us to program movement toward a goal by the use of words. But the cybernetic approach does more. It makes it possible for us to entertain change and chance in the largely unpredictable human situation that involves the use of words. An understanding of the cyclic process that is characteristic of cybernetics should give us, not only increased power in the planning of verbal *strategy,* but also control of that power under pressure. It should enable us to use tactics that will monitor and correct unfavorable consequences of our own words.

An understanding of the cyclic process in the use of words should give us, not only increased power, but also the control of that power.

**Power is dynamic. It has consequences. And today power is regulated by precise evaluation of its consequences.**

57

If the consequences of power are unfavorable to the pre-conceived goal, something is done about the control of that power. Power is *steered*—in the direction of the goal. Today, even the automated machine will correct its own mistakes if the consequences of its power are adverse to a programmed goal.[42] The process is not two-way. The process is cyclic and self-corrective. Can man do less than the machine he invents?

Man is, to be sure, a self-correcting animal on the physiological level, but Power-Steering with Words requires *conscious* attention to the process. If the consequences of our words are detrimental to our goals, we may use incoming signals as new information to guide us in our future verbal output. The process is a cyclic continuum that comes to rest only when the desired goal-state is reached. Students who are familiar with cybernetics will understand the title *Power-Steering with Words* to mean just that.

## WHY MANPOWER, UNLIMITED?

There are several reasons why Manpower is unlimited.

We know that no person can achieve his complete potential. There is power left over and to spare.

At every moment in time, for each one of us, our words are the measure of our incompleteness. As we mature, the configuration of our incompleteness acquires new dimensions that make possible new and more demanding goals. The surge of life within us is the process of *becoming* what we may be, but this is an ideal never to be fully achieved. We are born to become, but we die striving, wanting, reaching—we are always a system in search of everything and anything that will augment our completeness.

If there is peace on earth, it is not that kind of peace that comes from complete self-realization. When we cease to

58

strive, too completely At Rest, our dreams are buried with us. The joy is in the struggle. We can have it no other way. We would have it no other way.

**The power within us is never exhausted.**

### "COMMUNICATION IS A *BINDER*"

There is another reason why the power within us is un-limited. It spreads in all directions! It is multi-dimensional. No less.

Every organization, whether it be a family or a nation, is held together by communication. The ability to transmit and receive and react to messages *makes* an organization. A hospital would fall apart without communication. The laundry, the kitchen, the laboratory, the nurses, the medical staff, the administration, maintenance—everything is syn-chronized to achieve a single purpose, the care of the patients. A railroad would fall apart without communication. Every organization, large or small, is *unified by a purpose,* but whatever the purpose is, the operations of the organization depend upon the use of words—thought, said, or written.

The human parts of an organization adhere—or separate —because of words. If the communication channels are blocked, or jammed, or otherwise disrupted, the organization suffers. When an organization runs smoothly, we may say, with Robert S. Scott, Associate Director of Government Re-lations, Aerospace Corporation, "Communication is a binder."

To be a member of an organization is to be a part of a patterned process in which every member has a stake. This means that there is a common goal. To put this in the lan-guage of Scott:[26]

**A purpose + a human being = a direction and a force.**

To reach a common goal requires the combined competencies of all members of an organization, not as separate units, mind you, but as interdependent units. Each member is a focal point, with his own connections both in the group and outside the group. This pooling of competencies in an organization is much more common than appears on the surface.

To say of a person that he has good connections is to rate him highly. Can you see your self as the center of your field, however circumscribed it may be, connected with others who are, in turn, connected with others, who are, in turn, connected with others? The human being who is *open* to such conections may avail himself of Manpower Unlimited.

To be open to such connections requires a well-organized, highly integrated character-structure, as well as the ability to enter into cross organization with the world. This happens, of course, in the communication process. The self is organized. The environment is organized. The highly integrated personality relates himself in cyclic cross organization —in a kind of dynamic superstructure—to others. Together, they become as one, in concerted action toward a common goal.

To say, then, that a person has good connections is to indicate that he has resources beyond himself.

That communication is binding is well understood. When I talk to you and you listen and when, as a result of our interchange, we move along productively toward a common goal, our words bind us together. This binding happens on a grand scale. Telephones, for instance, are linked in an international network. But the telephone is only the channel. It is man's voice that is the means; it is man's voice that is heard around the world.

**Man's voice may become a binding energy—on the grand scale.**

Perhaps you think that to speak of binding energy in the communication process is to take a flight into the unknown, into the unknowable. But the psychologist Floyd H. Allport tells us that the encounters in a cycle of an ongoing event can be regarded, not only as a unifying pattern, but also as units of energy. "Events as happenings in the physical world," he says, "always involve energies."[27] I'll buy that. When we are contributing members of a communication process—you and I—the cycle of energy is binding. I use your energy; you use mine! Communication is a giving and a receiving. This is one of the miracles of life. Ours to enjoy—and to use.

Think of yourself at home. Your thoughts are heavy and lethargic. You speak to your wife, or to your husband, and the world is changed. One person may affect another in ways truly mysterious. Nonverbal and verbal communication rebounds with incoming energy. Regardless of the word-form that the response takes, this incoming energy redirects your forces into channels that may have been hitherto unnoticed, unseen, perhaps even unknown.

As a communicator, you may be open to verbal stimuli that rekindle your very self. Speak to a child or to a student. The questions he or she raises will excite *your* curiosity. And steer you in new directions! This is *binding energy*. Wherever there is talk, the binding energy of all participants is power compounded. The process is not additive. It is generative of

61

something new, something different. The words that you hear yourself say seem not to belong to you, so surprisingly dynamic are they in their effects on others—*and on you!*

When we communicate, we give and we receive energy, the capacity to do work. We need food and water and sunlight and air to sustain life, thus to defer decay and to outwit entropy, at least temporarily. Just so, we need the ideas of others to revitalize our own resources. A two-way communication process could leave us both untouched. The cyclic communication process is at once the expenditure of force and the generator of force.

**In Power-Steering with Words, the cyclic binding energy of all participants is imponderable in its potential.**

Only an *open self*—perceptive and receptive—can engage in the cyclic communication process. The open self thinks of communication, not simply as a means of getting what he wants, but as a means of giving as well as of receiving. Communication is a kind of sharing. For those rare ones who will look and *see,* who will listen and *hear,* who will perceive in every possible human way, words are Manpower, Unlimited.

## "A WORD IS . . . THE SKIN OF A LIVING THOUGHT. . . ."

I would be remiss if I did not point out, too, that words have their limitations. Words have, of course, stability as public conveyors of information and ideas, but words sometimes take wing and leave meanings behind as we follow inspiration.

Words and the ideas they express have their own destinies. A new word—a new idea—has its own struggle for survival. Its fate depends on its compatibility with the established structure of ideas. And this is natural. "Wisdom" says Professor Otto Wirth, Dean of Arts and Sciences in Roosevelt University, "is the integration of the known and the unknown." For man, to know is not enough. The quest for more knowing is never-ending. A quest is a wanting; not only a thinking, but a feeling and a willing, as well.

When we think of words as Manpower, Unlimited, we know that this is at once our joy and our defeat. For even as we become, we realize more fully our insufficiency. What power we have is in the thrust of the self beyond the self. The search is eternal. To know more is to know our ignorance the better. There is a kind of anguish in the search—and even in the finding.

Words encompass what we are in our very incompleteness, and our words are always, it seems, inadequate—bare. We grasp what we know, or think we know, and put this knowledge into vessels we call words. But the meanings of these words are very like the color of the chameleon—changeable and apparently without permanence. Justice Oliver Wendell Holmes brilliantly described the changing nature of words in a single poetic sentence:

A word is not a crystal, transparent and unchanged, it is the skin of a living thought and may vary greatly in color and content according to the circumstances and the time in which it is used.

The changing meaning of words is one of the natural hazards in communication. This obstacle may, in some instances, be circumvented. In other instances, the obstacle itself may be used as a force to help us reach our goals. This happens when your meaning and my meaning somehow coalesce to generate something more than either of us could project or experience alone.

63

*Power,* as everyone knows, may be used as a beneficent binder, but it may also be used to threaten and to destroy. Power-Steering with Words is ours to use, first, in the recreation of our selves, but, more especially, as a binder by which to achieve the common goals of mankind.

*Chapter III*

# Steer That Power!

## *POWER,* THE WORD

What does the word "power" mean when we are thinking, not about electronic hardware, but about a human being bent on the accomplishment of a goal by the use of words? What does it mean when we are concerned with Manpower?

*Power,* for us, means the "strength" to stay with it. To resist opposing forces. To move strategically toward the pre-determined goal with all the energy we can muster.

*Power,* for us, means also the generation of force, of energy, by which to counter opposition, by which to entertain the new and the unexpected in such a way as to turn it, if possible, to our advantage.

**Power is the strength to resist force; yet power is the dynamic generator of force by which to move toward a goal.**

*Feedforward* is the semantic device that provides power as strength to resist opposing forces and yet to move forward *strategically* toward a goal.

*Feedback* may be positive or negative. Positive feedback is feedforward without check, without controls. Negative feedback is the tactical control mechanism that counteracts unfavorable consequences of positive feedback.

**Feedforward and feedback, together, establish and maintain stability in the cyclic goal-seeking communication process.**

I know. When you speak under challenging circumstances, your heart pounds, your breathing becomes shallow and fast, your voice quavers, your hands shake, and your knees rattle. This happens to all of us. We call it "tension," and hate ourselves for our "weakness."

*It is far better to designate it properly as "tensile strength" and use it as a positive force in goal-directed behavior.*

Dr. Abraham Mannes Max, one-time professor of the "hard" sciences, and now researcher (still in the hard stuff) for the Radio Corporation of America, defines tensile strength as the point of greatest resistance to force—before whatever it is disintegrates, before it goes to pieces.

At what point will you disintegrate? At what point will you go to pieces? Is your tensile strength high or low?

Without doubt, you can shadowbox in two-way communication without getting hurt. But when you have to tangle with a genuine and vigorous opponent, at what point will you blow your top, or split a gut, or fold?

In the communciation process, tensile strength is at once the dignity and the power of self-maintenance, of strategic self-realization. It is the steadiness, the sturdiness, the relentlessly stubborn refusal of man to soften to the punch. For us, it is the use of manpower against opposing forces in the competitive struggle for self-realization.

Power-Steering with Words is not something that you can learn in "ten easy lessons." It asks for the moral courage to be prepared to be unprepared—to meet head-on with change and chance in the risky unpredictable human situation. It asks for tenacity, stamina, boldness, spirit, *nerve* to achieve something that must be won by interdependence and not by independence.

Sometimes it seems as if we must explode under the pressure. Sometimes the lid does come off. Who has not said, "What price glory!" Better this than flaccid impotence. Why do you suppose you are scared stiff when you face a mad dog? Fear is nature's way of making it possible for you to run like hell or to climb a tree. The nervous system is your most powerful ally. Trust it.

Kurt Goldstein, a psychiatrist and neurologist in New York City, has this to say of the nervous system:

The organism has definite potentialities, and because it has them it has the need to actualize or realize them. The fulfillment of these needs represents the self-actualization of the organism.[28]

Goldstein assumes only one "drive," the drive for self-actualization, the drive for making *actual* the potential of the self. But here is the point that must be stressed:

67

*Normal behavior corresponds to a continual change of tension, of such a kind that over and over again that state of tension is reached which enables and impels the organism to actualize itself in further activities, according to its nature.*[29]

In the sick individual, Goldstein contends, the tendency is to *remove* any arising tension. In sound life, the tendency is, rather, toward the process of *formation* of a certain level of tension—a level that makes further activity possible.

Tensile strength is the measure of our power to resist force. In the communication process, this means that we cannot easily be pushed around. We will maintain our strategy in the face of opposition. This we associate with feed-forward, and when tactical adaptation is required, Operation Feedback provides the flexibility that enables us to remake our selves and our world in preferred design.

This is not to imply that the communication process is a waltz. It is struggle. It is exacting. It requires the greatest vigilance. It is the kind of struggle that healthy human beings call *life*.

When you stand before an audience, struggle though you must to present your case, I can promise you this: the minute you begin to speak, something happens to you. The opposing forces (real or imagined) suddenly take the form of human beings—like you!—who are willing and ready to sit there and listen to you. You look at them. You see, not a sea of faces, but eyes. You have established contact with them! Somehow you respond, intuitively and warmly. That deep sigh that comes from your innermost being is the physical sign that you have made it.

You will not go to pieces!

You are now in control.

Tensile strength is augmented by cyclic incoming dynamic energy.

To say this differently, feedforward and feedback are now in operation, and Power-Steering with Words is effected.

To summarize:

FEEDFORWARD

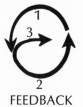

FEEDBACK

Tensile strength and dynamic energy are mutually complementary. Inseparable and together, both sustain life. Just so, feedforward (Arrow 1) and feedback (Arrow 3)—the two semantic devices we shall use—are mutually complementary. Both feedforward and feedback are essential to goal-directed behavior that involves the use of words.

FEEDFORWARD and FEEDBACK = PS/W

Inseparable and together, feedforward and feedback are in cyclic *trans*action. Communication becomes an *action* that *crosses over*. There is cross organization between speaker and listeners. The situation as a whole becomes a field in which speaker and environment—together—form a superstructure. Feedforward and feedback may thus become the components of Manpower, Unlimited, whenever words are involved.

## INTRODUCTION OF THE WORD *"FEEDFORWARD"*

When a new idea is born, it is sometimes necessary to invent a new word to signify the idea. *Feedforward* is such an idea. I. A. Richards coined the word and used it at the Eighth Conference on Cybernetics, held in New York City, on March 15 and 16, 1951, in a talk entitled "Communication Between Men: The Meaning of Language."[30]

By now, you have your own definition of feedforward, because I have been feeding forward to you intentionally. Feedforward means just what you think it means. If I say something that activates you in such a way that your thoughts jump ahead of me, I have fed forward. Otherwise not.

If I say to you *Are you hungry?* and you answer *Yes* or *No,* I have not fed forward. But if you should say *No, I'm not hungry, but I'll sit with you while you eat* or *Come on, I'll buy you a hamburger,* I have fed forward. Because, you see, I want something. And not just information. My purpose is to find eating-company. I do not like to eat—or drink!—alone.

When we feed forward strategically because we want something, it is imperative that we evaluate the consequences of our words. If feedforward meets with an obstacle, *the obstacle is information.* If feedforward is successful, *the success, too, is information.* As we move through life, we learn by trial and error what strategy is useful with specific listeners and under specific circumstances.

If, when I ask *Are you hungry?* you say *No* period, you may be sure that next time I will try another strategy. Or someone else!

In his talk before the Conference on Cybernetics, as recorded in *Transactions,* Richards is thinking about feedforward as a means of teaching (transmitting knowledge) and learning (gaining knowledge). "Teaching" and "learning" are two terms that I like to hyphenate: teaching-learning. A teacher learns; a student teaches. The process is cyclic as is every communication process. Where there is change in *any* aspect of the situation as a whole, there is change in *every* aspect of the situation as a whole.

Richards seems to be telling about the idea of feedforward for the first time, for he admits his difficulty in finding the right words to explain it clearly. But from what he does say, it is quite clear that feedforward is possible only by the use of verbal patterns ("enclosure series," he calls them) that are both cohesive and progressive. Only such a verbal pattern will catch up the listener or reader in its movement and set up expectations of what is to follow.[31]

Richards says, too, that there must be some kind of relationship between feedforward and feedback.[32] And there is, as you will soon see, in PS/W.

**The word "feedforward" symbolizes activity that feeds a verbal pattern forward. The verbal pattern represents the strategy by which a communicator hopes to reach a goal. The process is such that, once the pattern is started, the listener or reader is able to anticipate what is to follow.**

You want something. You have a plan, a program, a strat-

71

egy. You must enlist the interest and the collaboration of others. So you speak to them. Like this:

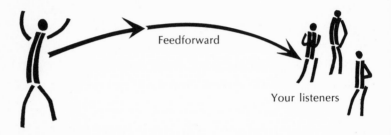

Feedforward

Your listeners

Do you go into details about your project? No! You shave down the strategy until it is as bare as bones. What is left is stark essentials. What is left is a verbal pattern.

Pattern is one of the words that I have already used, but without explicit definition. Though I have fed forward, I must now explain a fundamental semantic procedure that is comparable to programming in the computer processes: pattern-making.

## *PATTERN*, THE WORD

Everyone has used a pattern at one time or another. A woman will use a dress pattern; a boy, a mechanical toy pattern. A designer of anything, from a barn to a cathedral, will make a pattern.

Patterns are called by various names. The architect may call his pattern a blueprint; the businessman, a graph; the accountant, a financial report; the dentist, a model; the scientist, a mathematical model; the artist, a sketch; the computer engineer, a program; etc.

Regardless of the kind of pattern that you have used, you know that it is made up of *parts* that, together, make something *whole*. Each of the parts is essential to the whole. Lose or eliminate one part and you are left with a puzzle. Regardless of your understanding of the separate parts, the pattern is worthless unless you know how to put the parts together.

And this is as good a place as any to define "analysis" as we use the term in this context. Those who think analysis is the operation of breaking something to pieces to discover what is on the inside of it delude themselves.

**Analysis of anything—an object, an event, an idea, a problem—is the discovery of its pattern. It is not enough to discover the parts; it is essential, also, to understand the relationship between the parts.**

Anyone can pull a machine apart. The trick is to put the machine together again. And for this it is necessary to understand its pattern.

Here is the important point:

**The parts of the pattern must be put together in invariable order to make something whole—whatever that something is. To juxtapose the parts of a pattern is to destroy its value. The parts of a pattern are cohesive. They fit together like the parts of a jigsaw puzzle.**

Anyone whose purpose it is to make a blouse must be careful how he puts the parts together. Random connections are disastrous. Did you ever put a sleeve in backwards? I did.

We can find no better definition of the word "pattern" than that used by Norbert Wiener in *The Human Use of Human Beings:*

One of the most interesting aspects of the world is that it can be considered to be made up of *patterns*. A pattern is essentially an arrangement. It is characterized by the order of the elements of

73

which it is made, rather than by the intrinsic nature of these elements. Two patterns are identical if their relational-structure can be put into a one-to-one correspondence, so that to each term of the one, there corresponds a term of the other; and that to each relation of order between the several terms of one, there corresponds a similar relation of order between the corresponding terms of the other.[33]

This precise definition is well worth understanding. What Wiener is saying is this: If a tissue-paper dress pattern is put on a table and the cut-out cloth parts of the dress are placed on top of the tissue-paper parts, and if there is complete correspondence between the two—part for part and notch for notch (to indicate the connections)—then the two patterns are identical, even though one is made of tissue-paper and the other of velvet. What is important is that the parts correspond and that the relationship between the parts corresponds.

*A pattern . . . is characterized by the order of the elements of which it is made, rather than by the intrinsic nature of these elements.*

This definition means that a blueprint of a cathedral and the finished cathedral have identical patterns if the cathedral is built in accordance with the blueprint, part for part and order for order, even though you can put one in your pocket, whereas the other can hold thousands of worshippers.

**A pattern is an arrangement.**

When two patterns are identical, they are isomorphic; that is, they are equal in form. Equal in structure. Equal in pattern. The words "form," "structure," and "pattern" are used synonymously in this book. I prefer the word "pattern" to the others because everyone who has ever used a pattern knows without being told that the pattern is made up of parts that *must be put together in invariable order*.

"Isomorphic" (say it ice-o-mor'fik) is a very useful word. We need it. It is a short cut for many words and is basic to the logic of communication, as you will see.

The question *Are you logical?* confronts you in every argument. This question must be answered.

When are you logical?

**When a verbal pattern is isomorphic with an actual pattern —a "real" pattern in the world—the verbal pattern is not only logical, it is also true.**[34]

Such a verbal pattern is a statement of fact.

## THE *VERBAL PATTERN* IS A LOGICAL CONSTRUCT

To speak of a verbal pattern as a logical construct is to speak of a statement that is consistent, first, with basic assumptions (expressed or implied) and, second, consistent within the thinking process itself.

We have already said that a verbal pattern that is isomorphic with an actual pattern in nature is both true and logical. Such a pattern is, of course, subject to verification and accurately designates *what is* or *what was*.

But we are concerned with something more than assertions that are subject to proof. Because we are goal-seeking creatures, the logical construct frequently looks to the *future*. Such thinking may be said to be logical because it is consistent with what is known, because it uses what methods of prediction are available, and because it projects from these evidential bases a plan of action that is calculated to move in the direction of a new state of affairs, *i.e.*, a goal-state.

Where human operations are involved, such a projected logical construct cannot be said to be true (or false) because the essential operations of the plan are not subject to complete control. If the plan does, indeed, terminate as hoped, even then the logical construct cannot be said to be true because there is no way of knowing what fortuitous circumstances have intervened in the operational process.

**The logical construct may be said to be both true and logical when it is isomorphic with an actual pattern in nature. Such a logical construct is a statement of fact.**

**The logical construct that has a future reference and projects human operations may be consistent and valid but it cannot be said to be true. Such a logical construct is a statement of opinion.**

## WHEN WE MAKE A VERBAL PATTERN, WE ARE DOING WHAT COMES NATURAL

Remember that our past experience is not a chaotic assortment of odds and ends. Remember, too, that the structured self represents our input from the day of birth. But remember, also, that no thing, no word, no action, no event, has significance for us unless we can relate it to something in the pattern of our experience that already has meaning for us.

There is evidence from all the biological sciences that man is a patternmaking animal. The nervous system is just that—a system. And a self-organizing system! A perceived stimulus finds its place in an hierarchical structure, so that ultimately, ideally, a unified idea-system is at the peak of the pyramid.

We shall be going into this subject to explore its usefulness in the creative advance into novelty through PS/W, but it is important to point out here and now that the quality of your *input* and *storage* of information must necessarily affect the quality of your *output*. Computer engineers are quite aware of this, so much so that they have invented a word for it. "Gigo" (say it guy-go) is the word. Short for "garbage in, garbage out."

So, if you have lived the good life and paid conscious attention to the process of intake and storage of information, you are an invaluable man or woman—wherever you are. Your thinking takes the form of logical constructs. When faced with the necessity to make a decision, you manipulate and control your stored information through logical calculations in the interest of your goals. *You can make up your mind*—and know why. Because it is organized. *Structured!*

## THE VERBAL PATTERN *MOVES* UNDER ITS OWN STEAM

If you do not feed forward, no one knows what you are driving at. If you do feed forward, your listeners or readers are likely to jump ahead of you and anticipate what is coming. The reason is that the parts of a verbal pattern hang together in invariable order to make something whole. A pattern is an *arrangement*. To refer again to Wiener's definition, a pattern is "characterized by the order of the elements . . . rather than by the intrinsic nature of those elements."

Since the verbal pattern is made up of parts that hang together according to a principle of organization—an arrangement—the pattern determines what is to follow. There is nothing for the speaker to memorize. And once started, listeners are caught up in the arrangement. The verbal pattern is both cohesive and progressive. It hangs together—yet it *moves*, because the parts are dynamically related to each other.

Here are some of the molds into which verbal patterns are likely to fall:

Time pattern
Space pattern
Sectional pattern
Cause-to-effect pattern
Means-to-end pattern

## CHARLES MORRIS GIVES US THE SEMANTIC DEVICE BY WHICH TO MAKE VERBAL PATTERNS

Morris revived the word "formator" in his *Signs, Language and Behavior* to fill a semantic gap.[35]

Formators are terms that establish form. Formators are terms that epitomize strategy in goal-seeking behavior. Formators are terms that are used in order to make verbal patterns that are both cohesive and progressive.

None of my current dictionaries includes the word "formator," but the *New English Dictionary on Historical Principles* (1901) defines "formator" as an obsolete and rare word meaning "a person or thing that forms; a creator, maker." The last example cited is dated 1794.

Morris defines *formator* (say it form'-a-tor) as "a word that creates form." He tells us that the only function of the formator is to systemize—to organize—a verbal communication *so that the responses of a percipient are organized.* A listener or reader cannot jump ahead of the communicator unless his responses are organized.

We must, then, use formators in order to feed forward. We must, then, use formators in order to set up expectations of what is to follow in our listeners and readers. We must, then, use formators in order to make verbal patterns. Formators are, therefore, related by a principle of organization: time, space, sectional, cause to effect, means to end, etc.

Morris's title, *Signs, Language and Behavior*, makes use of sectional formators. He tells us by this title that the book is in three parts and, *in general*, what each of these three parts will cover. He tells us, also, by this title, the order in which these three parts will be developed. If we want to know more, all we have to do is look at the Table of Contents, in which we will find secondary and even tertiary formators.

**Formators are general terms, big terms, economical terms.**[36]

Formators will tell you nothing beyond how a book, an article, or an oral communication is systemized. They will set up expectations as to what you will find in the work, but that is all they can do. Their only function is to establish the *form*—the pattern—of a communication. Nothing more.

## THE *TIME* PATTERN

The simplest verbal pattern is the *time* arrangement. Lincoln's Gettysburg Address falls into a time pattern.

Past: "Four score and seven years ago. . . ."

Present: "We have come here to dedicate. . . ."

Future: ". . . that this nation . . . shall not perish from the earth."

*Past*, *present*, and *future* are formators. Together they make a verbal time pattern. Within the frame of reference (the Civil War) these formators make a cohesive and progressive strategy for the development of that address. Once started, *the pattern moves*. Listeners are caught up in the momentum of time. Their responses are organized, systemized.

Lincoln spoke for about three minutes. He could have

used precisely the same verbal pattern to speak for three hours. He could have used precisely the same verbal pattern to write a three-volume work. A pattern is a skeleton. Bare. We dress it up in words to keep it warm. The pattern tells us nothing beyond what form the Address will take. But it represents our thinking—our strategy—regardless of the depth of the development.

You don't have to be a Lincoln to make a verbal pattern that flows. When Wendy was about four, I asked her to tell me about the family trip up the river. She launched into her story:

"The first thing we did was to get into our car and go down to the dock. Then we all went to the bathroom and then we got into the boat. Then we rode for a long time and ate our lunch and then we all got off the boat and went to the bathroom. Then we went back on the boat and mama lost her hat. We had to fish around for it. And then we ate again and then we all got off the boat——"

"Yes, yes, Wendy," I interrupted. "I know. And then you all went to the bathroom."

Wendy had fed forward. And so had I. My responses were organized. Wendy had set up expectations of what was to follow. How could I miss? But I did.

**We can never predict exactly the consequences of our own words. Nor can we predict exactly what another person will say.**

Wendy looked at me soberly, shook her head, and drawled, "No, Gram, there wasn't any."

I was interested in knowing how she had remembered all the details. (And believe me, it was a long story.)

"Oh," she said. "That was easy. First this and then that."

STEER THAT POWER!

Not only had Wendy made a pattern, but she had recognized the fact that it was a time pattern. And that it was easy! The parts of a time pattern stick together like glue and they keep moving. It is impossible to get lost. And no amount of opposition can undermine the strategy.

Had Wendy stopped in the middle of the narration, I would have asked, "And then what, Wendy?" In the time pattern, the communicator transmits the nature of the dynamic relationship between the parts by the use of words that designate time. Words such as "first," "then," etc., cause listeners to expect (anticipate) further developments in time.

## THE *SPACE* PATTERN

In my work with industrial engineers, I found that the *space* pattern of formators was extremely useful in explicating economy of time and motion.

Every housewife has looked speculatively at the old sofa with a view to pushing it from here to there. Her mind is busy with a space pattern. An interior decorator is concerned almost entirely with space arrangements that have to be designated by words.

No one can get lost when the communication process is stabilized by a space pattern. The verbal map, if correct, stays with the territory. The listener has no trouble staying with the communicator. Nor does he have difficulty in anticipating what form the narration will take. Words such as "here," "there," "up," "down," "north," "south," "left," "right," etc., will catch up the listener and carry him along.

## THE *SECTIONAL* PATTERN

The sectional pattern is useful when we want to look at different facets of the same thing. The *different facets* make

81

up the parts; the *same thing* is the frame of reference, the whole under which the parts fall.

I set up a sectional pattern like this:

*Education:* Public Schools and Private Schools

This is a working-title, not a literary title. It is the title that the author or speaker *works* from. It prescribes and delimits the scope of his development.

"Education" is the frame of reference; "Public Schools" and "Private Schools" are the primary formators.

The terms "Public Schools" and "Private Schools" are the primary formators because they are the most general terms in the pattern. (The development cannot go beyond these terms in scope.) They are big enough to include secondary formators. In this case, we can use identical secondary formators under the two primary formators: Faculty, Curriculum, Methods, etc. These secondary formators will require supportive tertiary formators. What we have, then, is a verbal pattern that takes the form of a pyramid that rises from the least general, to the more general, and finally, to the most general (as is the case in all verbal patterns).

Here, then, is the sectional pattern:

WORKING–TITLE: *Education*: Public Schools and Private Schools
A. Public Schools
    1. Faculty
        (a) Requirements
            (i) Academic
            (ii) Experience
    2. Curriculum
        (a) Academic

   (b) Vocational
  3. Methods
   (a) Standard
 B. Private Schools
  1. Faculty
   (a) Requirements
    (i) Academic
    (ii) Experience
  2. Curriculum
   (a) Academic requirements
   (b) Electives
  3. Methods
   (a) Variable

Here is the important question to ask in the case of the sectional pattern: *Is this pattern open or closed?*

If the pattern takes in every aspect within the frame of reference, the pattern is *closed;* if it does not, it is *open.*

This working-title establishes an open sectional pattern because the major formators do not cover every aspect of education. Informal education is omitted. The open sectional pattern is very provocative. The "mind" darts in all directions to supplement the pattern. And since everything within a frame of reference is related to everything else in it, such elements as are *not* included in the pattern illuminate those dimensions that *are* included. For instance, I heard it said of a certain man that he never interrupted his education to get a degree. A more inclusive working-title would be:

*Education:* Formal and Informal

Under Formal, then, both public and private schools would fall logically. Under Informal, such secondary formators as travel, reading, on-the-job training, etc., would fall logically.

When you answer the question *Is the sectional pattern open or closed?* the frame of reference is illuminated in ways you can hardly anticipate. Ideas are generated that amplify your thinking.

**Closure is accomplished only by completing a pattern that is otherwise incomplete.**

The sectional pattern, whether open or closed, thus becomes far more meaningful to you.

The sectional pattern may also be used to compare two things, two systems, etc., which have similarities in their patterns but which yet exhibit differences. Such a verbal pattern is an analogical sectional pattern.

**Analogy means limited structural correspondence.**

The great analogy of our time is that between man and the machine, between the human organism and the electronic computer. The inept phrase "the mechanical brain" attests to this analogy; nevertheless, the analogy holds, for there is a limited structural correspondence between the two. Both, for instance, use feedback. The important thing to be stressed in such a comparison is the degree in which the structural similarity holds and the aspects in which it does not hold.[116]

The science of bionics has shown that the exploration of the analogy between biology and electronics extends knowledge of both systems. Engineers can control data and repeat operations in an electronic computer in a way that psychologists and physiologists cannot in the human body. Biological scientists are, therefore, extremely interested in the findings

84

and mathematical computations of engineers. Conversely, engineers use the physiologists' studies of the human brain to discover new ways by which to refine and amplify their mechanical systems.

The analogical sectional pattern has great utility. Perhaps there is no other verbal pattern in which design—pattern—plays so important a role in the advance of science. And, for that matter, in the advance of knowledge in social areas.

The businessman can, for instance, explore the question *Why is Branch A losing money and Branch B making money when they seem to be similar operations?* The answer to this question must be found in a comparison of similarities and differences in the two systems. And it is highly probable that both systems will benefit by the analogical investigation.

**Wherever comparison of two systems is essential to the analysis of a problem, the analysis turns on the investigation of similarities and differences in the structure, in the patterns, of the two systems.**

The sectional pattern has neither the cohesiveness nor the progressiveness of the time and the space patterns. The sections are relatively independent of each other. They find their unity within the frame of reference. In the analogy of Man and the Machine, the frame of reference may be Self-Organizing Systems, or better, perhaps, Bionics. In the case of Branch A and Branch B, the frame of reference is the corporate body that operates them, the industrial organization.

The frame of reference of the sectional verbal pattern is, at the same time, inclusive and exclusive. Such things as belong within the frame of reference may be included. Such things as do not belong within the frame of reference are irrelevant, and are therefore excluded. For this reason, it is

85

necessary always to indicate the frame of reference in the sectional pattern.

The sectional pattern has many uses. It is, for example, indispensable to a business organization, which, of necessity, must examine the operations of its departments (each distinct but all within the same frame of reference). That the sectional pattern is used as a logical construct is attested by computers that are programmed to make the same logical distinctions that a businessman must make on the verbal level.[37]

You don't have to be an electronics engineer to make a sectional pattern. When Pamie was five years old, she turned to Wendy, then four, and Jill, then six, and said, "Grandma's hands make wonderful spoons." A simple analogical pattern! Grandma's hands are shaped like spoons, but they are different, of course. Both hands and spoons are so *structured* as to be useful in making meat balls.

When we make a verbal pattern, we are simply doing what comes naturally, it seems.

## THE *CAUSE–TO–EFFECT* PATTERN

The *cause-to-effect* verbal pattern designates the *If this, then necessarily that* logical construct. If the verbal logical construct accurately represents a pattern in nature, the verbal pattern and the actual pattern are isomorphic and the statement is both true and logical.

When the cause-to-effect verbal pattern accurately represents a recurrent relationship in nature, it is trustworthy when it is necessary for us to make predictions. The *If this, then necessarily that* relationship is the mainstay of knowledge.

But the cause-to-effect verbal pattern is sometimes used when the relationship might be more properly expressed as

86

*If this, then probably, or maybe, that.* In human affairs, can we go beyond this? As Professor Anton Carlson of the University of Chicago was wont to say, "We yust don't know."

I recall an instance in which an executive was discussing a problem in his canning plant. There was spoilage. It is, of course, possible to investigate probable causes of spoilage in the laboratory. A series of tests was made and the conclusion was reached that there was an imperfection in the sealing of the lid of the can. This executive could say on the basis of repeatable and controllable operations *The present method of sealing cans is imperfect and is the cause of spoilage* (undesirable effect).

This logical construct can be tested; it can be shown to be either true or false. If true, it is a bona fide cause-to-effect relationship. Testing is fine, when it can be done. But, more often than not, it cannot be done. Many of the problems we face are not subject to precise investigation because we cannot control either data or operations. We cannot put a race riot under the microscope, and we cannot figure it out mathematically. Nor is there repeatability in the process of investigation. We must, therefore, be satisfied with imputed cause-to-effect verbal patterns in many instances. Because there is no way to attack a problem short of an attack on causes, we must, in these cases, *attribute probable causes* to an undesirable effect. Where we cannot determine causes experimentally, we ascribe probable causes as an initial point of departure in the hope that further investigation will sharpen our understanding of the problematical situation.

We cannot dispense with untestable cause-to-effect patterns. But we can and should differentiate sharply between the bona fide causal relationship and the imputed causal relationship. In the one case we deal with fact; in the other,

87

opinion. Perhaps informed opinion, but *always* opinion—because, where human beings are concerned, *all* the facts can never be in. But we are obliged to leap beyond the facts when we are faced with a pressing human problem. We cannot sit down and say *We can't be sure.*

Power-Steering with Words makes use of both bona fide and imputed causal relationships. The user of words handles himself differently in each case. When dealing with a bona fide causal construct, he maintains his position rigidly. He cannot deviate from a construct that is demonstrably true and logical. But when dealing with an imputed causal relationship, he is open and receptive to other opinions.

**An opinion is always open-end and subject to revision on the basis of incoming information.**

## THE *MEANS–TO–END* PATTERN

In a problematical situation, the cause-to-effect pattern tells us why we are having trouble. The *means-to-end* verbal pattern is the strategy calculated to rectify the undesirable effect. Obviously, it is necessary to know the causes of trouble (an undesirable effect) before we can attempt to get rid of it.

In the problem-solving situation we have a two-stage operation.

The first stage is to analyze the problem. This takes the form of a cause-to-effect logical structure.

*Cause*: Imperfect sealing. *Effect*: Spoilage.

This is a working-title. Notice that the working-title is "economical" (to use Morris's sharp term) in that it tells *everything,* and yet *nothing,* about the details. It gives us the formators, and it gives us, also, the principle of organization (cause to effect). This working-title meets all the requirements, therefore, of the dynamic verbal pattern.

The second stage is to solve the problem. The solution takes the form of a means-to-end pattern.

*Means*: Correction of imperfect sealing. *End*: No spoilage.

Again, this is the working-title—the title from which we proceed to develop strategy. The working-title is simply the summation of formators. Nothing more.

Again, notice that the working-title is economical in that it makes a place for everything we will say and yet tells nothing about the *how*—nothing about the details. Again, it gives the principle of organization (means to end). Again, this meets all the requirements of the dynamic verbal pattern.

Let me set up this verbal pattern for you because this is the formula you will have to use every time you are faced with a problem.

We cannot avoid penetration to the causes of trouble if we want to get rid of the trouble. Too many of us set up a goal and head for it without so much as a glance at the present state of affairs. To penetrate to the present state of affairs is to find the causes that give rise to it.

The two-stage strategy is indispensable to PS/W in the face of a problematical situation. No decision can be reached about the means of achieving a desirable goal-state until the present state is analyzed.

PROBLEM: *Cause*: Imperfect sealing; *Effect*: Spoilage.
SOLUTION: *Means*: Correction of Imperfect sealing; *End*: No spoilage.

89

*1. Problem
   **a. Cause: Imperfect sealing
      ***(1)
      ↓     etc.
   **b. Effect: Spoilage
      ***(1)
           etc.
*2. Solution
   **a. Means: Correction of imperfect sealing
      ***(1)
      ↓     etc.
   **b. End: No spoilage
      ***(1)
           etc.

I have indicated the primary, secondary, and tertiary formators by asterisks. In this case, it will be the tertiary formators that provide for the *specific* informative supportive statements.

Let me interpolate here an analysis of this complex verbal pattern. Because the primary formators are Problem and Solution, we have here a closed sectional pattern. Notice that the secondary formators under Problem are related as cause to effect; those under Solution are related as means to end. The pattern as a whole gets its name from the principle of organization of the *primary* formators (hence, in this case, the pattern is sectional). In general, secondary formators and tertiary formators may be related in any way that suits the purpose of the communicator. But in the case of Problem and Solution, the secondary formators are those given above.

My friend, the canner, had no difficulty at all in proceeding from his bona fide cause-to-effect pattern to the means by which to get rid of his trouble. All that was required, of course, was to attack the cause; that is, to rectify the imperfection in the sealing of the cans. The correction was made in the laboratory. A pilot run of the result showed no spoilage. The experiment was repeated again and again by qualified researchers with identical results.

In this particular case, the means-to-end hypothesis can be converted into a cause-to-effect pattern (*If this, then necessarily that*). The correction *caused* the elimination of the spoilage. But this is rarely if ever the case when human beings are involved. You and I do not live in a laboratory. The problems we face in our everyday lives are not scientific problems. The solution, in such a case, must take the form of a means-to-end pattern.

Students are frequently confused about the distinction between the cause-to-effect and the means-to-end patterns.

First, the bona fide causal relationship designates a recurrent pattern or, at least, a relationship in which both data and operations are subject to control. The point of reference of the causal pattern is *right now with a backward look*. And the result is a demonstrable fact, at that date.

The means-to-end hypothesis looks to the *future*, and where human beings are concerned, the future is far from predictable. It is *opinion*.

It is true, the cause-to-effect *imputed* relationship is also opinion, but, again, it looks *backward to causes*, whereas, the means-to-end hypothesis looks always to the future.

Concerning, now, the means-to-end pattern in goal-seeking behavior, data are not controllable and operations are not repeatable. The means-to-end hypothesis can never be proved to be true or false, because all the relevant facts can never be in.

As John Dewey points out in *Logic: The Theory of Inquiry*, even if the desired goal does ensue, we have no way of proving what made it happen.[38] Any number of fortuitous circumstances may have intervened to alter the course of events about which we know nothing!

I remember sitting with a group of company executives who were discussing a merchandising problem. The end in view was to increase profits in the foreign market. Everyone was, of course, agreed on the desired goal. But each one had a different opinion about how to proceed. One argued for an advertising campaign; another, for diversification of products; another, for increased sales force, etc. No two agreed on procedure. Eventually a compromise decision was reached.

A compromise decision is sensible in a means-to-end project. (Compromise would be witless, of course, when the fate of the means-to-end project could be settled in a laboratory or by the computers.) When the procedure is a matter of opinion, every sane person will *listen* to everyone else. The compromise decision in the case cited was implemented and the profits of the firm increased beyond expectations. But how could the executives know that the attainment of the goal was the consequence of their means-to-end strategy— and of that strategy alone? What about the general state of the economy? What about the competition? A competitor on the other side of the world might have dropped dead for all they knew. And what about the random happenings over which no one has control?

The means-to-end strategy is an opinion because it involves human beings and because it looks to the future. There is always an element of risk—even of gamble—in the means-to-end verbal pattern. The means-to-end hypothesis might be called a "speculative model." No one has said this better than Harold D. Lasswell:

Speculative models . . . [make] no claim of "inevitability". . . . Events in the future are not knowable with absolute certainty in advance; they are partly probable and partly chance. Developmental constructs are aids in the total task of clarifying goals, noting trends, and estimating future possibilities. . . .[39]

Yet the means-to-end strategy is not a shot in the dark. In the fluid world, it is our life line. It is based, always, on the information available, on statistical trends, and on carefully planned imputed logical constructs. But we know that an opinion is not right or wrong, true or false. An opinion is only better or worse, depending on the relevance, the inclusiveness and the quality of the evidence that supports it.

If the means-to-end strategy is so risky, how, then, shall we proceed to program action toward a goal?

Those who have lived the good life, those whose input and storage of relevant information over the years has been a conscious as well as an unconscious process, will find appropriate alternatives in the face of a problem and decide, ultimately, on a means-to-end hypothesis that is most likely to advance toward a desired state of affairs. Every means-to-end hypothesis is just that—a guess, a hunch, a hope. Every means-to-end hypothesis is a blueprint of action toward a goal-state. When that goal-state is achieved, the communicator has effected his desired change—change in a preferred design. He has, in short, created a desired *actual* construct.

In *Human Nature and Conduct*, John Dewey states that the means-to-end hypothesis is always open-end—always

93

tentative and subject to revision in the light of incoming information. He advises us to set up a series of *immediate* ends, or short-term goals, instead of a long-term ironclad strategy.

The means-to-end pattern becomes, in this way, a series of *What nexts?*—one small specific step at a time. Before each successive step, Dewey says, it is necessary to look around and appraise the actual state of affairs with respect to the projected end-in-view. What he is saying, of course, is that the means-to-end pattern is risky and that the strategy should, therefore, be subject to correction on the basis of change and chance, and certainly on the basis of new information.[40]

In life, aren't we always trying to go from *here* to *there*? This is the very meaning of life. Human beings are *purposive* creatures. But I have known persons who have knocked themselves out trying for an impossible long-term goal in the face of circumstances over which they had no control whatsoever.

Although the means-to-end verbal pattern is the second stage of the problem-solution situation, it is also man's invitation to life. We utilize the means-to-end pattern when we are inspired to reach out beyond our selves into the more. But even here, is it not necessary to know where we are (*and why!*) before we get going? Sometimes we skip the preliminary investigation of the *status quo* in our impatience to advance toward new goals. If we expect to change the present state of affairs, it is necessary to understand that state of affairs. Why don't we like it? What's wrong with it? And why? *How did it get that way?* When we are able to set up a verbal pattern that describes the causes of the present undesirable *effects*, we are in a position to attack those causes by the projection of a means-to-end strategy. We can then evaluate the mismatch between the goal-state and the actual state of affairs. We can then evaluate incoming signals with a view to correcting any deviation between what is going on and what we want.

We can then feed our aims forward. And this is possible only so far as we can construct logical patterns that light the way for us—and others.

## FEEDFORWARD? OF COURSE!

If you are smug, if you tell yourself complacently that you are smart because you are always ahead of a speaker (no matter who), you should settle down to this cold fact: Because you are endowed with a fabulous nervous system—one so magnificent that it makes the computer seem feeble-minded—you can think very much faster than anyone can talk. When words flow orally at an intelligible rate (say about 125 words a minute), you, as a listener, are thinking about four times faster than the oral flow.

What do you do with your spare time? Any number of things. You can think about last night's date or tomorrow's housecleaning. But if you are interested in the subject and have a personal stake in it, your mind undoubtedly will move ahead to complete the pattern the speaker has begun.

As speaker or listener, we can hardly avoid feedforward.

Tell the delivery boy that you want him to sweep the floor the first thing in the morning. The next thing he is to do is to straighten the shelves. The phone rings, you answer, and the boy waits. When you give him your attention again, he asks *And then what?* He has never heard the word "feedforward" and would rather not. But you have fed forward and so has he. He knows he must do certain tasks on schedule. The time pattern picks us up and carries us along.

So with the space pattern. Start one, and your listener is

soon far ahead of you. He is around the world and back before you hardly have started. He is bored stiff. He pats himself on the back and wonders why you are such a slow thinker.

Start a causal pattern by discussing the cause and your listener will move ahead to the effect. Start with an account of your troubles and your listener immediately asks himself *Why? How come?* He is back to causes.

Start a pattern by talking about something you want and your listener is asking himself how you expect to make it. Ends dart back to means; means dart ahead to ends.

As a listener, watch for formators and put them together in a verbal pattern. When you have discovered the verbal pattern of a speaker, you understand him. You know what he is driving at and you are in a favorable position to appraise what you hear. Because you have time to think, you yourself may set up an alternative logical construct. This is intelligent responsiveness. And discussion that follows such listening is rewarding. Productive conference rests upon just this semantic procedure.

As a speaker, you will be wise to feed forward consciously. You can feed forward by deliberately introducing formators that hang together according to a principle of organization:

*I'm having trouble, and let me tell you what I think the causes are.* (Cause-to-undesirable-effect)

*We have a plan I'd like to tell you about. Our objective is better relations between line and staff in our organization. This is what we propose to do . . . but I'd like to have your opinion of these procedures.* (Means-to-end)

And because your listener has time to think, he will probably make a logical construct that is isomorphic with yours. And you will be off to a good start. There is understanding between you.

As a speaker, it will be necessary for you first to gain the attention of your listener and then to maintain his interest. The time disparity between speaking and listening compounds this difficulty. How can you draw your listener into the moving verbal pattern that will take him with you? If you do not want his thoughts to wander, you will have to use every possible human means to find a common interest—a common need, a common activity—that is projected toward a common goal. There is no other way.

To repeat, then, in summary:

The word "feedforward" was coined by Richards to symbolize activity that feeds a verbal pattern forward, such that, once the pattern is started, listeners are able to anticipate the whole pattern.

Feedforward may be defined as the communication of a verbal pattern. The essential terms of the verbal pattern, the primary formators, are related according to a principle of organization—time, space, cause to effect, means to end, or as sections within a unifying frame of reference. There are as many kinds of verbal patterns as there are patterns in nature—actual, possible, or even plausible.

**It is the dynamic relationship between the formators that makes feedforward possible. It is the movement—the cohesiveness and the progressiveness—of the parts of the verbal pattern that sets up expectations in the listeners.**

It is apparent, then, that the process of feedforward, so brilliantly analyzed by Richards, requires the semantic apparatus initiated by Morris to give it maximum utility. We need the formators, the big words, in order to feed forward. Feedforward is impossible without formators.

97

But feedforward is not enough. Richards speculated that there must be some natural connection between feedforward and feedback. And there is.

## *FEEDBACK*, THE PROCESS

I have said that we are goal-seeking creatures, that we are embarked on a lifelong series of means-to-end projects in the process of becoming. But, as Lasswell says, the means-to-end logical construct may be called a "speculative model," partly probable and partly chance. And never referable to an actual pattern. Therefore never subject to verification.

You may now be at that point where you are beginning to argue with me. I can hear you say *But you said*—— I know. If you are not now in a semantic daze, I am afraid you have not been reading carefully. Right now you want to know *Where do we go from here?*

Operation Feedback takes over. Power as tensile strength is not enough. Power must be controlled and steered. Man has the power to use change, expected and unexpected, to promote his interests. Man will, and does, initiate change. He becomes a maker of change if it will help him get what he wants!

**Operations Feedforward and Feedback—together—generate and control power that steers us toward objectives by the use of words.**

We are endowed with a system of controls, physiological as well as psychological, that we use as much on the unconscious as on the conscious level. The system of controls is built-in. The operation of these controls is as natural as life itself.

A five-year old uses Operation Feedback with the greatest sensitivity. She wants something. She feeds forward:

"Skiing is like flying like a bird, mama. I want to." (Feed-forward)

*No,* you will say. *You are too little to ski.*

"I can take lessons." (Feedback)

*You will get hurt, I am afraid.*

"No, mama, I'll fall easy in the snow." (Feedback)

*You can't fall easy when you're going down a steep hill.*

"I'll take the little hills first." (Feedback)

All this without effort. Without premeditation. The child gets what she wants. And skis like a floating angel.

Goal-seeking behavior sets up automatic controls.

A woman uses Operation Feedback over a cup of coffee with masterly skill. She wants to know something. She feeds forward with a question. When the answer is evasive, she may detour for a round of gossip—but be assured that she will veer back again to her objective. She uses every subtle means to elicit the desired information. And she gets it. She did not learn this in school. She just does what comes natural.

A salesman uses Operation Feedback with naïve dexterity. The responses of a potential customer do not throw him. He counters—and delivers. Don't ask him how.

A labor leader uses Operation Feedback in the shop, in the front office, in Washington—everywhere—in an effort to get what he wants. He may never have heard the word "semantics," and he couldn't care less. His semantic skill is in his genes, and his experience has refined it until it approaches a fine art. If you should ask him how he does it, he will tell you honestly that he doesn't know.

But it is only when we use Operation Feedback and *know* what we are doing that we can move ahead to progressively higher goals. I shall now try to explain the process of feed-back in order to refine your skill, perhaps to the point where you will say:

"Say, lady, have a heart. All I wanted was to learn how to speak just a little bit better."

To which I can only say, *The worst is over*.

To which I can only add that I have heard this same wail for over two decades. But every now and then I hear one of those same voices (now controlled, yet dynamic) speaking to thousands from the highest places.

## *FEEDBACK*, THE WORD

When I was vacationing in Arizona not long ago, wallow-ing in the sunshine as only a frostbitten Midwesterner can do, an intelligent attorney broke into my heavenly peace with this:

"Say, what's this 'speedback' I've been hearing about?"

I groaned. "Can it be possible that you are thinking about 'feedback'?"

The answer was *Yes*.

I did the best I could to explain, without exerting myself too much. He kept interrupting. Somehow, the idea excited him. But every now and then he used the word "speedback." I became more and more irritated and finally gave up. "Speedback" it was—for him.

Later, after some reflection, I concluded that maybe he wasn't so stupid after all. Maybe he was thinking of that quick comeback, as, for instance, in the case of a sudden and un-expected upset in court. Maybe he was thinking of his ready response to a question when the less skilled might have been stunned into silence. Obviously, speed was, in his opinion, an essential to tactics. I forgive him now for his intrusion into my solitude because, if feedback is any one thing, it is efficient control—*on the spot*. Not later *but right now*. And quick!

Because of its history, the word "feedback" is uniquely expressive of the system of controls that we must use to make our verbal way under interference. When there is opposition of any kind, the important thing is to maintain direction toward the desired goal. The communicator must be a steersman. He knows where he wants to go. He wants to make that goal. He must not be pushed off course.

When I titled this book, the word "feedback" was close to the surface and ready to spill over. Power-Steering with Words fell off my lips as if it were waiting to be called. I was not thinking about the sleek automobile that can be steered with a finger tip. I was not, for the moment, remembering my difficulty in steering, when parking, under the power of my own inadequate muscles. I was thinking of that fabulous control mechanism in both man and machine that is referred to as feedback. I was thinking of the *power* of words to steer us toward the goals we hold dear. I was thinking of those semantic skills that permit us to *steer* toward those goals in the face of opposing forces with ease, with assurance, and with confidence in the power at our disposal. I was thinking of man's unique power, *words*, which become Manpower, Unlimited, when used with conscious skill.

The title of this book has, indeed, literal significance!

When the title PS/W was born, it was my hope that I could develop the concept of feedback as a useful means of control in word-produced behavior.

In the literature of communication, some authors have used the word "feedback" to designate only what comes back to the communicator from a listener. What comes back to the communicator from a listener is the listener's response, his *output*, which is the *input* of the communicator. If a listener yawns in my face and looks at his watch in boredom, this, in itself, is not feedback. His boredom is his response, and insofar as I *perceive* it, it is my input.

**Only when the response changes my behavior in such a way that I use my control mechanism, words, to correct the deviation between the unhappy state of affairs and my desired goal-state do I exercise feedback.**

Feedback is a corrective semantic device used by the communicator to *negate*, to offset, to counteract, the unfavorable consequences of his own words.

Because the operation *opposes* the present undesirable state of affairs, this corrective semantic device is referred to as *negative* feedback.

## *YOU*—A PROJECTILE NODE IN AN INTERDEPENDENT *FIELD*

You need something.

There is a goal that is calculated to satisfy that need. You do not proceed by trial and error. You are prepared. You have weighed possible alternatives. On the basis of available relevant information you believe that your logical construct is the most promising and the least risky. Your logical construct is both cohesive and progressive. You trust it. You speak. You feed a means-to-end pattern forward. This is your output. Like this:

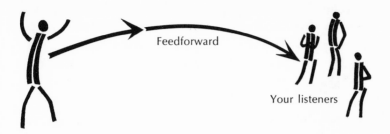

Feedforward

Your listeners

You have memorized nothing, of course. You have no
need to memorize. All that is required is understanding of
the verbal pattern. And the pattern is yours. You made it.
The logical construct is of your own design. You cannot forget it.

Your words may come haltingly, and they probably will,
because you are thinking. But they will come, because you
know what you are talking about. The rhythm of your thinking is projected in the structure of your sentences, your
phrases, your words, even your silence. Your pauses will be
loaded with meaning.

Your timing is perhaps the best means of transmitting your
logical construct. You are concerned with your listeners and
your thoughts, and not with yourself. You experience a concentration of energy that enables you to focus sharply on
your target, your goal. And your words seek that target.

You know that you cannot move forward alone. You need
others. You need those listeners. Your whole being is open
and alive to the consequences of your own words. You are
alert to every sign that indicates the responses of your listeners. You are a speaker-listener-observer. You strain your
every sentient fiber to relate to your listeners. And they respond. You come alive to the verbal and nonverbal signs that
come back to you. This is the output of your listeners. Your

103

perception of their output, their responses, is your input. Like this:

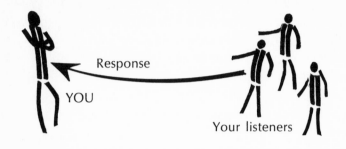

Response

YOU

Your listeners

If your preference system, your interest system, evaluates the consequences of your own words as favorable to your goal, you continue to feed forward. On the basis of such evaluatory signals, the system—strategic feedforward—continues without change of controls. There is no need for adaptation, because your input has added nothing to your information. Your input has in no way altered or augmented your understanding of the situation as a whole. You have anticipated and hoped for such responses, so you maintain strategy without interruption.

**When the difference reading between the state of affairs and the desired goal-state is zero, there is no necessity to alter the controls. When feedforward continues as planned, this is positive feedback.**

In the presentation of a logical construct, continued favorable responses are rare. The means-to-end pattern, as you know, is an opinion, and is partly probable, partly chance. You struggle to make mere words form a dreamed-of design that is calculated to reach your desired goal, but which is never completely predictable. Even when the goal-state is recognized as desirable by your listeners, they may quite naturally have other opinions concerning the best means of achieving that goal. No matter how carefully you may prepare your strategic pattern, it is impossible to anticipate every contingency that may confront you.

When an unexpected obstacle presents itself this is new information. In fact, the only new information that comes to you is unexpected. This is why I have said over and over again that the communicator must be prepared to be unprepared.

In the face of an obstacle, will you fold up in shock? Certainly not! You expect the unexpected. You are on the alert for new information. You have developed a healthy uncertainty tolerance.

**If you are wise, you will steer with the skid. You will go along with your opponent to explore his resistance.**

When you pause to consider an obstacle, this is your best insurance against overcorrection. An obstacle is likely to make us overreact. We move too quickly to corrective measures, with the result that we overcorrect. It is then necessary to correct the overcorrection! This is likely to put us in oscillation and upset our controls.

Analyze and evaluate an opponent's response *with him* and you are likely to convert the obstacle into an advantage. Here your logical construct is your life line. Your strength. In the chancy communication process, tensile strength, remember, is the ability to absorb the impact of opposing forces without going to pieces, and, like a spring, to bounce back to strategic feedforward and thence toward your goal.

But, in the face of an obstacle, feedforward must be supplemented by the corrective controls of negative feedback—

by the ability to adapt analytically and inventively to the new direction of the opponent (the opposing force) thus to redirect him to strategic feedforward and the desired goal.

**A tactical adaptive procedure that enables you to correct the degree of mismatch between the actual response and the desired response is negative feedback.**[41]

But, for this, we must presuppose several courageous personal characteristics.

What novice will steer an auto with the skid that is bearing down on a yawning ditch? The natural tendency is to steer in the opposite direction. Just so, with us. We are inclined to fight back. We forget that the verbal pattern has its own positive power. It doesn't depend upon anything beyond itself; its genesis lies deeply within the self. Trust the verbal pattern—the logical construct—and explore the obstacle until it is circumvented or absorbed.

Another fear of the novice arises from a distrust of himself. He wants to memorize something that he is obliged to say.

If you insist on memorizing your output, any obstacle will throw you off balance. Where there is controversy, the semantic procedure is to match your opponent's logical construct against your own. This is thinking. On the spot. On your feet. Controversy requires freedom to think and to speak and to interact with listeners—with opposing forces—without the constraint of memorized words.

**Your strength lies not in your memorized words but in your memory.**

Your memory is your reservoir of organized experience, reinforced by a lifetime of systemized knowledge and values. Your memory is there and ready to support your every output. You are not a mere verbal façade. You are a structured self with your whole-life-lived at your disposal. This structured self has created your verbal pattern—your logical construct. Trust it.

There is still another fear that few of us escape. We hesitate to express an idea on the wing—an idea in the making.

There are, of course, times when incoming information necessitates a change even in planned strategy. The words that spring to our lips emerge from a living present that we have never lived before and shall never live again. The inner self is stirred to its very foundation by the recombination of past experiences and by the combination of the old and the incoming new. Though the roots of an idea sink deeply into the past, its present and its future are alive with the ecstacy of surprise. This self is remade, transformed. The impulse to plunge into the new, into the never-before-experienced, is our invitation to creativity. For creativity, we must trust the self—the whole self.

So here, my friend, you stand; at the living center:

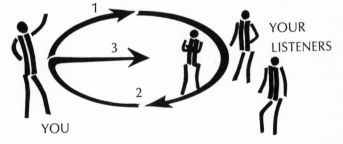

The communication process is cyclic and is never twice the same. Every communication process is unique, and it is *unique at every instant in time*. We are likely to forget the time dimension. We are likely to forget that the state of affairs *changes* as we move hopefully toward a goal.

We need power to maintain stability by strategic advance toward a goal. But we also need continuous control of that power to steer through or around obstacles under changing conditions. For control, we need *words*.

"Communication" (from the Latin *communicatio,* "a giving and a receiving") is a beautiful word. Communication is a kind of sharing.

The communication process is an output-input-output continuum for as long as we live . . . and want . . . and dream . . . and strive . . . and become what we would be. This is life-in-the-making. This is the moment in which we become fissionable material, not only to surpass ourselves, but to charge and recharge everyone around us.

**To be a self-made man is commendable, but to be a self-making man is glorious.**

*Part Two*

# Semantics

*Chapter IV*

# Words

## "...THE WORLD ALTERS AS WE WALK IN IT...."

What is new is new not because it has never been there before, but because it has changed in quality. One thing that is new is the prevalence of that newness, the changing scale and scope of change itself, so that the world alters as we walk in it, so that the years of man's life measure not some small growth or rearrangement or moderation of what he learned in childhood, but a great upheaval.

So says Robert Oppenheimer.[42]

If the world alters as we walk in it, surely nothing but a semantics applicable to process and change is adequate to goal-directed behavior. What is urgently required is a "science" of words that will keep pace with the natural sciences, that will keep pace with knowledge of the nature of the world and man.

In everything we want, in everything we do, words thought and said play the dominant role. The power of words is such that we must know everything we can about them, not only to move purposively and constructively into the future, but also to protect ourselves from other selves! We not only use words, we may be *used* by words, as Harry E. Maynard, Director of the New York Society for General Semantics, said at the International Conference of General Semantics in 1963. Our only protection against manipulation by others is an understanding of the uses and modes of language. This understanding is so important that Part Three of this book is given over to it. When we understand how to use words, we can guard against the misuses of words—by ourselves and by others.

A naïve belief in the power of words will carry us into a maze from which we will find it almost impossible to extricate ourselves. If words alone were all-powerful, we should not have to steer them; we could use words with complete assurance that they would find their targets and have the desired effects. But words are not all-powerful.

The world we live in has its own laws, and these laws are not man-made. Just so, human nature has its own laws. The use of words is man's unique achievement, but words, too, have their own laws.

**There is an unbridgable gap between the silent, unspeakable level of human experience and the descriptive level of words.**

Yet words are the medium of exchange of thoughts and feelings. Words thought and said are forerunners to human

e words we use are the meas-
of our freedom in the market
easure of our intrinsic worth
ught and said are the measure
:ompleteness which is on the
*ng.*

ORY OF SEMANTICS

is not newborn. It has had a
cause it is a social science and
ɔn the more exact sciences, it
has had its impetus and its inspiration from many seemingly
incongruous branches of knowledge. Of those authors already mentioned, for instance, Alfred Korzybski was an engineer; Ivor A. Richards is distinguished primarily as a literary critic; and Charles Morris, as a philosopher.

More recently, semantics has been strongly influenced by
mathematicians, telecommunication engineers, electronics
engineers, etc. Few persons have not felt the influence of the
mathematicians Norbert Wiener, Claude Shannon, and Warren Weaver. British scientists cross the Atlantic and leave
their imprint on the thinking of American semanticists. No-
table among these scientists are the physicist Donald M. Mac-
Kay and the mathematician, electronics engineer, and psychologist Colin Cherry.

In the immediate present, bionics, a new science nurtured
by the Aeronautical Systems Division of the Air Force Systems Command of the United States Air Force, has frankly
explored the relation between the biological sciences and
electronics in the study of communication systems, whether
in man or in the machine. A world-wide battery of mathematicians, biologists, and physical scientists now collaborate
in the exchange of information and research in communica-

tion theory. Most semanticists stand on the shoulders of these giants. Never before has the study of semantics been so richly endowed with collateral scientific information.

But semantics, the science of words, is not a cold, disembodied science. It is a warm social science with its roots in the biological sciences. Because both biological and physical scientists now collaborate in exchanging knowledge in communication theory, semantics has become so complex as to be virtually without limit.

Though the inventions of man are fantastic, we shall not depreciate man, the inventor. Human resources are fabulous. Man, himself, is the greatest mechanism ever invented, so great that we call his inventor *Creator*.

Man comes alive to his own power only when he allies himself with the universe in which he lives. Human nature is part of Nature.

## THE SEMANTICIST IS NOT NAÏVE

We have spoken of *process*.

Process, as we know, means inevitable and unrelenting change in all of nature. But it is not in the nature of words to capture change. If we used all the action-words available to us, even these verbs would stop life.

As I passed through the corridor of the Drake Hotel in Chicago one Monday morning, I saw the sign "Fresh Fish" at the entrance to the Cape Cod Room. The room was closed and dark, with not a person in sight, for it does not open until noon. But promptly at noon, every manner of fish is served on order. The sign, I am sure, is not meant to mislead, but my thoughts went straightaway to the sign "Live Bait" that I had seen on a deserted shack in Wisconsin in the dead of winter.

We are not gullible when we see the sign "Fresh Eggs."

We may wonder when the eggs were laid, how long they were in transit (and under what conditions), and how long they have been in the box in the corner grocery store. Process and change and time prod us into what, I am afraid, are foolish questions. The merchant's answer is always the same: *They just came in.*

But we forget about process and change when someone we trust says *Mary is a sloppy housekeeper* or *John is a poor workman.*

The word "is" is the culprit. Mary *is* a sloppy housekeeper —yesterday, today, tomorrow, and into eternity. The " 'is' of predication," as Korzybski calls it,[43] is sometimes a time-stopper.

As listeners, we know nothing of the circumstances of John's or of Mary's work. Maybe Mary was tending a sick neighbor and did not get to her own work. Maybe John had trouble with his machine tools and had to finish the job at hand as best he could. If, automatically, we would make a mental note to date such appraisals, we could counteract the permanence that inheres in words.

We are not always concerned with process. This is true, usually, when we speak of *things*, such as a house or a mountain. But on a hillside in California, even a house may succumb to gravity and cataclysmic change. When the semanticist talks about a human being, he remembers the fourth dimension of life—time—and revalues the state of affairs at that date. Revaluation of appraisals is probably the only way to maintain an awareness that words have a tendency to stop the clock.

**The semanticist is always "date-conscious."**

We have spoken of *uniqueness*.
We know that everything in nature is unique. But we also

115

know that words *omit* uniqueness. Every word is a class word that encapsulates the samenesses of the class of objects, persons, or events it represents. We remember uniqueness by remembering the subscript, the index, that reminds us of the differences left out.

We may, of course, be interested in the samenesses. In such a case, a class word such as "typewriter" will do. We may find it useful to move to a lower lever of abstraction and speak of a portable, or of a Royal, or of an IBM. Even here, although we have reduced the class word "typewriter" to a subordinate level, the new word designating the new class tells us nothing about any typewriter in that class that is different from any other typewriter in that class. Yet any criminologist can tell you that typewriter$_1$ *is not* identical with typewriter$_2$.

Because words can never capture uniqueness, the semanticist is careful to discriminate between similarities and differences. With human beings, the great concern of the semanticist is to remember the differences left out. After he has described a human being as carefully and as fully as he can by the use of words, he should add, always, Korzybski says, a silent *etc.* to remind him of the differences left out.

The semanticist will weigh the differences of human beings high, the similarities low. And because words can never capture uniqueness, he will never forget that white man$_1$ *is not* white man$_2$, that American$_1$ *is not* American$_2$, that Protestant$_1$ *is not* Protestant$_2$, etc.

**The uniqueness of a human being is a matter of fact— not opinion.**

We have spoken of *relatedness*.

Nothing in nature is isolated. Nothing stands alone. But

116

words tend to isolate elements that in nature are dynamically interdependent.

To overcome the isolating tendencies of words we may use hyphens to connect them. We know that Power-Steering with Words connects two operations, feedforward and feedback. For this reason, the words "power" and "steering" belong together. We write them with a hyphen, "power-steering," because we acknowledge and emphasize their relation, their interdependence.

Korzybski insists that such words as "emotion" and "intellect," "body" and "mind," belong together. These pairs of words represent a very complex organism-as-a-whole-in-an-environment, to use Korzybski's fundamental hyphenated phrase. When we put a hyphen between "body" and "mind," we indicate that there is no separation between the body and the mind. The hyphen in "body-mind" acknowledges their inseparability.

The word "body" is not likely to give anyone any trouble, but psychologists handle the word "mind" gingerly. Even the eminent biologist Edmund W. Sinnott qualified his use of the phrase "the human mind" by saying, "if psychologists will allow us to use the term!" The safeguard is necessary, and useful. Too many persons speak of the "mind" as something that exists mysteriously inside the skull, something that has no connection to a brain or a nervous system.

At this time, it is not necessary to stress the fact that "we hardly think of consciousness or physical activity of any sort without associating it with a nervous system," as Sinnott says.[44]

What must be stressed is the less recognized fact that any word—every word—is an itinerant wanderer unless it is anchored by other words. A word by itself is "a point at which very many different influences may cross or unite . . . hence its dangers . . . and treacherousness." So says Richards in *Practical Criticism*.[45]

The semanticist will put quotes around such a word as "mind" to indicate that he knows what he is doing. Korzybski had a device of his own. If, when speaking in a seminar, he used a word that should not properly stand alone, he would raise his arms and crook his index fingers to indicate quotes. Korzybski explained that when he did this, he was communicating on the nonverbal level *Keep your shirt on. I know what I'm doing. I am using this word in a special way. Keep still and listen.*

**The semanticist thinks words together that belong together.**

Process, uniqueness, and relatedness are grounded in *order*. A discrete word is an isolated bit in limbo.

When we think of order, we think of patterns—patterns in physical nature, patterns in life, and patterns in words. In goal-directed behavior we construct means-to-end verbal patterns that are strategic blueprints of adventurous works of the imagination; and although these means-to-end verbal patterns are grounded in cause-to-effect patterns of the *status-quo*, which may, indeed, be isomorphic with actual patterns in nature (*If this, then necessarily that*), the means-to-end verbal pattern that is necessary to goal-seeking behavior leaps ahead toward a new and preferred design.

**When the semanticist thinks of order, he thinks of language in which the function of words is to create design.**

To recapitulate:
(1) *Words stop the clock.*

118

The antidote is to make a mental note to date everything. Date a fact. Date an opinion. Date a policy. Date a principle. Date your loyalties (some would call them prejudices). Date an appraisal of a person, of a group of persons, of a nation, of the United Nations, etc.

*Date everything!* Because "the world alters as we walk in it" and as we talk in it!

(2) *Every word is underdefined. A word can never capture uniqueness.*

Because every word is a class word that must, necessarily, leave out all the differences of the members of the class it represents (chairs, boys, Negroes, Christians, Americans, Jews, Russians, etc.), every word is underdefined. We know that all any word can do is to encapsulate the similarities of the class of objects, actions, etc., that it describes.

Since every word is underdefined, get rid of the notion at once that understanding between human beings is ever complete. Understanding is always approximate. It is never complete.

Because words are underdefined, think of the snare we step into when we make generalizations. We cannot tell *all* about any one thing, and yet we presume to tell *all* about groups of persons.

What can we say about all Negroes? That they have dark skins? Even this generalization is questionable.

What can you say about all Russians? Only that they are born in Russia? Anything more?

What can we say about all anything? Very little that would stand up under investigation.

What can we say about all boys? *Boys will be boys.* That's about all.

Some persons do not use the word "all," but they make statements like this:

*Blonds are man-eaters.* (This means whatever you think it means.)

These persons believe they evade the fallacy of allness by simply saying *blonds*. What do they mean? *Some* blonds? If they do, why don't they say so? Or do they mean *Jane Doe*? If they do, why don't they say so, and give the date and the place and the horrible details?

Such generalizations lead to nonsensical "reasoning."

IF *all blonds are man-eaters*, and

IF *Jane Doe is a blond* (bleached or otherwise),

THEN it follows necessarily that *Jane Doe is a man-eater.*

But this is, of course, nonsense, because the major premise of the "syllogism" is nonsensical.

Charles Morris says that we can avoid this semantic snare by qualifying our statements and by holding them to such proportions as can be supported by respectable evidence.[46]

The index, too, insures against overstatement.

If Negro$_1$ *is not* Negro$_2$, what can we say about all Negroes? Nothing, except the tautological statement that all Negroes are Negroes.

(3) *A word by itself is likely to be an ambiguous noise that sends us in all directions.*

Look at the simple word "field." Where will it take you? To the baseball field? To a battlefield? To a cornfield? To the field of anthropology? To an infected field in a human body? To a magnetic field? Where? What?

We *think* words together that belong together. And if we construct a verbal pattern made up of parts that together make something whole, we are able to communicate precisely on the verbal level.

*Chapter V*

# Language

## THE EXPLORER NEEDS A *MAP*

I do not need to tell you that language is the fount of every idea that was ever expressed, that words can take man wherever his imagination leads him. For this, we need language.

Thinking is to man what simulation is to the computer. The computer can simulate operations—try them out—to compare the utility of possible means-to-end hypotheses. The human being can *think ahead*, and he must, indeed, think ahead in order to arrive at a *decision* as to the most promising and the least risky strategy by which to reach a goal.

*What does the semanticist do?* He uses language to make new compounds, so to speak. He puts words together in what is, for him, new and unexplored ideas.

121

The basic function of language is to organize knowledge. Language makes it possible to relate new data to what is already known. In this sense, language becomes a map of the territory it represents at a date.

This is what Korzybski says about language as a map:

> The only usefulness of a map or a language depends on the *similarity of structure* between the empirical world and the map-languages. If the structure is not similar, then the traveller or speaker is led astray. . . . If the structures *are similar* then the verbal . . . or map-predicted characteristics . . . are applicable to the empirical world.[47]

A map is worthless to a traveler unless it accurately designates the territory. A good map makes it possible for the traveler to plan a journey intelligently. Just so, the worth of a map-language, at its best the language of fact (the recurrent causal *If this, then necessarily that* pattern), lies in its usefulness in predicting the future.

As goal-directed creatures, we are dependent upon prediction. We know, of course, that absolute prediction in human affairs is impossible. But this is all the more reason for conscientious search into probable and possible recurrences in human behavior. If we move ahead without attention to available verifiable and statistical information, we move without direction, and we must inevitably end where we never intended to go.

Who will not listen attentively to the person who charts his course on the basis of available "consequentially" relevant information? Such a person is trustworthy. We willingly and confidently make him our leader. The image he has created causes us to say, *"He knows where he's going."* If leadership in business or in public life means anything at all, it means just that.

**The leader is the person whose map-language is isomorphic with the nature of the world and man and whose map-language looks to the future with a high degree of predictability.**

## *AUTOMATION*—IN THE NERVOUS SYSTEM

Psychology is concerned ultimately with the wholeness of the self, with the completeness of the self, with the unity of the self, with the integrity of the self in the literal and basic meaning of this word. Psychologists use the word "integration" to refer to the process of organizing the various traits and tendencies of the human being into one harmonious whole. The history of psychology is the history of investigations into the process by which the organization of the self takes place.

How does this organization take place?

The one fact on which there seems to be agreement is that there is a natural organizing principle of the nervous system and of the brain. We are, it seems, made that way. The mechanism is built in. In this respect the nervous system is without question our most powerful ally. The integration of the self is as much the result of the self-organizing principle of the nervous system as it is of conscious effort.

The psychologist Gordon W. Allport, author of that exciting little book entitled *Becoming: Basic Considerations for a Psychology of Personality*, says:

Now whatever else learning may be, it is clearly *a disposition to form structures.*[48]

What does Allport mean? Simply this: Every increment of knowledge is selected, understood, and stored in your memory system only because you relate it to something that

123

is already there—in the reservoir of your experience. The new has found its niche, with the result that a pattern is amplified, reorganized, recombined, rearranged, by the inclusion of the new. These relationships make more and more complex patterns. And smaller patterns coalesce to make larger patterns until, ideally, your self is one unified synthesis of everything you know and everything you believe.

**Human beings have this disposition, this natural tendency, this self-organizing principle!**

## BUT HUMAN BEINGS ARE *STEERSMEN*

There is ample evidence that we are self-organizing systems on the physiological level over which we have no control. Biological evolution has provided us with inherent powers so great as to be even now in the realm of mystery. Nature will do its share. Of this we may be sure.[49]

But we have reached that stage in the evolutionary process, we are told, where we can steer our selves consciously in the direction of personal unity, in the direction of successively higher levels of intellectual and spiritual organization. This is the thesis of the distinguished biologist Julian Huxley and others in *The Humanist Frame*.[50]

But how?

Richards provides the answer in his provocative book entitled *Speculative Instruments*.[51]

Words, Richards says, are instruments; and they are speculative in that they may go beyond the present, tentatively yet creatively, into the future.

Words are the instruments by which to unify all the strands of experience within a single life.

124

Words are the instruments by which to synthesize all the seemingly disparate areas of human experience within the community of mankind. Until science, art, and religion are brought together in one idea-system, Richards contends (along with Huxley and others), man's intellectual and spiritual evolution will be retarded.

There is a growing belief among scholars that knowledge and values can be unified on a higher level of organization. But, for this, we must speculate on the *conscious* level, and on the highest level of organization. For what is required is the unification of ideas and ideals. The leaders in science, industry, politics, and ethics must be concerned with map-languages—with map-languages not only of *what is* but also of *what may be*.

**When man moves consciously from what is toward what may be he becomes a steersman. And, for this, he needs language.**

## THE LANGUAGE OF *WHAT IS*— OF *KNOWLEDGE*

Why is the *If this, then necessarily that* verbal pattern the mainstay of knowledge?

Nothing in nature is isolated. Knowledge is understanding of causal (recurrent) relationships in nature. An *If this, then necessarily that* verbal pattern sets up a cause-to-effect relationship that can be verified by comparing it with an actual pattern in nature, again and again, with identical results to all qualified observers. Such a verbal pattern is either true or false. When the verbal pattern and the actual pattern are isomorphic, the statement is said to be true and logical. There is no argument.

Ogden and Richards put it this way in *The Meaning of*

125

*Meaning*: When the psychological (linguistic) context "hangs together" in precisely the way the external (physical) context "hangs together," we have a true and logical statement.[52] And they wrap it all up in this pithy conclusion:

**"Meaning . . . becomes according to this theory a matter open to experimental methods."[53]**

This statement of Ogden and Richards is incontrovertible when applied to scientific statements.

In *Science and Sanity* Korzybski corroborates the earlier thinking of Ogden and Richards when he says that "the only possible link between the objective world and the linguistic world is found in *structure, and structure alone.*"[54] To say this in our language: the only possible link between thinking and the external world is isomorphic patterns. When we remember that words cannot tell *all* and that definitions give us the run-around, we take heart that verbal patterns make PS/W possible of achievement in this world of flux and chance.

Again, Korzybski gives us the punch-line that strikes at the heart of the matter when he says that "two relations of similar structure have all their logical characteristics in common."[55]

If the word "logic" throws you and if you have never heard the word "syllogism," relax. The logic of Power-Steering with Words is the logic of patterns.

## HOW, THEN, DOES JOHNNY *LEARN?* HOW DO *YOU* LEARN?

If nothing is isolated and if knowledge is understanding of causal (recurrent) relations, learning is not memorizing.

**Understanding replaces memorizing.**

If you have ever despaired when listening to the Quiz Kids (young or old), recall what Einstein says about thinking in his "Autobiographical Notes."

Thinking is not merely the emergence of a series of "memory-pictures" in which "one calls forth another." Only when a memory-picture acts as a *connecting* element in such a series do we have thinking. To say this differently, it is only when a memory-picture becomes "an *ordering* element" and *connects* series "which in themselves are unconnected" that we have thinking. So says Einstein. And Einstein calls such a series of connected memory-pictures "concepts."[56] This is the kind of thinking that is expressible in a verbal pattern. Such a pattern, once started, will catch up a listener or a reader in its momentum.[57]

Unless bits of information are coordinated to make a unified idea-system, the bits are like the pieces of a shuffled jigsaw puzzle. The meaning of a part cannot be known in isolation. When the bits form an integrated pattern, any single part has multidimensions, because each part illuminates every other part, as well as the pattern as a whole.

The human being whose information is coordinated has a natural aptitude for learning. Incoming information finds its niche, its place, its connections. And the idea-system as a whole acts as a powerful magnet in attracting and storing new information. Anything that fits into the idea-system is absorbed to become an integral part of it. Coordination thus exhibits both structural integrity and plasticity through growth.

If, indeed, learning is, as Gordon W. Allport says, "clearly a disposition to form structures," then nature collaborates with us in the learning process. When you speak and a listener responds, when you link his thinking with the pattern of

SEMANTICS

your past experience, you understand him. And you change. You think. The structure of your inner self has been amplified or modified.

This is how Johnny learns. This is how *you* learn. And this is why you remember.

## AND HERE IS THE PLACE TO TACKLE THAT TROUBLESOME WORD *"INTERPRETATION"*

As early as 1923, and before that in their lectures, Ogden and Richards defined interpretation in *The Meaning of Meaning* as the basis of all learning, of all thinking. Never fully put to use before, their words fit now[1964] into accepted theories of perception and of personality at its highest level of complexity. Ogden and Richards say, "In all thinking, we have interpreting" of words, things, events, etc. "Our interpretation of any sign is our psychological reaction to it. . . ." And interpretation they say, "is only possible thanks to recurrent contexts."[58]

Have you ever heard one person say to another *I don't get the connection?* This is a highly sophisticated statement. When we do not see "the connection," we do not understand. The words of another are meaningless to us. They add nothing to our knowledge. They just do not fit into the pattern of our experience.

When you ask *How do you interpret it?* the question usually refers to a work of art—a painting, a poem, etc. What you really want to know is *What does it mean?*

Not so long ago, I saw a work (I hesitate to call it a painting) that might have been a design for linoleum. Little swirling circles, gray on gray. *What is it?* I wondered. *What does*

128

*it mean?* I looked for a title. There was none. (I was to make up my own, I supposed.) The word "incongruous" popped into my head. Why? Because there was nothing, it seemed, to link this design with anything in the pattern of my experience—except linoleum. Yet this was art. And it had won first prize!

I looked again. (I am not one to give up.) The tiny swirling circles seemed to be seething, trying desperately to lift themselves above the flat surface. My thoughts raced. Could this painting be saying something to me, something that I understood? *Are we not all patterns,* I asked myself, *so stable that we live, it seems, in the monotony of routine, habitual experience? Am I not a boiling seething cauldron attempting to rise above habit—above "security"—to escape from the flat surface to some beckoning height? Shall I give the painting a title?* I pondered. *Shall I call it "Emergence"? Or "Escape into Freedom"?*

I tell you this because, whenever you entertain a stimulus object, you must find its meaning by relating it to a psychological context in your past experience in which it has a place. And this is interpretation.

Interpretation is, in every sense, a discovery. When you "place" an incoming stimulus in the pattern of your past experience, the structure of your self is now different—augmented, reorganized, changed in some way.

Words, then, have this fabulous power to recreate us. To transform us. We are like persons reborn with exery experience of discovery through interpretation. Speakers who spark discovery in us, we call "interesting," "exciting," and "stimulating." They have our avid attention.

Interpretation is thinking.

Interpretation is learning.

129

Interpretation is advance in the process of becoming.
To repeat:

**"Our interpretation of a sign is our psychological reaction to it."**[59]

If words, a work of art—anything—is not a linking member of a psychological context in your experience, it is irrelevant to your thought-feeling. For you, it has no meaning.

In the case of my interpretation of the work of art, it is hardly likely that anyone else in the whole world would interpret it as I did. What the designer meant, only *he* can say (if he can symbolize it in words). What the judges perceived when they awarded the prize, only *they* can say.

Who is to say that my interpretation is "right" or "wrong." The terms "right" and "wrong" are not, in my opinion, relevant here. An interpretation can be said only to be "better" or "worse," depending on the relevance and quality of the past experience of the interpreter of the stimulus object.

We should not limit the meaning of the word "interpretation" to such personal adventures. The word has far greater significance to PS/W. But the immediate lesson seems clear.

**When we interpret a stimulus—word, object, event, etc. —we relate it to a psychological context in the pattern of our past experience.**

Interpretation is subject to verification in varying degrees. At the lowest extreme is the strictly personal interpretation of an art object. At the highest is the interpretation of a stimulus that has reference to controllable data, to repeatable operations, or to the body of scientific knowledge. Put differently: some interpretations are private; others are public.

Between these two extremes is a vast area of experience in which interpretation is partly public and partly private. This in-between area is not to be depreciated, because in it lies human behavior—both individual and social. In it lies Power-Steering with Words, in which thought-feeling is an inseparable unity.

If you look inside your self, you have an awareness of organic unity, living and indivisible. You cannot chop yourself up into a body and a mind, a head and a heart, a spirit and the flesh. You cannot know where your wanting ends and your thinking begins. Beneath every clear, structured idea, there is desire. There is needing. There is wanting. There is purpose. Goal-directed behavior activates the whole man.

Goal-directed behavior begins with a decision to move in one direction rather than another. How does the whole man, a composite of knowledge and values, a composite of everything he knows and everything he believes, arrive at his decisions?

## LIFE IS A *DECISION–MAKING* CONTINUUM

**A decision is a choice among possible alternatives by which to reach a goal.**

When you make a choice—a decision—you do not start from scratch. Every day of your life you make small decisions automatically, almost unconsciously. Your integrated self is a composite of everything you know and everything you believe. You have made some fundamental big choices in the past that eliminate the necessity of examining certain categories of action.[60] You know what you want with respect

131

SEMANTICS

to long-term goals. You know what you like. Your preference system has reached a kind of peak that was erected by
a life lived. The reservoir of your experience is a hierarchical
structure of your knowledge and your values, in which priorities dominate choice.[61]

The making of a decision frequently involves conflict and,
perhaps, imponderable risks. Every decision is a means-to-
end logical construct that looks to the future. Its outcome
cannot be predicted exactly. Every decision involves multidimensional consequences, many of them far beyond our
knowing. Every decision involves sacrifice: to say *Yes* to one
course of action requires us to say *No* to others.

What, then, is a good decision?

A good decision is one that promises the greatest possibility of achieving a desired goal.

A good decision is one that entails the least sacrifice of
competing wants.

A good decision is one that is least wasteful of human
possibilities.

A good decision is one that provides a course that avoids
collateral detrimental consequences, and should, above all
else, avoid the risk of irrevocable disaster.

A good decision is relevant to the dynamic process world
—at a date. The time dimension, so frequently overlooked, is
of paramount significance in the decision-making process.

But how?

**A good decision will have a built-in self-correcting mech-
anism.**

A good decision programs strategy (feedforward) and
leaves elbow room for tactics (negative feedback). A *strategy*

132

is a program that is calculated to effect the reconstruction of a present unfavorable state of affairs. *Tactics* is the control that provides for the entertainment of intervening and unexpected variables. Strategy (feedforward) and tactics (negative feedback), together, maintain stability in goal-directed behavior.

### Power-Steering with Words is the answer to How?

There are, I believe, three stages in the decision-making process.

### First, it is necessary to clarify the goal specifically and definitely.

If we do not know what we want, how can we make a choice? Having set up the goal, we then construct a verbal pattern of *what is*. We then look around and attempt to survey the territory that is relevant to the accomplishment of the goal.

Remember, now, that Korzybski said that "the only usefulness of a map or a language depends on the *similarity of structure* between the empirical world and map-languages." And map-languages should, Korzybski adds, provide map-predicted characteristics [that] are applicable to the empirical world."[62]

Clear enough. To make a map-language of the existent state of affairs from which we must move toward a goal-state requires that we make a verbal pattern that is similar *in structure* to the present state of affairs. We must investigate the *Now* with a backward look. This means that we must construct a cause-to-effect verbal pattern. Such a pattern, if designative of a recurrent pattern in nature, will have value

133

for us insofar as it can help us predict the future. The causal pattern of the present state of affairs should at the very least provide information as to *how to change it*.

To look at a complex situation and attempt to penetrate to causal factors calls for something like omnipotence. But this does not mean that we must give up and say *It can't be done*.

**Goal-seeking behavior starts with a present state of affairs and moves toward a goal-state.**

Obviously, it is imperative to understand the present state of affairs so that, as we move strategically toward a goal-state, we may evaluate the mismatch between the actual state of affairs and the goal-state.

The medical man must know causes before he approaches a goal-state. The political aspirant must know causes before he approaches a goal-state. Only attention to and manipulation of causal factors can make it possible to move toward a more desirable goal-state.

In human affairs, the best we can have in most cases is an imputed causal relationship attributed on the basis of what information is available. We cannot be sure *which* imputed causal factors are decisively relevant to our problem. Many factors are relevant but "inconsequential." Their consequences are insignificant with respect to the attainment of the goal-state.

**The determination of causal factors that play a decisive role in the present state of affairs which must be changed is necessary to the decision-making process.**

The second stage is the determination of the most promising means-to-end hypothesis. We do not have a crystal ball.

We cannot predict the future with exactitude. *Why shall we choose this hypothesis and not that?*

Because we are now attempting to use the causal factors of the present undesirable situation as a point of attack, we are not entirely at loose ends.

There are some things we can know, not positively, but with a high degree of probability. *What does past experience tell us about the present problematical situation?* "History" is the resource here. There are records. Some provide statistical trends that are ongoing with greater or lesser regularity. Sometimes the facts in the case may be in doubt or in dispute. We are, let it be understood, in the area of opinion. This is an *imputed* relationship, ascribed on incomplete information, and, therefore, tentative. It is not a bona fide verifiable causal relationship.

When we have assembled the consequential information, we are ready to prognosticate—to evaluate the competing hypothesis with a view to choice. *But how?*

The third stage in the decision-making process depends on you, because it depends upon the degree of integration of your knowledge and your values, and even more, on the breadth and quality of your knowledge and your values.

If you are an "indecisive" individual, you have probably paid little conscious attention to the organization of yourself. Nor have you had the advantage of rigorous discipline. But if you are systematic, if you are well-structured, if your past experience is well organized, you are probably now in a professional or business situation in which decision-making is a primary function.

*But how do you make your decisions?*

135

**This third stage in the decision-making process is one in which your whole self participates over and beyond your knowledge of the why or the how.**

In the winter of 1962, I participated in a Conference in the State of Washington. It was my good fortune to be in the audience to listen to a speaker who was head of research of one of our largest producers of space craft. I listened avidly, for here was a man who was obliged to make decisions that affect the security of our nation, of the world, and of all who live in it. I thought *Decision-making here must indeed be refined to the highest point of excellence.* I listened.

The speaker said much about the decisions that had been made, but not one word about the decision-making process. After the speaker had finished, I was the first to rise to ask a question.

"Would you care to discuss the nature of the decision-making process?" I asked.

This was easy.

"We have computers that can screen out the less relevant from the more relevant data. These computers can simulate operations and assess their comparative worth. They are indispensable to the decision-making process."

"Then the computers make your decisions," I said. I was still asking.

There was a long pause and then a very quiet *No.* He turned away, but I was still standing there in the shape of a living question mark.

"Would you care to tell us, sir, how you arrive at these decisions that affect all of us—all mankind?"

There was a deep sigh. I thought he would shrug and turn away.

136

"Please, sir," I ventured. "You can tell us something we need to know. For years, I have been asking this question and have met with evasion." I smiled and added, "I put my trust in you, sir."

When he next spoke, it seemed the words were torn from him.

"First, I assemble all the available relevant information. Some of this comes from the computers, but not all. Some of it comes from associates. And with judgments, you might call them. I steep myself in the factual data and these judgments." He paused. Finally: "And then I pray to God that every fragment of my past experience that has bearing on my problem will somehow coalesce and propel me into the way —the best way—to proceed."

Decision-making appears to me to be a three-stage process:

(1) Map-language of *what is*

(2) Map-language of possible strategies toward *what may be*

(3) Movement from this meticulously conscious process to reliance on the whole self—unconscious as well as conscious—to choice.

No one can say this better than Theodore C. Sorensen, an advisor to the late President Kennedy and, at the time, a member of the executive committee of the National Security Council:

The President may seek advice from the Congress, from the Cabinet, or from his personal advisors. He may seek the view of the press, the parties, and the public. But however numerous his counsellors, in that final moment of truth there can be no "multitudes, multitudes" in the "valley of decision." There can be only one lonely man—the President of the United States.[63]

In "How the President Makes a Decision," Sorensen says, "To begin with, White House decision-making is not a science but an art." I would disagree with Sorensen here because he himself says, "It is simply the interaction of desire and fact—simply a determination of what the national interest requires in a given situation."

To put this into our language, we have here:

(1) Purpose. Purpose is a desire for something new, something different. As Sorensen says, it is a desiring of "what the national interest requires."

This means that a specific goal is set up. A goal can be reached only by putting a means-to-end program into operation.

(2) Analysis. Sorensen is concerned with the "determination of what the national interest requires *in a given situation*." This means, therefore, that there is a need, first, to analyze the *status quo*. And this means the determination of causal factors—bona fide and imputed—of the present problematical situation. And this is, necessarily, the point of departure.

What we have here, is, therefore, in my opinion, both science and art. Science, in that when we attack a problem, there is need for the analytical reconstruction of the undesirable state of affairs. If this analysis results in a bona fide cause-to-effect pattern of recurrent relationships, we have, indeed, a scientific account of the *status quo*. But there is need, also, for art because the means-to-end strategic program is highly dynamic, complex, and largely unpredictable. Here it is necessary to advance *beyond what we know*. The decision-making process is the point at which man must surpass himself, for now he is engaged in creating a pattern in preferred design. That something new. That something different.

In the deliberate decision-making process man consciously exercises an exactitude that is the mark of the scientist, insofar as that is possible. There is that further step which is closely allied to inspiration—to the genius of the artist. This is something that happens to all of us, in greater or lesser degree, as a gratuity of life itself.

I like to remember here what Richards says of the artist:

He is the point at which the growth of the mind shows itself. His experiences . . . represent conciliations of impulses which in most minds are still confused, intertrammelled and conflicting.[64]

Can we say less for the scientist? Can we say less for any human being who advances creatively in the constantly emerging state of becoming?

**The decision-making process is the point at which the growth of the mind shows itself!**

I will tell you now what makes this statement credible and acceptable to me.

Korzybski refuses to separate the language system and the nervous system. For Korzybski, the nervous system is structure, and the linguistic system is a function of that structure. So he uses the hyphenated word "neuro-linguistic" to include both concepts.[65]

If our knowledge is such that the pattern of the neuro-linguistic system is similar in structure to the pattern of the world, we have a factual base on which to ground our goal-seeking behavior. The map-language is then isomorphic with the territory. The map-language is then both true and logical. This is the solid basis for predictability that will stabilize goal-directed behavior in this chancy world.

The reservoir of experience of a single human being is deep and impenetrable. When this reservoir is tapped both on the conscious and the unconscious levels, we assemble all the power with which we are endowed.

And now we are ready for *Communication* as PS/W.

*Chapter VI*

# Communication

### *COMMUNICATION* IS A *BIG* WORD

The word "communication" is the primary formator in this book. "Communication" will make a place for everything and anything we can say about the use of words in goal-directed behavior. It stands at the peak of the pyramid. It is probably the most inclusive formator in semantics.

Let me set this up for you with three subordinate levels of formators (abstractions) that will establish the order of my exposition. The function of the formator is, remember, to establish the form of a communication. Every time you use the word "formator" you are concerned with a verbal pattern.

The following pattern is sectional and inclusive (closed):

141

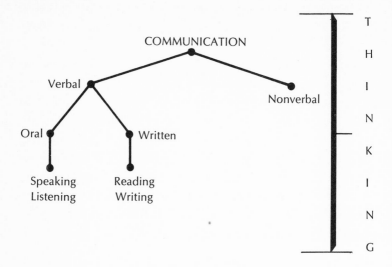

Communication is the primary formator
Verbal and Nonverbal are secondary formators
Oral and Written are tertiary formators
Speaking and Listening, Writing and Reading,
are fourth-order formators.

You will be interested in both verbal and nonverbal communication. Words have, in some instances, relatively explicit meanings. But over and above their literal significance words have overtones and undertones of meaning. How you *say* a word is often as important as the word itself.

Written and oral communication have some basic principles in common. You will want to know how to write a memo, a letter, a report, an abstract, an article, etc. You will want to know, also, how to converse with one person, how to speak to several at a conference, how to address large groups from a platform, or how to speak before a microphone.

If you will write and speak, you will be just as concerned with reading and listening. When we write, the reader looks over our shoulder. When we speak, we speak with a listener's ear, for every audience is different. In face-to-face communication we are speakers *and* listeners. Communication is a giving and a receiving. To break the cycle is to cut the communication line.

Finally, every use of words is dependent upon thinking. When we write, we may think at leisure and, if need be, rewrite. But when we speak, we are frequently obliged to make a decision on the spot—on our feet. Conscious use of systemic language, as explained in Part Three, will make this possible.

All these facets of communication depend upon some basic semantic principles. Everything you can learn about any one aspect of communication will have a carry-over value to every other aspect.

Everyone converses. As time goes by and we achieve "status," we use different words to describe "conversation," as I have already indicated. We use such words as "interview," "salesmanship," "counseling" (in or out of an attorney's office), "conference," "teaching," "consultation," "discussion," "debate," etc. And we use the archaic term "public speaking" to pretend that this speaking is something special or different. It is not. Whether one person or hundreds listen, the semantic principles remain the same. The skills that you develop around your own dinner table can take you anywhere.

**Power-Steering with Words is yours—wherever you are. And beyond.**

## NONVERBAL COMMUNICATION

If I look at any object in space—a cathedral, a space ship, a painting, a child—and entertain it as a stimulus object, I do something more than merely see it. I perceive it. The word "perceive" has a special meaning in psychology. Perception is the entertainment of a stimulus that causes some change in the behavior of the percipient. If there is no change, there is no perception.[66]

If I look at you, a silent object in space, and something happens to me, I have perceived you. I am a percipient. But *why*? If your very silence can establish a bond between us, perception is, indeed, a wondrous thing. That this does happen, all of us know.

I do not need to tell you that I am a lover of life, and especially of human life. Words are for me what song must be for the nightingale, a spilling over of the innerness of life. I know, too, that words that come must break through a silence that is replete in its inexpressible living fullness. There is always that unbridgable gap between life lived and the words we use to describe it.

I would say with Richard P. Blackmur, Professor of Literature in Princeton University, that silence itself is a language, because it communicates. I have a great respect for silence.

What does silence communicate? Blackmur says, "Rhythm is how we feel. . . ." And rhythm is what moves us—and others.[67]

Silence communicates the rhythm of life undistorted by words. You may say this is farfetched. But the rhythms of your brain are evidenced by the EEG (the electroencephalogram) according to the distinguished British physiologist W. Grey Walter, author of the epoch-making *The Living Brain*.[68]

Blackmur would say, and I with him, that the scope of language is as broad as the scope of life itself. Its realm extends from the pitiable efforts of men to communicate something experienced on the silent level—something that is unspeakable—to the precision and the accuracy of the mathematical formula. Between these two extremes, we exercise our fabulous Power-Steering with Words. But words are not enough. Words cannot tell *all*. When our thoughts cry out in words, when our joys, our anguish, our prayers cry out in monosyllabic sounds, it is as if we explode and shatter our silence. As Blackmur says:

**Meaning is what silence does when it gets into words.**

There are many ways in which the body expresses the inner self. We cannot will it. We cannot suppress it.

Cynicism is communicated as much by the curl of a lip or by a raised eyebrow as by the words said. Perhaps more significantly without words!

Skepticism fairly shrieks through words.

Tenderness is more a look than a word.

Curiosity, that gadfly that stimulates us all, singly and together, is in the pitch, the inflections, the pacing, the wordless breath control.

Joy looks out of the eyes.

Weariness and langour have their circumflex in the tone quality. The helplessness . . . the hopelessness. . . .

Every emotion has its own silent voice that affects the image we project to others.

Sadness is a thing apart. Words are powerless to express deep suffering. Yet how strangely communicative a profound emotion is.

145

After deep sorrow, I was scheduled for a series of TV broadcasts. I gave my whole heart to the series and I loved it. I was speaking about communication and somehow felt the responsiveness of those whom I never came to see or to know. One morning a friend telephoned me and asked with unmistakable solicitude, "How are you?" "Fine!" I answered briskly. "Why do you ask?" Her answer was hesitant and, I thought, troubled. "You looked so sad this morning. . . ."

How could I know that the whole of me was expressive when I thought that only that part of me which was relevant to my task was being communicated?

We cannot know how much the self communicates over and beyond the words we use. Whatever is on the inside somehow comes through. There is a pulsation that cannot be translated into words, for it is life itself. The rhythm that dominates the self is furious in its compulsion to express. We may repress our words, but we cannot repress the rhythm of life. Can we control the heartbeat?

We know, of course, that every thought-feeling, every idea symbolized, is something less than silent wordless living. Language is undoubtedly the richest personality clue that we possess, but we know that language cannot tell all. How can I reach you now with words alone to show you that your silence, unspoiled by your words, is your living life before verbal abstraction has whittled it down? So little of the rhythm of life—the momentum, the tempo, the voiceless urgency—gets into words.

Rhythm is the heartbeat of life. It is the time dimension—the fourth dimension—of life. When rhythm stops, life stops. And PS/W stops.

Wherever there is process, wherever human beings are involved, there is movement. Wherever there is movement, the

146

time dimension is of the utmost significance. Every human experience has a tempo, a momentum, a rhythm of its own. But can we capture it?

As a silent object, how do you manifest rhythm in movement?

I cannot pull you apart and say rhythm is your posture, your gestures, a raised eyebrow, a shrug, your walk. Or that it is something that looks out of your eyes. It is all of these, and more. Nothing I can say about you will touch that inner something that spills over without your knowing. Yet I have responded to it. I must try to know why.

Posture, gestures, your walk. Movement.

Is the rhythm of your self communicated by your movement? If the rhythm of your brain is evidenced in the EEG, and if your brain is the essential part of your nervous system, and if your nervous system is responsible for your every movement—why not?

Extrapolation can do no harm.

I heard it said of a woman that she wasn't much to look at, but that when she walked into a room, the whole place lit up like a neon sign. There must be something to the "body" and how it is presented.

Then there was an evening of tiresome variety "entertainment." A girl walked out on the platform. About sixteen, I judged. Skinny as a rail but pliant as a willow. Don't ask me why, but that yawning, squirming, bored audience applauded as one man, vigorously and affirmatively, before she opened her mouth. She was worth it. But how did they know?

We know a person by his footsteps. Why?

The momentum of a living thing stamps it, actually, as being alive. But sometimes there is so little animation that we have to feel the pulse to be sure.

A person is recognized by his characteristic rhythm. It

may be regular, like the ticking of a clock or the dripping of a faucet (a means of torture, we are told). This smooth steady rhythm is predictable, it arouses the expectations of others about the tempo of future behavior. To this extent, at least, movement affects the image that others have of you.

The rhythm of your personality is, I believe, an important aspect of your self as a silent object. Your movements characterize the vigor, the tempo, and the variability of the rhythm of your personality. Variability that is coincident with a rapidly changing scene bespeaks decisiveness and flexibility—an excellent combination in this unpredictable process world. When variability of rhythm is synthesized with the life situation as a whole, it would seem that a cyclic transaction between self and world has been effected.

How can you move expeditiously if you do not feel expeditious? How can you swing it if your pulse rate is sluggish? How can you synchronize efficiently with a complex life situation if you are not sensitive to it? The body is a unity, and it is an integral part of the immediate environment. Does it fit into the moving changing scene? Are you running when you should be treading carefully? Are you askew when you should adapt purposively to sudden change?

Your body is, I believe, a physical clue to the rhythm of your personality, and, as such, it is a factor in the image that you create.

On the nonverbal level of communication, I have often thought that the appearance of a person is expressive. Although clothes do not make the man (or woman), clothes are an essential part of his physical appearance. How can we separate the clothes and the man? Clothes are at least a quick clue to the man who is inside them. And to how he is likely to speak.

148

The outside of the self is important because it expresses the purposive inner self. If I am being interviewed for a position as teacher, I had better look the part. (And answer questions briefly and very much to the point.) If I am auditioning for a TV show, my appearance should leave nothing to the imagination. (And I had better watch my pronunciation, my enunciation, and my choice of words. To say nothing of my voice.)

If you are parading a costume that is out of character with what you are and what you want to become, you are, I am afraid, covering up instead of exhibiting your personal attributes. And you are not happy.

I heard M. Albert Ramond, then President of Albert Ramond & Associates, Inc., Industrial Engineers, say to a group of executives:

"Every time a man comes into my office, before he says one word, something happens between us that is hard to undo."

That nonverbal communication is potent, no one will deny. That the human body is expressive, everyone knows.

When your eyes look out on the world, what comes through? *Your estimate of your self!*

If you do not respect your self, how can your eyes express candor, your words express confidence or self-assurance? If you despise your self, how can your eyes or your words disguise that bitterness?

A great deal has been written about self-love. This should not be confused with egotism, which is a bastard kind of self-love. The love of which I speak, which is so well defined by Erich Fromm, is reverence, awe, humility, gratitude, adoration, joy—all for the gift of life.[69]

Your self is the receptacle of all that you are and all that you hope to be. You are alive with memories and with hopes. That center which is you is steady yet dynamic. It is you who are the container of your many loves, each one different, each one nourished by that central fount that is your love of self, deep and inexhaustible. As the bird sings, as the trusting dog pleads, as the child dances, as the nun prays. Sounds. Colors. Smells. Things to touch. There is love everywhere. And made possible only by our first love—our love of *life* and of self.

Erich Fromm says that if we do not love the self, we cannot love another. The world is then bare and cold, unresponsive and dead. But love is contagious. Like this:

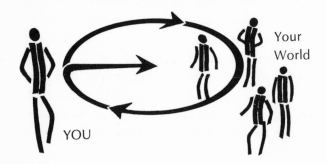

There is more, much more, to be said about nonverbal communication. We use words because we want something, something that has worth for us. *Value.* So we plan ahead. We think ahead. We formulate strategy. Then we choose words that we consider appropriate to the situation.

Expediency, try as we will to avoid it, affects our choice of words in our bid for attention, for interest, for understanding, for trust, and for acceptance.

Take the extreme case of the person who is highly "moral" in his personal life but "immoral" or "amoral" in his business relationships. He is honest with some, devious with others. He is reliable in some ways, irresponsible in others. He is meticulously trustworthy in certain situations, outrageously deceptive in others.

The many roles he is obliged to play in the normal conduct of his life are inconsistent with each other. Some of these roles overlap! Every problem becomes an indecisive struggle. Conflict paralyzes his activity. And, I am sorry to say, there is no way to hide the inconsistency of the inner self by the use of words. We cannot pretend to be whole selves when we are torn apart by antagonistic impulses. The ring of integrity cannot be play-acted. We might as well accept the point made by the eminent psychologist Gardner Murphy in *Personality, a Biosocial Approach to Origins and Structure.* Every time we open our mouths, we give ourselves away, whether we like it or not, whether we are aware of it or not. *What we are* speaks so loud, that it is sometimes impossible for listeners to hear *what we say.* Murphy says that "the intensity, pitch, timbre, and time relations vary not only with structure but with the energies, the rhythms of expression; the voice becomes 'self-expressive.' "[70]

This nonverbal communication—then which there is nothing more potent—is the silent partner of verbal communication. Beyond our control, nonverbal communication is honestly and deeply expressive of the self. We cannot restrain it. We cannot force it. It is a derivative of the self.

We can, ultimately, loose the full force of nonverbal communication to achieve our purposes only by indirection. As we achieve higher levels of organization, as we move toward unity, the self will speak for itself. Honestly, decisively, and powerfully. Our words always express something beyond the literal significance of the words themselves.

**Nonverbal communication is the power that augments Power-Steering with Words, for better or for worse. In order to communicate better, we must become better.**

As we become better, we become more human, more intuitive, more receptive—more perceptive—of the needs and wants and values of others. On the nonverbal level, communication becomes, in actuality, a giving and a receiving. And when this happens, empathy—that *feeling with* another—becomes that deep, stirring, and binding force between you and others.

## *VERBAL* COMMUNICATION: WHY SHOULD I LISTEN TO *YOU*?

Like you, I am a system in search. I want most of all to fulfill my self. I want, I need, I desire. I am a goal-seeking creature. Like you, a patterned decision-making process of becoming, I am on my way.

Why should I stop to listen to you? I am interested in you as a person, of course, but I have neither the time nor the inclination to listen to your detailed and circuitous account of anything that does not flow in the stream of my ongoing life. Although I respect you, I do my best to protect myself against your verbal intrusion. I just do not listen. We-ell, maybe with half an ear, but I take pains to be on my way before you can really be aware of my indifference.

In spite of everything I can do, my nervous system screens out what does not concern me. And the word "concern," incidentally, derives from the Latin *concernere,* which means, according to my dictionary, *"to sift,* hence, *to perceive."*

How can you catch me and hold me? How can you capture my willing attention?

I am sure you will think me incurably addicted to Gertrude Stein when I say, never more serious in my life:

**You can interest me every time you talk about something that interests me. Otherwise not!**

All this means is that my interest system is my preference system. And the interest system is the most zealous, the most stringent, the most uncompromising priority system the human world over.

So, I perceive what my nervous system chooses to perceive. Nothing else. When I am bombarded with words from all sides, my highly selective nervous system takes over. It works as a preference system—a threshold, high or low, to incoming demands.

## YOUR *SYSTEM OF INTERESTS*

The system of interests is another dimension of what has been described as your structured self, your *character.*

I have talked about you as an organized composite of what you know and what you believe. I have said that your symbolic system—the words you live by and which fall so naturally from your lips—is mysteriously but inextricably linked with your nervous system. When we emphasize goal-directed behavior, this highly complex, intangible hierarchical system may best be described as your *system of interests.*

Many of us are inclined to use the word "interest" loosely. When a student comes to my classes, I want to know why he comes. I ask him about his interests. Almost invariably the student will beam and say,

"Oh, I'm interested in everything!"

These are the students, I have found, who sit on their hands

153

and do nothing. Yet inquiries into their interests bring no end to their protestations.

In *Theory of Valuation*,[71] John Dewey strips the glamour from such personalities by his unforgettable definition of "interest":

**An interest is an activity that springs from a need and moves in the direction of a goal that is calculated to satisfy that need.**

Like this:

This pragmatic definition of interest pulls every aspect of the self together. Because one short-term goal is the stepping-stone to another, the system of interests is, like character, the growing edge of selfhood.

**Thought, feeling, and action coalesce in your interest system.**

A predetermined goal calls for prediction—for thinking ahead. *Which, among possible alternatives, is the most logical plan? The least costly in sacrifice of competing interests?* This is *thinking*.

A need is a wanting. A wanting is *feeling*.

And movement in the direction of the goal that is calculated to satisfy the need is *activity*.

*Thinking-feeling-doing*. That's all there is. There is no

more. When these three components of the self converge in goal-directed behavior, the output is a concentration of Manpower, Unlimited.

## YOUR INTEREST SYSTEM *DOMINATES* YOUR LIFE

Interests are organized: heads, sub-heads, and so on. A great many interests hang together—familylike.

You, for instance, are interested in words. This I know, because you are now *doing something* that springs from a need and is calculated to satisfy that need. Else why should you be bothered? Your whole self—thinking-feeling-doing —is involved in the reading of this book.

Because you are interested in words, I know, too, that you are interested in ideas. How do I know this? Because an idea is defined as anything that can be signified, anything that can be put into words.[72] And because the use of words characterizes the human species, I know, too, that you are interested in human beings and, especially, in their behavior as mediated by words. But I know more. I know that you are interested in personality, because personality is defined as our impact upon others, and what is more potent than the use of words? I know, too, that you are interested in psychology, because you are concerned with how you think, how you learn, how you can become what you hope to be. As I sit here and write and think about you, a veritable family of interests draws us together.

Just so with others. You can safely speak to an architect about art, to a trained musician about mathematics, to a priest about education, to a carpenter about forestry, to a lawyer about logic, to an advertising man about words, etc.

155

Within the self each specific interest is in dynamic inter-relation with every other specific interest. What affects one interest affects another.

At the peak of the interest system we find, of course, our primary interests. These exert powerful control over the levels of interest that are of lesser importance to us. On the lower levels we are likely to make what appear to be automatic decisions; but when conflict arises here, a higher and more stable level of interest is likely to take over to make the necessary choice, the necessary decision.

Your interest system dominates your life. It rules with inexorable "logic." You hear what you choose to hear. Your system of interests regulates the threshold that determines whether or not impinging candidates for your attention will be admitted.

Just so, with me. Just so with every human being who lives.

## WHY, THEN, WILL I STOP
## TO LISTEN TO YOU?

**I will listen to you only when your words survive the screening process of my interest system.**

*But what interests me? How can you know what interests me?* You cannot know for sure, of course. You cannot jump inside my skin and penetrate to my *needs,* and my words may be misleading. Nor can you be absolutely sure of my *goals.* I may profess to be headed toward one objective when, in truth, I am "programmed" for another. But there is one thing you can be sure of. *You can look and see what I am doing, consistently and happily.* From my activities you may be able to draw some correct inferences about my needs and my goals—about my interests.

156

**An interest is an activity that mediates a need and a goal.**

More, we cannot do.

As I now write[1963], the great question concerning the ratification of the test-ban treaty with Russia is:

*Can we trust the Russians?*

On the basis of Dewey's conception of the nature of interests, we might consider whether or not two opposing factions might *act* profitably in common accord for different reasons (different needs and different goals).

Is it not conceivable that Khrushchev would *act* in accordance with this treaty because of his desire to create a favorable image in the newer countries, because of his need to solidify his position with the satellite countries, because of his need, also, to ally himself with the Western powers as a deterrent to China? Or for other reasons? And is it not conceivable that although the needs and the goals of Russia may be different from ours, some benefits may nevertheless accrue to both Russia and the allied powers because of this common *activity*? I do not know. But it does seem plausible to argue that both sides may maintain an agreement about *actions* while differing about other components of interest. If this is so, the question, then, is not one of trust but of understanding of the nature of the interest *in all of its components* behind the agreement to *act*.

Concerning our personal relationships with others through the medium of words, again, the emphasis on *action* holds promise. One of my favorite questions of a new acquaintance is, "What do you do?"

I really want to know because the answer is my best clue to his interests, his character, his personality.

157

The other night I met a young man whose name is Kim Saedi. A Persian. "What do you do?" was, for me, the most natural question in the world. His answer would tell me something about his past experience, and also how he had made his place among us.

"I am an interior designer," he replied.

I liked the word "designer."

His answer showed that in his actions he touches the lives of many people. For who does not have a home, a home that expresses so much of the self on the silent level. We talked for a long time, he from his perspective, I from mine, until, as considerately as possible, I withdrew to speak to another. But not before Saedi had asked me, "And what do you do?"

This question is always a poser for me. Though my answer sums up my whole life and has multidimensional ramifications, I can, and usually do, answer the question in four words, "I am in communication." And then I stop. Saedi had used five words, and he had stopped. A short yet specific answer is an effective formula. Tantalizing to the interested, considerate of the uninterested. The speaking-listening process is not two-ways; it is strictly cyclic. Like this:

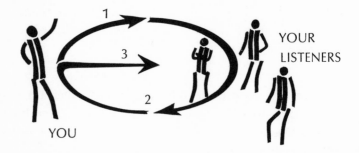

We must look for signals. We must look for signs, verbal and nonverbal, and use them as new information in our output.

## THE *FORMULA* FOR GAINING AND HOLDING ATTENTION

If, as Dewey says, an interest is indeed an activity that mediates a need and a goal, you have only to observe what others are doing (or if you do not have that opportunity, to ask) to be able to draw correct inferences about their interests.

The formula is self-evident. If you would interest others, it is necessary, somehow, to touch their needs, their goals, and their activities. This is almost impossible to do if *your* interest is strictly personal. The broader your interest, the more likely you are to relate successfully to the interests of others.

Try, first, to relate to a common need. (We are, after all, human beings.) Then the question of which goal will best satisfy the need will hold attention. Until there is agreement on goal, no further progress can be made. When need and goal are matters of common concern, the discussion will move naturally to activities. Expect differences of opinion when you discuss alternative means by which to attain the desired goal. Your position should now be open-end and subject to change on the basis of the cyclic transaction.

When you reach this stage, you become an active node— a center—in the interdependent situation as a whole. Nothing less than PS/W will be adequate to the attainment of consensus.

## WHAT IS YOUR *WQ*?

If we could weigh words by the ton or the pound or the ounce and classify the users of words by a numerical average, the first question on an employment application blank would

159

probably be *What is your WQ?* What is your Word Quotient?

The heavyweights would probably classify as verbomaniacs. The word "verbomaniac" is not in any of my dictionaries. Never mind. It was coined by Ogden and Richards in *The Meaning of Meaning* to designate the compulsive talkers.

Compulsive talkers abhor nothing so much as silence. So they talk, mostly in circles. They start something that reminds them of something else that reminds them of something else, and on they go, *ad infinitum*. In a seminar, when one such verbal wanderer took off for nowhere, Korzybski commented irritably, "You seem to be suffering from diarrhea of the mouth." Compulsive talkers never come to a point; in answer to the question *What are you talking about?* they should certainly say *I don't know*.

Every time we open our mouths to speak, we want something. We use words to inform others, to persuade others, to activate others. We must use words as conveyors of ideas with precision, clarity, and brevity. A good idea can be smothered and killed by words. When we initiate talk and direct it to a goal, we must pare the strategic verbal pattern until the skeleton of the idea is as bare as bones. Businessmen have learned that this semantic skill pays off in profits. For such precision, clarity, and brevity, formators are indispensable.

## NO ONE CAN LEARN TO SPEAK BETTER ABOUT *NOTHING*

When students come to me and say they want to learn to speak better, I say, "That's fine. What about?"

This comes to them as an unpleasant shock. On the non-verbal level they hiss *You darn fool! What business is it of yours anyway!* Then, as if to apologize for the unspoken thought, they blush and stammer, "Oh, about anything. Everything."

It doesn't work that way. We cannot learn to speak better about everything and anything. We can learn to speak better about *something,* and that should be our primary objective. Later, we find that our competency may be, and usually is, extended to related subjects.

To know something about one subject is all that is required to give anyone a sense of well-being and dignity, no matter what the occasion. I know a physician who would sit quietly all evening and listen to others talk about politics, economics, philosophy, and other complicated subjects. One day I asked him:

"Why were you so silent, doctor? Were you bored? Or tired?"

"Not at all," was the quick reply. "These are subjects about which I know little. I prefer to listen, especially when such well-informed persons are speaking."

I did notice, on other occasions, that whenever a discussion touched on medicine or a related topic, everyone deferred to him. And he spoke amazingly well. He is a contented man. He is not trying to be the best conversationalist in the world. He is not trying to speak well about "everything." All he wants is to be able to express himself well about a subject in which he is competent to speak. I admire him.

It can be, and usually is, a mark of self-respect to be able to sit quietly and listen to others. It is no disgrace, in this age of specialization, to say *I don't know. Tell me about it. I'm interested.* But it is essential for everyone to know enough about one subject to be able to initiate and to entertain conversation on that topic. This is the goal I set for my students. So I ask:

*What do you want to know more about?*

*What do you need to know more about?*

*What have you always wanted to study but have never had the time to put into it?*

*What? Tell me!*

The most surprising answers come back to me.

One beautiful Negro boy, about twenty-one, said: "I have always wanted to know something about philosophy. Could I read in philosophy and talk about what I read?"

I liked the idea. It is one thing to read in a new field and to think that we understand; it is another thing to be able to talk about what we read. We cannot paraphrase the ideas of another until we understand those ideas thoroughly. But to talk about them is to struggle through to understanding.

Curious about why the young man had this urge to know something about philosophy, I asked, "What do you do?"

"I am working for my Ph.D. in math," was the totally unexpected answer.

Then I understood.

I remember discussing with him how so many mathematicians came ultimately to philosophy, how the barren symbols of math describe timeless invariant relationships in nature and venture into space-time, and into infinity. He grinned, for he knew more about this than I did.

This young man began to read systematically in philosophy and to talk about what he read. He had a difficult time! Obviously, words were not his medium of expression. He could not pronounce "Aristotle." The polysyllabic words came laboriously. The class fidgeted restlessly. The air was filled with nonverbal hostility. *What is he trying to do? Learn some big words to throw around?*

In spite of everything the young man persisted. His voice was a drumbeat. Slow. Deep. Resonant. With a halting, broken rhythm; with the staccato of sudden discovery; with the slow, relentless measure of search. Before long he had earned the respect of every member of the class. He was expressing ideas with the decisive rhythm of march. I shall never forget him.

So it was with all the students. Those who were hopeful of advancing in their work or profession chose to read in the specialized journals in their particular fields. This was good. The periodicals carry current information long before such information finds its way into books, and articles in the journals are relatively short, well organized, and informative. A student can read many articles in the time it takes to read one book. What is more important, he may soon have a broad view of the topic of his choice.

Reading in a professional field lends itself naturally to the presentation of ideas in the classroom and to conversation and conference with associates. The newly acquired body of information, the students found, allowed them more choices when solutions to a current problem were being considered.

Other students, who did not choose to read and speak in an area in which they were competent, elected, rather, to explore a topic for which they had a yearning, a wanting, a need to know more. This, too, was good. The exploration became an adventure in ideas—and words! In every field of study the vocabulary is peculiar to itself; and because ideas depend on a specialized vocabulary, fully to understand the vocabulary is to understand the ideas.

163

As he read each new author in a single field, the student found that the authors used the same specialized words, but that each author immersed them in a different value system, discussed them from a different perspective. The joy of recognizing and understanding new words and ideas was augmented by surprise at the divergent opinions of the authors about identical facts. What was even more amazing was the discovery that an author chose those facts that supported his values! Soon the student felt impelled to consider all the facts presented by all the authors and to make up his own mind. As a result, he accumulated a body of organized information.

So every student carved out for himself an area of knowledge in which he enjoyed speaking. For me, the students' experiences were a revelation. Frequently, the scientist chose to read and speak of religion, even as the priest chose to read and speak of science. The M.D. spoke of art; the housewife, of psychology; the programmer, of the human organism, etc. All were searchers. All were intensely aware of adventure in their lives. All experienced a high sense of fulfillment that made itself manifest in every word they uttered. They had learned to speak better by *becoming* better. Is there any other way?

In order to speak better, we must have something to say, something that excites us. Nothing is so deadening as a warmed-over idea. When we learn, when we add to what we know and what we believe, the process of becoming grips us and activates us in the advancement toward what must necessarily be a receding goal. The search for more knowing is endless.

We cannot learn to speak better about everything or anything. What is required is a transformation of personality. What is required is a flank movement that will take us toward

164

the goal of more knowing. We can learn to speak better only by indirection.

## READ ALOUD. THEN *SPEAK*!

If you would learn to speak better, decide, first, *what about?* This is a momentous decision. It should spring from your need and impel you happily and actively toward your goal. Choose a topic that will add to your reservoir of information in an area in which you hope to excel—and to advance. *And to speak!*

Prepare yourself for the adventure of this new reading-speaking experience by reading aloud in the field of your interest. Your tongue will become agile in the use of a specialized vocabulary known previously only to your eye or to your ear.

I hope you have been reading this book aloud, preferably with a partner. Your every word, your every pause, will become meaningful to your collaborator. The rhythm of your voice will reflect the rhythm of my ideas. Grammar, especially punctuation, will, perhaps for the first time, take on structural significance. The rhythm of your voice will transmit the pattern of my thinking—and of yours.

When my words are read aloud by you, we come together. There is concert between us such as you may never have experienced with an author before. There are differences of opinion, of course, and perhaps even argument. No matter. Let us, first, have understanding. Then let the interplay generate something new, something different, something creative, for you. An idea—understood—is a pilot light, not an end in itself.

Now it is time to put the book down and talk about it. Try one idea. Paraphrase that idea, to be sure you understand it.

This may not be easy. It may be necessary to read aloud again —and try again. When you understand that idea well enough to restate it in your own words, take the next step. Evaluate the idea. Do you agree or disagree? Say why.

Now if you can converse about the idea with another, you will derive the maximum benefit from the exercise.

### *COMMUNICATION,* THE PROCESS = *PS/W*

I want, first, to draw a "picture" of your self. I wish I could penetrate to the cyclic, dynamic organization of your inner self, to that constantly emerging hierarchical structure of your knowledge, your values, your interests—to your brain, even to your heart.

Here you are.     This is your selfhood—humming within you.

Now I am going to draw a "picture" of you as you mesh with your world.

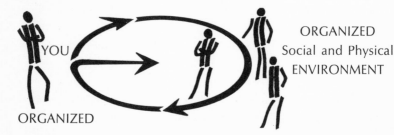

YOU

ORGANIZED
Social and Physical
ENVIRONMENT

ORGANIZED

You are, of course, still an object, sending out nonverbal signals. But inside your skin is that summary of your life lived—your self, your inner organization—and it is now in *trans*action—in cross organization—with your world.

Now you are what Gardner Murphy calls a "personality in a field."[73]

Now your organized self and the organized social and physical environment in which you are immersed—*together* —make a superstructure. You are a purposive center of a situation as a whole. Because *trans*action is a cyclic process, you affect the environment and the environment affects you. This is what Murphy calls "cross organization." What happens is not up, not down, not sideways, not two-ways, but cyclic.

**Your personality and the field in which you are immersed are inseparable.**

When you are in cross organization with the relevant environment, you are an actor whose role is only a part of the moving, changing interdependent scene. Maybe you are smiling—at someone else. Maybe you are speaking—to someone else. Maybe you are listening—to someone else. Maybe you are shaking hands, maybe working, maybe laughing, weeping, singing—with someone else. Your personality is at the highest level of complexity. You are a structured node—a vital center—within a larger organized field. Energy is a swirling force that binds every aspect of the field together, so that when one aspect of the field changes, every aspect of the field undergoes change of some sort—your self included. This is cross organization, and in cross organization PS/W becomes your indispensable resource.

I agree with Gardner Murphy when he says that the term "field theory" is fittingly and appropriately used to describe this conception of personality and communication theory if, as he says, "we expressly state that ['field theory'] is used as it is in physics; an electromagnetic field, for example, permits of no strict demarcation of a boundary and may change continuously as a result of varying currents."[74]

At this level, Murphy points out, "world and self flow into one another." And the boundary between them "is often vague or nonexistent."[75]

Your personality is, then, a relationship between your self and other selves every time you use words. You are a nodal region—a center, a point of concentration—in the cyclic, dynamic reciprocity of outgoing and incoming forces. This is reciprocal process and it is at its best in the face-to-face encounter: in selling, in conversation, in conference, in consultation, in teaching. But this is an *orderly* process because your activity is *purposive*. You want something. You use words to exert a measure of control over ongoing change to promote your interests. Because change is the very essence of the electromagnetic process, the situation as a whole is unique at every instant in time.

**In the communication process, there is cyclic transaction, uniqueness, relatedness, and order. And PS/W makes it possible for us to entertain randomness.**

The semantic devices are *feedforward* and *feedback*. It appears, then, that we have made an "equivalence" pattern:

$$\text{COMMUNICATION}^{1964} = \text{PS/W}$$

## MAN AND/OR MACHINE

The human being has a stream of consciousness that flows out of the past and into the future and that is permeated through and through with anticipatory thinkings-of and long-ings-for; with hopes, dreams, wants; with purposings. This the machine does not have. ("Not yet!" says a young computer scientist to whom everything is possible.)

That purpose is built into the human organism seems to be generally conceded, especially since the genetic code has been cracked.[8] The eminent biologist Edmund W. Sinnott says, "What . . . we call conscious desire or purpose originates in the unconscious and is part of the general regulativeness of living stuff."[76] In another interesting statement, he says:

Conscious purpose is the subjective experience of the operation of this regulatory activity in the brain. A purpose may be compared to the norm of a self-regulating machine, and presumably is effective through a feedback mechanism of some sort. There should be no objection to this conception of purposive activity, which may be interpreted as mechanistically as one wishes.[77]

Let's see. Every decision has a goal as its target. Every decision springs from a purpose.

In the decision-making process, where "consequentially" relevant data and operations can be fed forward (programmed) into the machine, the process may be said to be scientific. But it is agreed that the result can be only as reliable as the data and operations fed into the machine by the programmer.

In the decision-making process, the machine falls short of man in that, in man, the process is both science and art. Only man can function as a unity of thought-feeling, of "facts and desires" (as Sorensen puts it).[63]

**Man is purposive. The machine is a fantastic instrument that may be utilized in the accomplishment of purpose.**

**The computer program controls the machine. The speaker's purpose controls his behavior within a situation as a whole.**

No one denies that with the use of the electronic computers and, especially, the newer Perceptron, man is breathing into mechanical instruments a power that cannot be separated from the context of life and death. But Man *is not* Machine. And Machine *is not* Man.

Man is the maker of machines. Man programs the mechanism. Man sets the controls. A switch can be open or closed; an electrical pulse can be present or absent; a vacuum tube can be on or off: man plugs in the otherwise inert mechanism.

For those who would speculate on what future "generations" of machines might be, let me refer to the work of the physical scientist Jeremy Bernstein, who writes historically and analytically of the "emergent evolution" of the electronic machine. I give you here only his conclusion:

The history of electronic computers is only twenty years old, and they are still sufficiently simple for one to have a sense of understanding in detail how they work, and therefore of being in control. . . . But computers are already being used to design other computers, and it is quite possible that future generations of machines, which have been designed by machines, or which are not organized according to an entirely deterministic plan, may be beyond our complete understanding. . . . Alan Turing, a brilliant English mathematician, for one, seemed to accept this possibility as a foregone conclusion. "I suppose when it gets to that state," he said, "we shan't know how it does it."[78]

If, as you read, your blood curdles and a shiver runs down your spine, ask yourself *Who programmed the programmer?* If, like me, you can come to but one answer, you will, like me, take heart. If man can program the electronic machines with such unbelievable results, surely he can program himself. Surely he can move from his present self-image to his ideal self-image with equal skill—and with even better results.

**Man is not Machine. Man is a maker of machines. Man is a maker of his own destiny.**

170

We have considered communication as a process by which to exert a measure of control over the cyclic interdependent field in the interest of purpose. The process involves the use of words and requires that words be *selected and arranged* appropriately to a specific goal-state. In *Signs, Language and Behavior*, Charles Morris's exposition of the four uses and the four modes of language covers this culminating aspect of semantics. Morris's theory is a behavior theory. His uses and modes of language address themselves to purpose—to thinking, to wanting, to doing. In Part Three we shall turn our attention to his work.

*Part Three*

# Write It! Say It!
# Think It!
# Live It!

*Chapter VII*

# The Informative Use of Words

## THE VIRTUES OF INFORMATIVE LANGUAGE

When it is the intention of a communicator to *inform* his listeners or his readers, he will use informative language as defined in this chapter.

The virtues of informative language are precision (accuracy), clarity, and brevity. *Precision*, at its best, results from the use of verbal patterns that can be confirmed by actual patterns. *Clarity* requires emphasis on the essential formators and, perhaps, the secondary formators of the verbal pattern. *Brevity* is a natural consequence of emphasis on formators.

In the scientific use of informative language, statements are either true or false because they are subject to public verification. Informative language, at its best, is the language of recurrent patterns in nature.

The objectives of informative language are obstructed by two natural hazards. (A natural hazard is not a man-made hazard.) These natural hazards are inherent in human nature and in the nature of language itself. First, we speak because we have a need. Every word we utter is colored by *purpose*. Second, the meaning of a word is discoverable only in the past experience of the speaker and his listeners. Understanding is, for this reason, always approximate and never complete. These natural hazards must be reckoned with, if only to evaluate the consequences of our words intelligently. Semantics does provide some measure of control over the natural hazards, but they plague us even under the best of circumstances.

## WHAT WE *THINK–FEEL* AND WHAT WE *SAY*!

Because we speak with purpose, our hearts are in our mouths. Our feelings—our emotions—are always involved in lesser or greater degree. In this book, for instance, my primary intention is to inform you. The basic requirement of informative language is that it elicit *understanding*. Even if I wish to persuade you to an attitude response or to an action response, my informative language should be precise (accurate), clear, and brief.

**Understanding is neutral. This is a basic semantic principle. If we judge before we understand, how can we make a sound judgment?**

When you understand, it is your privilege, and your natural tendency, to evaluate what I say on the basis of that understanding. You may accept certain of my informative statements and reject others. You may want me to offer more evidence to support my informative statements.

176

You may even go so far as to pattern your future activity after my informative statements. Although my ultimate goal is to affect your behavior, what I think-feel must not distort my intention to inform. I must make a conscious effort to avoid this. A standard way of avoiding distortion in a book such as this is to use definitive quotations from others who cannot be accused of collusion with the author. Notice, for example, that the Appendix to this book does not paraphrase my sources. Nothing but a quotation will do. Yet you will be quick to recognize that I pick quotations that support my position.

When we speak or write, the subjects we choose to speak or write about are a matter of preferential selection. Our presentation is molded, always, by a purpose. Our strategy is directed, always, toward a goal.

Try as I will, I cannot separate thought-feeling. There is always an overlay of purpose—of needing, of wanting, of desiring. My preferential interest system dominates my life. And so with you. If we could separate our emotions from our thoughts in a clean-cut and precise fashion, our words would be unmuddied; words would be as specific and unequivocal and impersonal as numbers. But we cannot separate emotions from thoughts. P. W. Bridgman, Hollis Professor of Mathematics and Natural Philosophy at Harvard, sums up opinion on this point in *The Intelligent Individual and Society*:

I do not find the clean-cut separation of the emotional from the rational that the assumption of universal communicability would imply.[79]

The human being operates as a unity, as an organism. . . . This colors what we say and beclouds the meaning of our words. *What* we say is overlaid with *why* we say it. The subtle

177

overtones and undertones are part of our meanings. The description of a car by its physical features would be informative language, when we speak of a car as a "dreamboat" or a "crate" or even "a sweetheart of a car," we are way off the informative beat.

Some years ago an oil company ran a series of ads with the heading (which I paraphrase here):

*It's an OPINION whether fishing or hunting is the best of all sports, but it's a FACT that Blank Oil is the best.*

"Best" is, of course, an appraisive term and, as such, indicates an opinion.

Because we cannot penetrate precisely to the motives of those who inform us, understanding can be no more than approximate.

Both speakers and listeners, both writers and readers, are confronted by this natural hazard.

## OUR *PRIVATE WORLDS*

Words do not have *identical* meanings for different readers or listeners. If you are an engineer, a photographer, an advertising man, a foreman or supervisor in a factory, a mother and homemaker, a minister, my words insofar as you understand them, fall into some niche in your past experience. If they do not, my words are without significance to you. But if my words *relate* in some way to your life, you already are making applications of my words to your problems.

My life is different from yours. The words that roll off my fingers as I write for you come from a lifetime of concentrated interest in a specialized area of human experience. As I write, I am depending on you to fit my words into the pattern of *your* life. But I do not have the slightest reason to believe that the patterns of our lives are isomorphic—

identical in structure. Thus, even though you may under-stand me, your "meaning" and my "meaning" have different dimensions; *different connections.*

**We interpret words by referring them to the pattern of our past experience. There is no other way. If we cannot do this, the words are without significance to us.**

Your past experience is private. So is the experience of everyone else. Words are the medium of exchange between these private worlds. If this were not so, language would be without value. But even in the informative use of words re-member that words have varying degrees of communication value. The informative statement *The temperature is 90°* has a very high degree of communication value. That statement is universally understood. The informative statement *It is snowing* may have no definite significance to someone who has never seen snow. Of those who have seen snow, one may think of flurries, another of heavy flakes, and yet another of wet flakes.

Some informative statements represent public informa-tion.

The communication value of the language of science is, for example, very high, for meanings are explicit and well-nigh universal. To those who understand it, the language of mathematics reaches the zenith of precision, clarity, and brevity. The language that you and I use in the daily conduct of our lives is the nadir in comparison. And this is inevitable.

*What do you mean?* is probably the most intelligent ques-tion you can ask. Far from being a sign of ignorance, it is an indication of semantic awareness. No two human beings will respond *exactly* the same way to the words of another.

When I am puzzled, I have a habit of saying, "Please say

that in different words. I don't understand." Sometimes this helps. If it doesn't, I have another way of responding to a speaker whose words are not getting across. I say, "Let me see if I understand you."

Then I rephrase what I think he means. The restatement will alert the speaker to ways in which he may facilitate my understanding.

There are, then, two natural hazards in the use of informative language:

(1)  We speak because we have a need. Our words are the means by which we hope to satisfy that need. Our primary objective is to inform. But does the teacher inform her students with the circumscribed goal of bare understanding? Does the scientist present a technical paper with the hope of eliciting a response that indicates only a bare understanding? Information is the very stuff of experience—past, present, and future. The communicator must hope that the information he presents will augment and modify the pattern of experience of a reader or a listener in such a way that his future conduct will be different.

**A fact is never bare.**

The communicator is a human being. The listener or the reader is a human being. We select facts to promote our interests. How can it be otherwise? There is an arbitrary circumference around any fact[80] that is always determined, mind you, by a purpose. To know *all* about one fact we should have to know all about every related fact. *And all facts are related.* We should then have to know all about everything! We are selective creatures. Pity the man who screams: *Give me the bare facts!* There ain't no such animal.

180

How, then, shall we achieve uncontaminated language that may justly be called informative language, whose purpose is to elicit understanding.

(2) The words of a communicator originate in his personal perspective and fall upon the personal perspective of each listener or reader. Each percipient will entertain the communicator's words in his private world. There is no other way. It follows that meanings cannot be identical.

**The meaning of a word is discoverable in its relationship(s) to a structured life. And every life is unique.**

Korzybski said repeatedly that every word has multidimensional order. A word, depending on its purpose or emphasis, can be related in many ways to experience, even of the same human being.

How, then, shall we use words in such a way as to overcome the discrepancy between the intended meaning of the user and the percipient's meaning?

## WHAT DO YOU *MEAN*?

*The Meaning of Meaning* of Ogden and Richards was published in 1923. The "science of symbolism" advanced by them underpins the informative use of language as advanced by Charles Morris.

Ogden and Richards, mindful of the two natural hazards, provided a safeguard with respect to informative language that has stood the test of years: they drew a sharp distinction between two kinds of language, symbolic language and emotive language.

Symbolic language is defined by these authors as the use of words (symbols) to refer to some*thing* (objects, persons, events, etc.) in the world. The word "chair" is a symbol. We

181

can point to it out there in the world. But to speak of a "comfortable" chair is to introduce an emotive word that is, in their theory, "symbolically blank." Ogden and Richards do not depreciate the value of emotive language, but they insist that such language is irrelevant to the "science symbolism."

Symbols, as defined by these authors, are used to elicit an "understanding" response. Symbols are, therefore, in the informative use of language.

The very first thing that Ogden and Richards do is to unscramble the meaning of the word "meaning." Look at their "triangle" of meaning:[81]

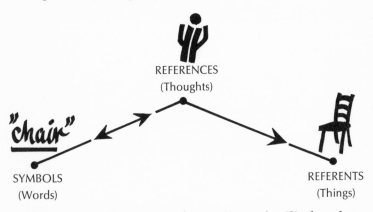

REFERENCES
(Thoughts)

"chair"

SYMBOLS
(Words)

REFERENTS
(Things)

Meaning has three dimensions: (1) words, (2) thoughts, and (3) things.

When I ask *What do you mean?* how can you know (1) whether or not your vocabulary is my vocabulary or (2) whether or not I follow your thinking or (3) whether or not I ever heard of the *thing* you seem to be talking about and would know it if I saw it.

So when I ask *What do you mean?* you will have to inquire into what is blocking our communication: your words, your

182

thoughts, or whatever it is that you are talking about out there in the world. When a discussion bogs down because the participants do not speak "the same language," it is futile to fish around aimlessly for the cause of the misunderstanding. It is so much simpler to inquire: *What don't you understand? My words? My thoughts? Or the thing I'm talking about?*

**Meaning is not simple. It is complex. It has three dimensions: words, thoughts, and the things referred to.**

(And my apologies to Ogden and Richards for the little man at the peak of the triangle. He is there! And every word he uses is filtered through and through by his nervous system. It is he who swings the lariat that pulls words together and *arranges* them in a pattern that is isomorphic with a pattern out there in the world.)

## THE *PUBLIC* USE OF WORDS

Ogden and Richards know that there is a certain "treachery of words," to use their phrase. They know, too, that there is no way by which your thoughts and mine can be directly compared. So they use the third dimension of meaning—*referents*—by which to ground a communication process and bring participants together.

As you see, I take some liberties, again, with their "triangle" of meaning on page 184.

Notice that there is play between your words and your thoughts. The arrows go in both directions. We think with words. But notice that another arrow brings your thoughts downward—outward—to the referent, to the things out there in the world to which your words refer.

Now notice that I am there, too. You are speaking to me. There you are, on your apex, a thinking-feeling creature.

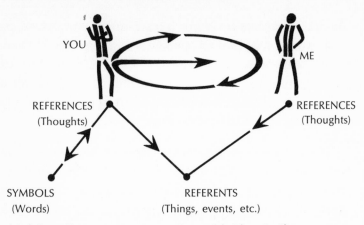

And there I am, on my apex, also a thinking-feeling creature. And I want to know what you are talking about: precisely (accurately), clearly, and briefly.

Say that you are talking about a "metronome" and that I don't know what the word means and that I wouldn't know one if I saw one. If you can direct my thoughts to an actual referent that the word "metronome" symbolizes (refers to), we can't miss. You can make it work for me and *show me* its utility in practicing exercises on the piano. We are together. You may feel one way about the usefulness of the metronome and I another. But this makes no difference. To quote Ogden and Richards, we can rid the communication process of "emotional, diplomatic, and other disturbances" by *looking at the thing*, quite apart from our personal reactions to the symbols or even the thing referred to.

This solution is no dodge. Ogden and Richards realize that there is no *direct* relationship between your words and the things they refer to. The "triangle" has no base! *The meaning of your words lies in your skull.* You have your skull and I have mine. When we converse, what happens? On the basis of our personal experience, you *interpret* my words and I

184

*interpret* your words. Words have meanings only as we can relate them to the pattern of our experience. There is always a difference in meanings in greater or lesser degree. The "triangle" of meaning recognizes the existence of differences of meanings but avoids the natural hazard by directing all participants to the referent. Out there!

**The symbolic language of Ogden and Richards is informative language. Words that do not refer to things are symbolically blank. Feelingful words are not symbols; they are irrelevant to the "science of symbolism" of Ogden and Richards.**

Symbolic language is either true or false. On this point Ogden and Richards are clear.

True reference is reference to a set of referents as they hang together. False reference is reference to them as being in some other arrangement than that in which they actually hang together.[82]

References (thoughts) are complex. (Incidentally, these authors use the word "reference" to emphasize reference *to* some*thing* out in the world. Thoughts may, and often do, live phantom lives with no reference whatsoever to the world of people and things. Thoughts can float, without landing.)

The language of Ogden and Richards has already been translated into the language of PS/W. However, because of the significance of symbolic language to the informative use of language as explicated by Morris, I shall recapitulate:

When a verbal pattern matches an actual pattern out there in the world, part for part and order for order, then we have a true and logical statement. The symbolic reference of Ogden and Richards gives us, then, informative language that is subject to verification.

185

Informative language makes it possible for all to *understand*—precisely, clearly, and briefly. *Precisely* and *accurately* when the verbal pattern and the actual pattern are isomorphic. *Clearly* when the verbal pattern is referable to an actual pattern in the world. And *briefly* when the verbal pattern is made up of essential formators that, together, make the pattern as a whole.

Symbolic language, as defined by Ogden and Richards, is, at its best, the language of science (*If this, then necessarily that*). Here, of course, we have recurrent patterns that are subject to verification. But symbolic language is used by all of us in making reports. A report that is isomorphic with the state of affairs described is both true and logical. And accurate!

The means-to-end hypothesis, as such, is not considered by Ogden and Richards. Since the means-to-end construct looks to the future in goal-seeking behavior, it is less amenable to the prescriptions of the "science of symbolism."

Let us turn, now, to Morris's *Signs, Language and Behavior*, which is our primary source.

## THE "SCIENCE OF SIGNS" OF CHARLES MORRIS

Ogden and Richards are concerned with two kinds of language, symbolic and emotive. Symbolic language refers to things. Words that do not refer to things are "emotive" and emotive words are symbolically blank. Morris's theory of uses and modes (kinds) of language differs from that of Ogden and Richards in that it is a *behavior* theory and, as such, recognizes the overlapping nature of the various uses and modes of language.

Whereas Ogden and Richards restrict meaning to symbolic language (Morris's informative use of language), Morris considers meaning within the framework of purpose. Morris explores the questions: *To what uses (purposes) are words put, and how are those uses (purposes) best accomplished?*

The accomplishment of purpose involves more than informative assertion and proof. The accomplishment of purpose is a complex feeling-thinking-doing behavioral situation that requires the systematic arrangement of these facets of behavior. Morris therefore explicates four *uses* of language: informative, valuative, incitive, and systemic. He explicates, also, the four *modes* of language that are appropriate to the four uses. Morris's uses and modes of language will be explained in this concluding Part of PS/W. In this chapter we are concerned primarily with the informative use in the designative mode.

Here is Morris's definition of *informative* language:

In the informative use of signs, signs are produced to cause someone to act as if a certain situation has certain characteristics.[83]

To say this differently, in the informative use of language the intention of the communicator is primarily to inform—to elicit an understanding response. He will be careful to select descriptive terms that refer to things and to omit valuative and incitive language.

*Valuative* language differs from informative language in that the intention of the speaker or writer is primarily to elicit a preferential attitude-response to something he values. Valuative language may, therefore, be used to elicit a preferential response to a goal-state.

*Incitive* language asks primarily for a specific action response.

The only function of *systemic* language is to *systematize* the other three uses. Systemic language is the language of *pattern*. It makes use of informative, valuative, and incitive formators so as to organize all the responses of a listener.

Unlike Ogden and Richards, Morris recognizes the overlapping nature of the informative, valuative, and incitive uses of language. Informative language may serve purposes other than to inform. If, for example, I wanted to persuade you to a preferential attitude toward my interests, I might decide that emotive language would be less effective in your case than strictly informative language that refers to things, persons, and events in the world. A salesman, for instance, would be unlikely to use predominantly valuative or incitive language to a discriminating buyer. The salesman would undoubtedly make use of informative language that refers specifically and definitely to the product, to competitive products, to service, etc., even though he hopes to excite enthusiasm and, ultimately, to get an order.

On the other hand, if I say to you *I've got a toothache*, my statement cannot be *referred* to anything or anyone outside my self. My toothache is so damn personal, it isn't even funny. And yet, I may want you to react to that statement, first, as if it were in the informative use. I do not want a valuative response. I do not want sympathy. I want to get rid of the toothache. Maybe you will consider the statement, first, in the informative use, and then in the incitive use. If you do, you will first understand me, and then you will take me to a dentist or give me an aspirin.

For Morris, in behavioral situations, the informative, valuative, and incitive uses of language, while sharply differentiated, tend to overlap.

188

## THE *INFORMATIVE* USE IN THE *DESIGNATIVE* MODE OF CHARLES MORRIS

Morris defines informative language as the use of signs produced to cause a percipient to act as if a certain situation has certain characteristics. For this purpose Morris uses words that he calls *designators.*

Designators "signify characteristics of the environment."[84] A designator does just that. It designates. It identifies. It indicates. It specifies. It names. It points out. It refers to "a certain situation." And "the primary use of designators is informative."[85]

**When a designator does, indeed, identify a characteristic of the environment, that designator is said by Morris to denote. A designator that denotes is true.**[86]

A designator is reliable, Morris says, when it denotes: otherwise not. A designator is reliable to the degree that it denotes in various instances of its appearance.[87] (This is a statistical account of recurrence.) Designators that denote consistently have importance because expectations based on them will not be disappointed. This, of course, has relevance to prediction.

## "... TO CAUSE SOMEONE TO *ACT* AS IF...."

Notice that Morris defines the informative use of words as signs produced to cause someone to *act* as if a certain situation has certain characteristics. This action is important.

**The emphasis in Morris's Signs, Language and Behavior is on the behavior that words in any use or mode tend to produce.**

Behavior is our interest, too. It is necessary to be able to use words in such a way as to stimulate the desired behavior in our listeners or readers.

We are, let it be repeated again at this point, goal-seekers. We want. We ask for change of some sort in the relevant environment. If our words can produce that change, then PS/W becomes an actuality.

We proceed now specifically to the uses and misuses of informative language. Morris's *Signs, Language and Behavior* is our grounding, but what forays we shall make beyond his basic theory are on our own heads. (Professor Morris, exempt and uncommitted, is nonetheless a multidimensional catalyst.)

## THE USER OF INFORMATIVE LANGUAGE IS ESSENTIALLY A *REPORTER*

The purpose of the reporter is to inform; his objective is to elicit an understanding response.

The virtues of informative language are precision (accuracy), clarity, and brevity.

The language of the report is, in general, I believe, best served by nouns and verbs. Informative language is neutral. Adjectives and adverbs are, therefore, not appropriate to the strictly informative report. Long and involved sentences are likely to obstruct understanding. The subject-predicate-period style has the virtues of simplicity and clarity.

In the informative use of language the arrangement of formators is extremely important. Remember now that *information* is defined as a symbolic pattern of relationships between objects, persons, events, etc. Since informative statements are, at best, confirmed statements, the structure of the

190

report should be isomorphic with the structive of an actual pattern.

**There should be correspondence, part for part and relationship for relationship, between the verbal pattern and the actual pattern it purports to designate.**

## IF YOU ARE *WRITING* AN INFORMATIVE *MEMO*

An informative memo takes this heading:

*Date*:
*From*:
*To*:
*Re*:

*Re*: answers such questions as *What about? Where? When?* etc. For example: *Re: Meeting of all foremen in Supervisor Green's office at 4 P.M., January 10, 1964.*

Information to answer the question *Why?* can be put into the body of the memo. For example: *Subject for discussion: Demonstration of automatic machinery.* Such a memo is precise, clear, and brief. Every word is strictly informative. It asks the reader primarily for understanding.

## IF YOU ARE *WRITING* AN INFORMATIVE *LETTER*

The informative letter may, and usually does, make use of the *Re:* caption as a heading. Example: *Re: Proposed changes to meet your repair service requirements.* Who would not give this letter careful attention?

The writer of an informative letter deserves a "thank you" from the recipient if the letter is brief and to the point. The

191

fewer the words, the better. Correspondence is now weighed by the ton. No one wants to search for an idea that is lost in words. The reader wants the idea sharp and clear.

Write as you would speak to the recipient, but always simply, directly, and briefly. Phrases such as *Your esteemed favor of the 13th ult., We beg to remain your faithful,* etc., are now archaic.

Reread your informative letter, very much as you would a telegram, to see if you have said what you must say in the minimum number of words.

## IF YOU ARE *WRITING* AN INFORMATIVE *ARTICLE*

The strictly informative article is written, usually, for specialized publications. Whether it is a scientific journal or a trade magazine, the reader will appreciate an abstract.

**An abstract is a skeletal statement of the contents of the article.**

Because the abstract usually precedes the published article itself, the reader can know in about one minute flat whether or not he wants to read the entire article.

Today, because periodicals pile up unread, more and more editors are insisting that authors write abstracts of articles that they submit for publication.

Here is a rule for the title of an informative article:

The title of an informative article should be a *working-title* that prescribes and delimits the scope of the article. The title should not be a literary title concocted to induce interest. An informative working-title is made up of primary formators that are related to each other according to a principle of organization. Here is such a working-title.

*Feedforward* + *feedback* = *PS/W*

The abstract that precedes the published article should amplify this working-title by the use of secondary formators. The abstract should require only one short paragraph.

FEEDFORWARD is the use of a strategic verbal pattern that is both cohesive and progressive, which, once started, enables a reader or a listener to anticipate what is to follow. FEEDBACK is the tactical semantic control which corrects any diviation between the present state of affairs and the goal-state. Feedforward (strategy) and feedback (tactics) maintain stability in goal-directed behavior. Feedforward + feedback = Power-Steering with Words.

The "article" itself you will find in Chapter III.

In an informative article, the title, the abstract, and the text itself should have identical form. The title, the briefest of the three, includes only the primary formators. The abstract is a short paragraph that amplifies the primary formators by introducing and defining the secondary formators (strategy and tactics). The text itself may be as long as necessary to develop every point carefully.

To say this differently: the title, the abstract, and the text are isomorphic.

## IF YOU ARE *WRITING* A *REPORT*

Few of us are required to write technical or strictly informative articles, but almost everyone is obliged to write a report now and then. Such a report is submitted for the record and should carry a heading:

REPORT: (The Working-Title)
*Submitted to*:
*By*:
*Date*:

Begin with a working-title. *What is the report about?*

Use your working-title to establish the form of the report. The formators may be related in time, in space, sectionally, or causally. Notice the omission of the means-to-end pattern here. A means-to-end pattern is a project, a program, and not a report. It must be classed as a "speculative model" or a "developmental construct."[39]

In the development of the report you will use secondary formators that fall logically under the primary formators. It is possible that you may need tertiary formators to report evidence, operations, etc. Be as brief as is consistent with completeness of essentials. Details are excluded.

I, personally, like to use "leads," or marginal subheadings, to alert the reader to the form—the pattern—that the report takes. Paragraphing is, of course, another device by which to make transitions. And it is helpful to the reader to introduce a transition by the use of the formator under which the part falls.

The conclusion of such a report is simply a restatement of the working-title, which, as you know, makes a place for everything in the report.

Sometimes a report is followed by the writer's recommendations. These will, of course, take the form of a mean-to-end pattern.

In the industrial report the preferred form is to keep the report and the recommendations separate. When this is done, each section has its proper heading. The report then designates facts; the recommendations express opinions about future procedures.

## DON'T READ IT, *SAY* IT!

In my opinion, every report should be written and stored as information. The written report belongs in a file where it can be retrieved when needed. But if you want to enjoy a dynamic relationship with your audience, do not read the report. If it is so word-dependent that it must be read, it is better to have it mimeographed and distributed and then open the subject to discussion.

When you read a report, you withdraw into isolation every time your eyes are glued to your paper. Before you have finished you are likely to be in the deep freeze.

If you memorize your report, you are lost. Before you have fairly launched into it, your glazed eyes will excite the pity of your listeners. If they are still listeners.

**The person who is qualified to write a report is qualified to say it.**

The form of an oral report is precisely the same as the form of a written report. The patterns are identical. We begin with a working-title that prescribes and delimits the scope of the report. We use the working-title to establish the pattern of the report as a whole. Primary, secondary, and tertiary formators, properly organized, automatically establish form.

Here is the cardinal rule:

**The pattern of the oral report must be fed forward because the pattern represents your strategy—your logical construct.**

As a reporter you will hit hard, first, at the working-title, which will call attention to the primary formators. As you feed this verbal pattern forward, your listeners will anticipate what is to follow. *You have organized their responses.*

I find that *timing* is the best device by which to feed a verbal pattern forward. Pauses—long and clean—between the primary parts serve the same purpose that sections serve in the written document. Shorter pauses can, in the same way, set secondary formators apart under each section.

Just as I use marginal topic leads in the written document, so in the oral report I introduce each successive part by specific reference to the formator under which it falls. At the end, I wrap up the whole thing by getting back to the working-title, which makes a place, of course, for everything that has been said.

As in the written report, we start with the working-title and we conclude with the working-title.

You will maintain your strategic pattern in spite of any kind of interference. The parts of the verbal pattern will stick together like glue, and yet they will move. You will not need to memorize *anything*.

**Understanding replaces memorizing. Remembering is a consequence of understanding the relationship between the essential parts of a pattern. The pattern is a dynamic relatedness that moves by its own power.**

You have made the pattern yourself. It is yours. And it will see you through. You will find your words as you go. Your delivery may be choppy, even as thought is sometimes choppy. You may grope for words, *but never for ideas*! The rhythm of your words will reflect your thinking, and your listeners will think with you.

By the use of Operation Feedback, you can entertain questions and interruptions without disrupting your logical progression toward the conclusion that has been epitomized in your working-title.

Until a speaker learns to report on his feet, he is not qualified to discuss anything on his feet, because all other uses of language hinge ultimately, on precise, clear use of informative language.

196

**The informative construct is the basis of our judgments and of our actions. The informative construct is the basis of the judgments and of the actions of our listeners.**

PS/W begins with the clipped, sharp, decisive patterns that designate information.

## WHEN YOUR *LOGIC* IS SHIFTY, YOU *MISUSE* INFORMATIVE LANGUAGE

We use the word "logic" to refer to relationships.

When a verbal pattern is made up of parts that correspond part for part and relationship for relationship to something in the actual world, we say the verbal pattern is both true and logical.

The recurrent *If this, then necessarily that* verbal pattern is both true and logical. We refer to such a pattern as a bona fide cause-to-effect pattern.

Maybe you are talking about the possible causes of a strike, a race riot, juvenile delinquency, or economic depression, inflation, disease, any one of the hundreds of problems that concern us in our everyday lives. In such cases we use the available data and operations to arrive at an imputed (possible or even plausible) cause-to-effect relationship. This is the best we can do. But it is illogical and incorrect to foist such a verbal pattern on listeners as if it were a bona fide cause-to-effect pattern in which all the relevant data and operations are controllable.

Nor are we logical if we present a means-to-end pattern as a recurrent *If this, then necessarily that* pattern. Where human beings are involved, there are too many variables over which we have no control. A means-to-end pattern is neither true nor false. It is "better" or "worse" depending on

197

the relevance and inclusiveness and quality of the evidence that supports it.

So your logic may be inadvertently shifty when your verbal pattern is not referable to an actual pattern in nature. Charlatans try this intentionally. Promoters sometimes try this. The semanticist who tries it is a downright fraud.

## OR MAYBE YOU DON'T KNOW
## WHAT YOU'RE TALKING ABOUT!

Informative language is subject to verification. If you do not have evidence to support your verbal pattern, the pattern is open to criticism, to refutation, and to rejection. In the informative use of language our words are referable to objects, persons, and events in the world.

Most of us are inclined to take "information" at face value when it is presented by an "authority." This is risky. Serious errors have been compounded and perpetuated because a respected and trusted authority has made a mistake.

The most embarrassing thing that can happen to a reporter occurs when someone gives the lie to his words. This is difficult, if not impossible, to live down. In everyday situations, now and then, we hear a person spout "facts" and we marvel at his comprehensive, almost encyclopedic, knowledge. Until he lets fall an obvious error. Then, quite suddenly, we get the distinct impression that he doesn't know what he is talking about.

## BUT MAYBE YOU WERE MISINFORMED!

It is one thing to be *un*informed; another, to be *mis*informed. Being misinformed can happen to anyone: someone who is supposed to know "just doesn't." But we take his word

THE INFORMATIVE USE OF WORDS

for whatever he says. Former President Eisenhower once presented figures to the public concerning our defense equipment. I listened. And I went to sleep that night comforted by the "information" the President had passed on to me and to the world. The next day, my morning newspaper indicated that the man in the White House had been "misinformed" about the status of our defense preparedness. Somebody had checked his statements. But I hadn't. I couldn't. So I possessed misinformation that I might have passed on to others without a qualm.

## AND DON'T WE ALL?

Informative language must be used at times in everyday discourse. When we are asked for the facts in a case, an informative response is indicated. We try to respond informatively. But, whether we will it or not, we are likely to select such facts as support a personal value system. There is always selectivity on the basis of preconceived ideas, on the basis of a preference system—conscious and unconscious.

No matter how conscientious we may be in our choice of informative language, there are always "hidden persuaders." That bias. That slant. That emphasis. That intrusion of the personal self that is directed toward the heart's desires.

We do not—we cannot—go all the way in our analyses. There is so much more beyond what we can perceive, beyond what we can know. And so one of the most innocent and yet most deceptive misuses of informative language is that innate pressure toward hoped-for goals that makes itself felt in subtle ways of which we know little.

When we have our eyes on a star, we are blind to everything else that impinges on our vision. We learn what we want to learn. We believe what we want to believe.

**The observer and the observed are as one. The knower and the known are as one.**[88]

When someone asks *What are the facts in the case?*

Why not try *From where I stand, this is how I see it. How does it look to you?* And then *listen*. The informant becomes the informed. The teacher becomes the learner. The communicator becomes the communicatee. *The speaker becomes the listener.* And there is Power-Steering With Words, such that we are all the wiser, all the happier—and all the more loved.

*Chapter VIII*

# The Valuative Use of Words

## WHEREVER YOUR WORDS GO, THERE *YOU* GO

In the *informative* use of language, the objective is to find a way to *report* as conscientiously as possible, with all due regard for precision (accuracy), clarity, and brevity.

In the *valuative* use of words, the urge is quite different. We are not reporters alone. We live. We take sides. We want others to take sides with us, and for us. If we would lead, we must not only say *where and how*, we must also say *why*.

Every word we choose to utter carries with it something more than the dictionary meaning. Every word is immersed in a value system. A dictionary definition can never give us a hint of the *attitude* of the user of words. If, for instance, I should meet you as I walk with a friend down Park Avenue,

WRITE IT! SAY IT! THINK IT! LIVE IT!

I may say *How nice to see you! I want you to meet my friend Leila Kingery.* Why am I so glad to see you? Have I missed you? Or is it that you are the very one to meet Leila and to become a friend to her? Korzybski knew what he was talking about when he said:

**Every word is $\dfrac{\text{over}}{\text{under}}$ defined; overdefined because it carries with it an attitude; and underdefined because every word is a class word—an abstraction—that leaves out all of the differences.**[89]

Valuative words may, of course, be obstacles to communication. Yet, sometimes they are aids to communication. At times we can "catch" a group, each individual with his own "attitudes," and somehow bring all listeners together, not on the basis of dictionary meanings, but on the basis of feelings, of wantings, of needings.

Now we dip frankly into values, into character, into the integrity of the self. A value is something—anything—that has worth for us, and the value system is the backbone of the structured self.

**The value system acts as a preference system that monitors everything we say or do.**

## TO CAUSE SOMEONE TO TAKE A PREFERENTIAL ATTITUDE TO SOMETHING

Following Morris, we shall define the valuative use of language as that use of words which causes a listener or a reader to give preferential status to a hope, a dream, a wanting. We use valuative language to affect a listener's or a reader's attitudes to objects, to persons, to events, etc.[90]

202

**We define an "attitude" as a disposition to act in a given way.**

To change the attitudes of another is to stir him to his innermost depths, for attitudes are gut-filling experience. Heated arguments will not budge attitudes. Our attitudes stem from our values, and our values spring from our needs.

A change in the value system is difficult to bring about. The value system is not directly approachable by feelingful valuative language alone, but there is evidence that change may be effected in the value system indirectly by "uncontaminated" informative language. When informative language is used as a base for valuative language, valuative language carries a powerful impact.

In an experiment that was made by the National Opinion Research Center of the University of Chicago some years ago at the Conference for Education in the Atomic Age a questionaire was distributed with the objective of determining attitudes toward a current problem. The answers were collected and collated. Afterwards, three speakers of consequence discussed the problem. Each speaker was a specialist in his field and introduced relevant information concerning the problem. The three talks represented three dimensions of the same problem. After the talks, another questionaire, using precisely the same questions as the first, was distributed. Answers to the second questionaire showed a marked change in the attitudes of the participants.

**That valuative language rests on informative language must be conceded. An attitude should therefore be dated and looked at periodically in the light of incoming information.**

## THE *VALUATIVE* USE IN THE *APPRAISIVE* MODE OF CHARLES MORRIS

The appropriate mode of valuative language is the appraisor.

An appraisor sets a value on something. Appraisors call things "better" or "worse," "beautiful" or "ugly," "interesting" or "dull," "useful" or "ornamental," etc. You can spot an appraisor immediately by its grammatical form. All adjectives, all adverbs, are appraisors. Any fifth-grade student who knows an adjective or an adverb when he hears one can say with confidence *That's the way you feel about it. That is your opinion. I'll make up my own mind.*

Although adjectives and adverbs are easily distinguished as appraisors, some nouns and some verbs have an appraisive coating. These are the sly words that puzzle us. And ensnare us.

When I talked to my butcher the other day, I asked, "What's the difference between a Boston cut and a pot roast?"

He could have said, "Well, professor, the difference is a semantic difference."

He did give me the impression that the price was hiked on the fancier name. I have wondered, too, why Hayakawa's "hunk of dead cow" becomes a *filet mignon* at about $4.50 and a *Chateaubriand* at something like $8.50. The other day I was asking about "chuck."

The butcher grinned and said, "It's all chuck."

I'll never learn. (And don't argue with *me* about this. I confess to complete ignorance of the anatomy of a cow.)

I'm not complaining. I am not a reporter when I sit before a steak. However, if the conversation should turn to serious things, you will find me taking sides. And warmly. For what

204

is a "fact" if it is not related to something that matters, to something that concerns us on the personal level? For me, appraisive language is that extra special "something" that puts the humanity into words. Appraisive language is our only way of showing involvement in cold facts.

Verbs, too, can dress up—or down!—an informative statement until you cannot recognize it as a conveyor of information. *She slithered across the room. He slouched in his chair*. Etc.

If you are one who thinks it proper to maintain a calm and aloof dignity, if you are one who thrives on facts, and if you wonder why nobody loves you, try blowing warm. You will find that those who formerly stood off in respect for you will come closer. As close as you will let them. And they will be eager and ready to follow where you lead.

Appraisors take a fact and look at it frankly to determine its value with respect to a purpose. Every writer of a report who is worth his salt will supplement the report with his opinions about the facts presented. If he is semantically wise, he will keep his report and his appraisal in proper order, and he will keep them separate.

Here is the rule when you wish to persuade:

**Designators first, and only then appraisors.**

If the appraisors are tightly linked with designators that denote, the opinion is supported by the evidence. An unsupported opinion is worthless.

## FEELING, THE BASIS FOR PERSUASION

A means-to-end pattern springs from a need. Words are persuasive only when they touch the need of a person.

The word "need" is a feelingful word. A need is a wanting,

a desiring; it is a craving for the attainment of a goal that will satisfy the need. A goal is not a lure unless it gives promise of the satisfaction of a need.

If your need is strictly personal, valuative language is likely to go unattended. If you can relate your need to that of others' needs, you have a basis for persuasion.

Some persons are well aware of their needs. They know what they want. Others are not sure. First, the goal must be clarified. Then the spark must be struck and the torch lit to illumine the way toward concerted action in the direction of the desired goal. This is not so difficult as it sounds.

A salesman has no difficulty in determining the needs of a customer. The categories of needs are limited. The customer's needs relate to products, to equipment, to service, etc., at the right price. The salesman does not address himself cold to a potential customer. He knows, in general, what the customer wants, and if he is wise, he investigates the customer's specific needs. This done, he sets up a means-to-end program that is calculated to satisfy those needs. Now he has a good "prospect."

The minister has little difficulty in determining what the members of his congregation want. In general, they seek security—personal security, the security of the family and of the state. They want to know what affects that security, and what they can do about it. They need more. They want to believe. They are tormented by their incompleteness, and they want, somehow, to ally themselves with more—with the Infinite More.

The lawyer knows precisely what his client wants—a favorable settlement of a problematical situation. The goal is clear. Only the means must be clarified.

The physician knows precisely what a patient needs: health and a sense of well-being.

206

The salesman, the minister, the lawyer, the physician, each must stir the hearts of those who listen. Facts are always a solid support to appraisive language that calls out for attention, for interest, for hope, for courage, for willingness to act. The warm words are warming. They are the blessed cover of cold facts.

In *Philosophy in a New Key*, Susanne K. Langer speaks of a morphology of feeling as a basic form, a basic pattern, within the human self.[91] Think of this! It means that human beings are endowed with certain universal longings, feelings, passions, that are common to everyone who lives. So general are the "laws" of feeling that they make a place for your sorrows and mine, your joys and mine, your fears and mine, your hopes and mine. Works of art, Langer says, express these general "laws" and invite, not an emotional response, mind you, but a kind of insight into a universal understanding of human needs. And this insight, she says, may be and usually is below the threshold of consciousness. It is a kind of wordless knowledge that is never explicit, a kind of unconsummated pattern that, in essence, represents eternal human striving.

We are feelers as well as thinkers. We are filled with the warmth of living. Appraisive language may stir the responsiveness that causes human beings to band together, to work together, to sing together, to march together, to weep together, to pray together. There is that indefinable, that indescribable, that unspeakable, dynamic pattern of feeling that somehow embraces us all.

Valuative language has perhaps its greatest potency in the feelingful response everyone experiences on hearing it—but each response is different. When I use the words "sorrow," you respond. But only because you are thinking of the sorrow that *you* know and that is yours alone. The meanings of valuative terms are pervasive, so pervasive that they may touch us all.

**If we would kindle warmth in others, we must experience warmth within our selves. And we must dare to be expressive of that warmth. Valuative language in the appraisive mode will make this possible.**

## EVALUATION IS *CRITICISM*

A valuative statement may be called criticism. The word "criticism" is a neutral word, because criticism may be positive (favorable) or negative (unfavorable) or a combination of positive and negative statements. The term "criticism" is often misunderstood as negative evaluation only.

Valuative language that is unsupported by designators is powerless. When we relate our appraisors to designators that denote, we have a powerhouse of persuasiveness. The combination of appraisors and designators has the compound appeal to both thought and feeling. "Criticism" is an excellent word to describe this thought-feeling.

**Keep appraisive language close to designators that denote. Appraisive language must have its foundation in designative language.**

Frequently, a reporter is asked for his opinion of the state of affairs he describes. In my work with industrial engineers I found this to be common practice. For the purposes of the engineers, the approved form separated the report of facts from the evaluation of facts. In some instances, a separate document was required, but, in all cases, the procedure was *facts first, then evaluation.*

Almost everything we read today is a combination of reporting and evaluation, but there is rarely a sharp division between the two. A semantic awareness of the uses and modes of language is our only protection against naïve responses. An editorial may, for instance, begin with a single factual sentence and give the entire remaining editorial space to evaluation. The intelligent reader should keep that factual sentence before him as he reads, for the whole editorial is grounded in that one fact. He might then ask himself *Are there any other relevant facts—facts which have been omitted? Or How would I evaluate that fact on the basis of my own value system?*

Appraisive language that stands alone is suspect. A percipient wants some designative support of valuative statements. A second important consideration is the relationship between designators and appraisors. That relation must be established and evaluated.

## CRITICISM AS A *GENERATOR* OF *FEEDBACK*

Those who appraise what they read and what they hear go beyond analysis to evaluation. This critical process augments the value system. Nothing could be more important to goal-directed behavior.

*Negative feedback* has been defined as "the control system that corrects the mismatch between an actual state of affairs and the desired goal-state."

*How do you know there is a mismatch? And how do you know the degree to which it occurs?*

A mismatch is indicated by the evaluatory mechanism. We know what we want, but we need to know also how we are

209

doing. So we appraise the present state of affairs by stacking it up against the goal-state. *How do we like the present state of affairs? Is it moving toward the desired goal, toward what we want?*

**Negative Feedback has been defined as "activity under correction of evaluatory signals."[41] This means that Power-Steering with Words is possible only when incoming responses are appraised by the value system.**

Evaluation flows from and returns to the value system of the communicator. Evaluation is his means of measuring the degree of mismatch between the present state of affairs and the goal-state. Evaluation is his means of determining the tactical corrections that must be made in the face of interference of any kind.

Some persons would speak of facts as having precedence over values. But a fact is nothing unless it has *value* for us in goal-directed behavior. Negative Feedback is "activity under correction of evaluatory signals," but it calls as well for thinking, for the making of decisions with respect to corrective action. Facts and values are two dimensions of PS/W.

**Never underestimate the importance of the valuative use of words in the appraisive mode.**

BUT WORDS ARE NOT ENOUGH!

When we write, we may infuse our words with something of the self. This is especially true of personal letters. And of poetry, too. In more formal writing—in expository writing, for example—we do the best we can. Something of the human being is discoverable, if not in the lines themselves, then between the lines. As we read, we come to know the author. If he keeps us at arm's length, we know our place. If he in-

210

THE VALUATIVE USE OF WORDS

vites confidence and collaboration, we read as if he were a friend.

Opening *On Human Communication* by the British scientist *Colin Cherry*, I found this dedication: "To my dog, Pym." Here something, apparently, happened to me. I saw a man. And a dog. I sensed love, respect, loyalty, and even understanding between them; I sensed the relatedness of all living things. Some months later I had occasion to write Dr. Cherry. Later, when rereading our correspondence, I found, to my surprise, that I had written, "Dear Dr. Colin."

We were friends. And how could it be otherwise? To a woman whose family of children had midwifed and raised three generations of dogs, each with its own "personality," Pym was a feelingful "connecting element" (to use the language of Einstein).

I also remember reading a scientific article written by the celebrated chemist Dr. Karl Paul Link. The effect of the article was electric, as much because of the writer as the ideas. Something does come off the page. But it is nothing compared with what comes through unsought, unbidden, in the living face-to-face situation. Here we know that words are not enough. Over and beyond the literal significance of our words, the value system comes through, whether we will it or not, whether we like it or not.

I believe the most important use to which we can put valuative language is in self-appraisal. It is not easy to evaluate the self, because we are so inclined to protect the self, to make excuses for the self, to see the self only in the best possible light. Evasion of self-evaluation seems to be the only way we can live with our selves. We see the *ideal* self-image, not the *actual* self-image.

Because appraisal has its roots in understanding, the first task is to examine the pattern of the self, that composite of what we know and what we believe. It is then necessary to examine also the relationship of the self to others.

To know your *character* is to understand that composite of your knowledge and your values, insofar as you can. To know your *personality* is to determine how you relate to others. *Do they trust you? Respect you? Like you? Are they willing to go along with you in your plans?*

Only through an understanding of your character and your personality, your structured self and your relation to other selves, can you move to an appraisal of your whole self. This will be an appraisal of your self-image. There is, too, your ideal self-image, that self toward which you strive. So that what we have is not a static evaluation of the self. If the self-image does not move in the direction of the ideal self-image, we cease to be goal-directed. We renounce the future. And there is then no need for PS/W.

But is not your self the most interesting thing of all that the world holds? Why not really try to know it, for in it lies your power. Who would be so reckless as to run a power machine without understanding it?

## OUR APPRAISALS ARE TOO PAT

When we appraise, we rarely look at the various dimensions of the thing, the person, the event appraised. An examination takes time and we are unwilling to delay our reactions.

In *Permanence and Change* Kenneth Burke points out that if we could develop a "perspective by incongruity," we would see things more wholly, more truly.[92] A friend of mine, a young minister, disrupted a dinner meeting by saying:

"I am for secular religion. I would have it divorced from the church [small *c*, I am sure] and put it in the home, in the courts, in the market place, in the international forum—wherever there are human beings."

This is "perspective by incongruity." The words "secular" and "religion" would seem to many persons to be irreconcilable. Yet notice how this juxtaposition of words apparently incongruous broadens the perspective. Notice how it throws light on many hidden dimensions of religion.

"Perspective by incongruity" is, I believe, an interesting formula. Burke says that if we put incongruous *words* together, we may throw a light on situations that we have been appraising patly. This is precisely what Morris suggests in *The Open Self* when he says that we should experiment with new *word compounds*, which may create new ideas. Who knows where word compounds will take us?

**Every thing, every person, every event has multidimensions. The semanticist will look for them. This action will automatically delay his reactions and thus improve the quality of his appraisals.**

## WE FORGET THAT APPRAISAL IS *THOUGHT*-FEELING

If we jump impulsively to a feelingful appraisive response, we omit two important steps, observation and inference.

Observation will give us information. We cannot see everything, of course, but we can, at least, try to discover salient facts.

From observations we make inferences. An inference is a "logical" procedure that results from our knowledge of recurrent patterns. This knowledge sets up expectations. If I see a group of teenage boys wearing leather jackets labeled

"TIGERS" surrounding a sports car, I can draw several inferences:

I can infer that they are admiring the car.

I can infer that they intend to make off with it.

I can infer that one of the boys owns the car and that the others are envious of him.

All three of these inferences may be incorrect. As Bertrand Russell says, "non-mathematical inference . . . is always only probable."[93] And yet we are inclined to appraise the boys, on the basis of our inference, either as a group of respectable young men or as a gang of delinquents.

The whole procedure is fraught with possible error. Actually, the first step is the only one that I can describe by designators. All I know about the boys is that they are wearing leather jackets labeled "TIGERS." That's about it. All I can honestly say about these boys is "These boys are wearing leather jackets labeled 'TIGERS.' " Hardly enough as the basis for a reliable inference from which to move to appraisal.

The moral is that those who are positive about their appraisals as derived from inferences (even those which rest upon designators that denote) are naïve. At its best, an appraisal is an informed opinion, and it is better or worse depending on the relevance and the inclusiveness and the quality of the evidence that supports it. *Directly, and not inferentially.*

### An appraisal should not be divorced from thought.

If you will listen at a dinner party or at a cocktail party, you will hear a preponderance of floating appraisors. Something like this:

*I didn't like his talk.*

*I thought it was terrific.*

214

*What he said was obvious and stale.*

*He was anything but a bore. I liked, especially, his choice of words. He was so dramatic.*

*He didn't say anything worth listening to. He was lousy.*

On and on they go.

What did the speaker say?

What ideas were common knowledge?

Listen to a business meeting or a legal or political conference and notice the insistent demand for supportive designators that denote.

**Power-Steering with Words requires alertness to the danger of floating appraisors.**

## SIMPLE SEMANTIC *ANTIDOTES* TO FLOATING APPRAISORS

There are two simple semantic antidotes to floating appraisors: (1) Appraisors are more effective when they are anchored to designators. When the designators *denote*, the appraisor is anchored in evidence. (2) An appraisor is an opinion and, as such, should always be *dated*.

We say of a fact that it is true at a date. Until Copernicus, it was generally believed that the earth was a center around which the sun revolved; Galileo discovered a new and correct definition of force that changed the whole of Aristotelian physics; Einstein's Special Theory of Relativity supplemented Newton's mechanics. The history of knowledge is the history of discovery. It follows that an appraisal should be tied to designators that denote and should be dated.

Because our appraisals are freighted by our values, we can hardly budge them. We maintain our "principles" and

215

our "loyalties" unquestioningly and without regard for change. Our appraisals of persons and groups of persons are static, rigid, fixed.

The semanticist says: A report is worthless without a date. An appraisal rests upon designators that denote. It, too, is worthless without a date.

When we date an appraisal, we are likely to take a fresh look tomorrow.

Two appraisals that have disturbed Americans in recent years concern "national sovereignty" and "State rights."

National sovereignty was an accepted principle until our world became small, so small that what were formerly thought to be strictly national concerns have now become world-wide concerns. Unilateral decisions are impossible now because of overlapping responsibilities and interest. The conservative individual, he who is bent on conserving what he considers to be the best of the past, is out of step, for "the world alters as we walk in it. . . ."

Just so, State rights are now under examination. Federal laws that provide redress for inequalities of citizenship and of opportunity now supersede State laws. Here, again, the conservative wants to maintain the *status quo*.

We live in a process world in which change is inevitable. But change has taken on a new quality and new dimensions. Yesterday's appraisals are no longer suitable to today's designators.

We have now taken two consecutive steps, following Morris.

(1) The informative use of words in the designative mode aims to cause someone to *act* as if something has certain characteristics. If the designators denote, that something

216

does, indeed, have the characteristics ascribed to it. Then the designators are true, and, therefore, they are reliable. Such informative words are convincing.

(2) The valuative use of words in the appraisive mode aims to cause someone to *act* with a preferential attitude toward something, in the cause of goal-seeking behavior. When appraisors are firmly linked with reliable designators, the appraisors are effective.

The second step rests on the first step.

Designators and appraisors are used to cause a behavior response in others, but this response is mainly preparation for a specific *action* response that is desired by the communicator.

A third step is now necessary.

*Chapter IX*

# The Incitive Use of Words

## THE *INCITIVE* USE
## IN THE *PRESCRIPTIVE* MODE

We shall, following Morris, define the *incitive* use of words as that use which directs action into *specific* channels.

The persuasiveness of incitive language is very closely linked with the convincing and effective use of designators and appraisors. The percipient of incitive language must be convinced that the information is reliable and that the appraisors warrant the preferential status given them.[94]

The incitive use of language is difficult to achieve. A listener is willing to sit still and listen sympathetically to designators and appraisors as long as he is not asked to bestir himself. A specific action response calls for a deep conviction of the value of the action in question. Before a percipient commits himself to an action, he must be thoroughly involved. He must think-feel with the communicator before he will act.

**The appropriate mode for the incitive use of language is, in general, the prescriptor. Prescriptors are imperatives.**[95]

Again, the grammatical form of the prescriptor alerts us to the intention of the communicator. Imperatives say *Do this! Don't do that!*

## THE INCITIVE VALUE OF A *QUESTION*

Interrogation is a subtle yet powerful form of incitive language.

A question is incitive because it asks for a specific action response. It asks for an answer. It limits the answer, because the answer must be directed to the question. The question, therefore, puts a circumference around the response. In this sense, the question directs the thinking of the percipient. The question may, however, be answered in a way favorable or unfavorable to the goal-state of the communicator.

The objective of the question is "to evoke in the mind of the receiver something which the originator has in mind." But the objective is more. The objective is that "of evoking in the receiver a state of readiness in some desired respects similar to that of the originator." In this sense, the intention of the communicator is not "to *depict*" information but to cause a percipient "to *select*" information at the receiving end.[96] So says Donald MacKay, physicist-semanticist.

**The question is open. It is not a telling. It is an asking. The question is a device par excellence to cause a desired selection at the receiving end.**

219

What happens to you when someone asks you a question? *You begin to think.* Now, if you can ask a question that has a strong bearing on an interest of yours, this is good. But something more is required.

The question must not be trivial. It should have wide appeal because of its general significance. It should, I believe, have relevance to the making of a decision. Your objective, remember, is to induce a specific action response. This, in itself, will call for a decision. For these reasons a question should relate to *policy*.

Policy is to business what a value system is to an individual. Policy concretizes a value system. Policy is the operational value system. Policy puts values to work. Policy reflects itself in procedures. Policy reflects the integration of a complex organization whose operations are synchronized and unified by purpose. Just as the value system of an individual will determine the major decisions he will make, so the policy of any organization affects future decisions about the conduct of its activities.

The word "policy" is probably one of the most important in economic theory and in business practice, as well as in the conduct of every and any kind of organization that is goal-directed. As Consultant in Communication to the faculty, I sat with professors who taught policy in their classrooms. It became apparent that policy is the concept that pulls our economic system together, that pulls an industrial organization together, that determines the decisions with respect to any business problem.

Why should this be so?

A specific business problem is not an isolated problem. It concerns the business as a whole within an economic structure. It is impossible to isolate such factors as production,

220

distribution, finance, administration, etc. The whole organization is affected by any important decision.

A proposal for action to an individual or an organization will be referred to the policy of that individual or that organization on both the conscious and the unconscious levels (if, indeed, we can separate the two). When, therefore, you ask for a specific action response, you do well, indeed, to concern yourself with the policy that will affect the decision of your listener(s) to act with you and for you.

Let me pause with this concept of policy. A volume entitled *The Policy Sciences* and edited by Daniel Lerner and Harold D. Lasswell contains seventeen articles by scholars in different fields. When this volume was published by Stanford University Press in 1951, I experienced a high sense of elation because of its relevance to communication theory as I understand it. I quote from Lasswell's introductory article:

The word "policy" is commonly used to designate the most important choices made either in organized or in private life. We speak of "government policy," "business policy," or "my own policy" regarding investments and other matters.[97]

So much for the word "policy."

What methods are used to achieve the goals in the policy sciences?

The policy-science approach . . . calls forth a very considerable clarification of the value goals involved in policy. . . . For purposes of analysis the term "value" is taken to mean "a category of preferred events. . . ." The policy sciences must proceed as speculative models. . . . Speculative models . . . can be called "developmental constructs." They specify the pattern *from* which we are moving and the pattern *toward* which we are going.

. . . developmental constructs are not scientific hypotheses. . . . A developmental construct refers only to the succession of events, future as well as past . . . No claim of "inevitability" can be accepted. Events in the future are not knowable with absolute certainty in advance; they are partly probable and partly chance. Developmental constructs are aids in the total task of clarifying goals, noting trends, and estimating future possibilities.[98]

This excerpt in part has already been referred to; I call it to your attention again because of its relevance to incitive language. The "developmental construct" as defined by Lasswell is our means-to-end pattern which emanates from the causal pattern of the *status quo*.

I ask you now *Is it not important to place your need, your wanting, your plan of action, within the context of the policy of your listener or your reader?*

**Your question, then, will have to do with values, with goals, and with the consideration of the possible means by which to achieve a goal.**

Such a question will have a high incitive potential.

It is your listener's policy, remember, about which you ask. His answer will help you understand the values that motivate him when he is confronted with an important decision. You will relate that answer to your present problem. You will present your means-to-end pattern that is calculated to reach your goal. He will think-feel with you because your words will be relevant to his interests as well as to your own. If you are together on policy, you can move from a firm base to collaboration.

Say that you are an employer whose policy it has been to employ only white personnel. Your chief competitor now employs only white personnel. If you can discuss this policy and agree that Negroes should be given fair employment treatment, it will be simple for you to introduce a project

222

that will have his support in the advancement of industry-wide employment of Negroes.

When there is agreement on policy, the specifics are automatically disposed of.

## *IMPERATIVES* WILL NOT GO DOWN EASILY

I have heard parents shout at children in the prescriptive mode. Bare. Without preparation. Children do not like it. They are human beings.

I have heard employers use imperatives to employees. Strangely enough, the employees offer little or no resistance to prescriptors that concern the routine maintenance of a plant. The reason, it seems to me, is clear. Imperatives are imperatives (to sound again like Gertrude Stein) in a machine shop, in a shipping room, on the production line, etc. And the imperative must be designatively clear to avoid fouling up the synchronized action of the plant. The men themselves monitor the prescriptors necessary in the accomplishment of their jobs. When one worker steps out of line, the other workers suffer. And they move in on the culprit!

The industrial plant will print instructions and glue or paint them on the wall. There is no mistaking the action that the worker must take. Every word in the instructions is an informative prescriptor; there is not an appraisor in sight.

*Maintain time schedule as per specifications.* (When all the workers are out of step but Jim, Jim gets the ax by common consent.)

*No smoking anywhere in this plant.* (Who wants to be blown to kingdom come?)

To get back to the children: if parents and children would together formulate the imperatives of running a household smoothly, there would be, first, an understanding of the prescriptors and, second, a desire to give them preferential status because they protect the rights of the children as well as the rights of the elders.

Just so, imperatives of the law of the land maintain the rights of all citizens: the weak and the strong; the young and the old; the rich and the poor; the bosses and the workers.

**Prescriptors are more readily acceptable when those affected have a voice in framing them and when the prescriptors protect the well-being of all concerned.**

## THE *TRAINING PROGRAM* CALLS
## FOR PRESCRIPTORS

There is an economical way and an uneconomical way (in time, effort, and precision) to perform a routine task. The economical way is determined by experts. There is no need for the learner to use the trial-and-error method.

Here prescriptors are set down (usually in writing) in orderly fashion and, usually, in chronological sequence. The learning process is a step-by-step procedure. Each step must be mastered before a further step can be undertaken.

When informative prescriptors are linked with designators that denote familiar objects, operations, etc., the instructions are clear and definite. One appraisive word can destroy clarity. Words such as "hot," "cold," "smooth," "loose," etc., must be replaced by designators that denote.

**Informative prescriptors are strictly impersonal and have a common value for all. They exemplify incitive language at its best.**

224

## *"RECOMMENDATIONS"* IS A GOOD WORD

An old horse chestnut is this: *You can lead a horse to water but you can't make him drink.* He has to *want* water. Maybe this is what is meant by "horse sense."

Natural leaders seem to sense this intuitively and are adroit in their relationships with others when decisions must be made.

There are times, of course, when a salesman will say, "Sign here, sir." But remember that this statement is the culmination of a series of designative and appraisive steps that make it more informative than prescriptive. "Right here, sir. This is the place to sign."

In the business world life is a succession of decisions of what to do and how to do it. When there is a problematical situation, the industrial engineer will take three steps:

(1) He will investigate the present situation. *What is going on? What is the cause of this problematical situation?* The answer to this question calls for informative language in the designative mode, the language of the report.

(2) He will evaluate the report. *What features of the situation are satisfactory? What features are unsatisfactory?* The words "satisfactory" and "unsatisfactory" are appraisive terms. There may be differences of opinion here, but the answers to these questions must be sought before *action* can be taken.

(3) The industrial engineer calls the third step "Recommendations." This is a good word because it is only implicitly imperative. It is not a prescriptor. It is not explicitly incitive. It does not say *Do this!* It does not ask for a specific action response, but it suggests one which is open to discus-

sion and to evaluation. What it means is *In my opinion, this is a course of action worth considering before you make a decision as to what course of action to take.*

**The decision for action should flow logically from the preliminary steps. If your listener makes the decision himself, you can count on his follow-through.**

The objective is *to help the other fellow make the decision.*

Give the other fellow good and legitimate and sufficient reasons for making the decision that will coincide with your plan. This should not be difficult of achievement. You yourself have reached your decision by a painstaking process:

(1) Analysis of the problematical situation

(2) Evaluation of the relevant factors

(3) Study of the plausible means-to-end hypotheses by which to overcome the problem, with eventual decision

If you are able to communicate your thought-feeling convincingly, effectively, and persuasively on the basis of designators that denote, appraisors that sink deeply into the informative base, and implicit suggestions as to means, you will probably find that your listener will be ready to make up his own mind in much the way that you did.

Explicitly incitive language, although it has important, though limited, uses, is likely to set up resistance in conference situations. Progressive advance from preparatory informative and valuative language to implicitly incitive language is likely to be far more effective.

Remember this: the man who makes the decision is a thinker, a feeler, and a doer. He has all the components necessary to intelligent action, but he will not do what he does not *want* to do. He, too, is endowed with "horse sense."

Touch him at his needs if you would incite him to action!

226

## *APPRAISIVE–INCITIVE* LANGUAGE DEFEATS ITS PURPOSE

Explicitly incitive language must be specific. To say *Pack that box tightly so the bottles won't break* doesn't mean a thing to an employee. "Tightly" is an appraisive term. What is tight for him may be loose for you—and the bottles. *Put twelve bottles in that box* is explicit. Informative-incitive language is specific. And incitive language, remember, calls for a *specific* action response.

Just so, *Be a good boy!* is meaningless to Johnny. Nothing he does is "good," he will tell you.

*Behave like a lady* is just so much blah to Sally. *What lady? What kind of lady? An old lady?* Tell Sally what to do under certain circumstances.

*Set the thermostat low* is meaningless. Where there is a thermometer, indicate the preferred reading.

**If you want to be explicitly incitive, it is necessary to omit all appraisive terms and to substitute strictly informative language.**

## SOMETIMES *LISTENING* IS BETTER THAN TELLING

One of the most interesting experiments in human behavior was made by Dr. Carl R. Rogers, psychotherapist, and reported in his *On Becoming a Person.* Patients came to him mostly because they appraised themselves as failures and even as neurotics.

When a troubled person called on him, Rogers did not "direct" the interview. Instead, he let the patient talk. So successful has this method been that it has now become common practice.

Rogers asked no questions. A question is incitive because

it calls for a specific action response, an answer; and because it calls for an answer to a specific question, it is *directive*. One thing Rogers did not want to do was to direct the interview.

Rogers did not wish to *steer* his patients. His objective was, of course, to help them steer themselves.

How did he accomplish this?

Rogers listened while his patients talked. His listening was not passive, because he evidenced his constant interest by his noncommital but receptive comments. Some critics have referred to Rogers's method as the "Uh-huh" method. But Rogers listened with a difference. There was no hint of evaluation in his comments or in his manner. His comments were a kind of "giving-back" to the patient of what the patient had said to him. But the giving-back was not one of mere understanding. His effort was to understand, of course, but his effort also was to *feel with* the patient. This is listening as we define it in PS/W. The *what* a person says is important for the *why* he says it. We can hear words, but unless we feel with the speaker, we do not really understand him.

Everything that the patient said to Rogers was accepted. Rogers's attitude was entirely permissive, an attitude in which the therapist experiences a positive regard for the patient, without reservation of any kind. Rogers says that it means that the therapist *cares* for the client, in a non-possessive way.

This honest speaking-listening-speaking continuum is precisely what is required in PS/W. The results of the process are far-reaching. Let Rogers say it:

In regard to feelings and personal meanings, the [patient] moves away from a state in which feelings are unrecognized, unowned, unexpressed. He moves toward a flow in which ever-changing feelings are experienced in the moment, knowingly and acceptingly, and may be accurately expressed.

The process involves a change in the manner of his experiencing. . . . From remoteness he moves toward an immediacy of experiencing in which he lives openly *in* his experiencing, and knows that he can turn to it to discover its current meanings.

The process involves a loosening of the cognitive maps of experience. From construing experience in rigid ways . . . the client moves toward developing changing, loosely held construings of meaning in experience, constructs which are modifiable by each new experience.

In general, the evidence shows that the process moves away from fixity . . . toward fluidity, changingness, immediacy of feelings and experience, tentativeness of constructs, discovery of a changing self in one's changing experience, realness and closeness of relationships, a unity and integration of functioning.[99]

This is the dynamics of change. This is the open self toward which we strive. This is the process of becoming what we hope to be. The honest speaking-listening-speaking continuum has far-reaching consequences, indeed.

When we deny a speaker our honest attention—thought-feeling attentiveness—we implicitly reject him. The best salesman I know is a young man who does little talking, but a great amount of honest listening. He makes a person like himself, respect himself. And his customers react warmly to him.

When we desire a specific action response from someone, we are inclined to be impatient with him. We push. We prod. We try to put words into his mouth. Such impatience is obstructive.

**Power-Steering with Words may sometimes best be accomplished by listening to the words of others.**

*Chapter X*

# The Systemic Use of Words

## MORRIS'S DEFINITION
## OF *SYSTEMIC* LANGUAGE

Systemic language is the language of pattern and the appropriate mode is the *formator*. The purpose of systemic language is to organize all the responses of a listener or a reader.

Morris makes it clear that the other three uses of language —informative, valuative, and incitive—and their three corresponding modes—designative, appraisive, and prescriptive —tend to overlap. This is what Morris says:

Designators do always inform, and hence it is natural that their primary use should be the informative one, even though it remains true that they may be used for other purposes and that other kinds of signs may be used informatively.[100]

230

And again:

> . . . a designator may give information without being used to inform.[101]

It appears, then, that the mode is only a clue to the intention of the user.

**Only systemic language in the formative mode can help us penetrate to the principal and overriding purpose of a speaker or a writer.**

The words of a communicator are selected to advance his purpose. The responses of a listener or a reader can be organized only when he is aware of the communicator's purpose. Only then does he have some basis for evaluating the communicator's selection of facts, his appraisal of those facts, and his suggestions for action.

How does systemic language help us determine the intention of the communicator?

Let me quote, first, Morris's definition of systemic language:

> In the systemic use of signs [words] the aim is simply to organize sign-produced behavior. . . . This may be done with respect to all kinds and combinations of signs, and by the use of signs in the various modes of signifying. . . .[102]

Say that a commentator describes the state of affairs in an underprivileged area. He will give us statistical facts concerning population (birth and death rates), income, etc., in the informative use and the designative mode of language. He will, then, undoubtedly, describe living conditions, health conditions, etc., in appraisive language. He might say, for instance, *The living conditions are squalid; the children emaciated; the elders haggard and old before their time; the medical facilities desperately inadequate*, etc. He may then use the one incitive word "help" (and, then, informatively, give the address of CARE).

The organization of the essential terms of a communication takes the form of a working-title. I use the term "working-title" to *systematize* all the essential formators of a verbal pattern.[103] The formators are joined together according to a principle of organization, in the case of this example, as sections:

*Facts re area X; evaluation of facts; and proposed action*

The whole of this presentation is directed toward the word "help." Is the talk predominantly informative? Predominantly appraisive? Predominantly incitive? The working-title would seem to indicate that the informative and valuative language is preparatory for that one word "help" and that the talk is, therefore, predominantly incitive.

Just so, in the political field, a speaker could use this working-title:

*Biographical facts about Candidate X; qualifications of Candidate X; proposed action*

Systemic language puts the designative, appraisive, and incitive modes in their proper relationship. This enables the percipient to make a judgment concerning the *primary* intention of the communicator. Knowledge of the primary intention colors the entire communication. Facts, we know are *selected* to achieve a given purpose. Even if the facts that are presented are true, we have no way of knowing what facts have been omitted that may be detrimental to the purpose at hand. The purpose of the speaker is then a clue to his selection of facts and to possible omissions of facts.

232

**Systemic language is the use of words to organize all of the responses of the listener or reader.**

Even though the primary intention of the user of words is to incite the percipient to a specific action response, designators and appraisors may be used effectively to contribute to this purpose.

Is a young lady who tells a poor but promising professional man that when she comes of age she will receive a sizable trust fund using informative language? Maybe and maybe not. We cannot know for sure. Perhaps she doesn't know!

Much that is called information is persuasion. Any salesman can tell you that. But an appraisive statement may be informative. *Her "statistics" are 38–23–38.* No one will deny that this statement is both appraisive and informative.

**Systemic language permits us to see the parts in relation to the whole, since its function is to organize all of the responses of a listener or reader.**

## THE *SYSTEMIC* USE IN THE *FORMATIVE* MODE OF CHARLES MORRIS

Much has already been said about the utility of formators in establishing order in feedforward and feedback. A formator is a big word, a general word, that makes a place for secondary formators of a lower level of generality and for all the details that fall logically under them. Like this:

WORKING–TITLE: *Biography, Qualifications, and Recommendation for Action re Candidate X*
1. Biography

    a. Family

    b. Education

    c. Political history

2. Qualifications

    a. Character

    b. Personality

    c. Ability, experience, etc.

3. Action

    a. Vote for X

This closed sectional pattern presents the primary and secondary formators under which all the details will fall. Note the economy of this pattern. As Morris says, formators are especially economical and trustworthy signs for the systemic use. Formators organize all the responses of a percipient. They have no other function.[36]

**The economy of the systemic use of language in the formative mode is perhaps the most important characteristic of Power-Steering with Words.**

When you stick your head into the office of a superior to tell or to ask him something and you use the bare pattern, you will find a willing ear. Today everyone budgets time very much as he budgets dollars. No one wants to listen to details about anything if the essentials do not interest him.

The pattern represents our thinking, regardless of the time we expect to put into the development. One of the most important things a communicator must learn is *The time must be right*. He must use only as much time as the percipient is willing to give. The communicator should be extremely sensitive to any cues, any signals—verbal or nonverbal—that indicate how fully he may develop his pattern.

The economy of the systemic use of language in the formative mode is an asset in every aspect of communication, whether written or oral.

## IN *WRITING* EXPOSITORY WORKS

Systemic language is the bare skeleton of a verbal pattern.

It has been said that "information" means, not isolated events, but a patterned relationship between events. In order to communicate information, then, a formula by which to transmit relationships is necessary, and the systemic use of language in the formative mode is that formula. Systemic language is made up of *parts* that are *related* to each other *according to a principle of organization*. The systemic use of language is the most economical of all uses because it is concerned with essentials and the relationship between essentials.

A communication may be as brief as is consistent with the purpose and the occasion. But however brief, however lengthy, a written expository work may be, it will maintain the order established by systemic language in the formative mode. In anything we write, whether a memo, a letter, a report, an article, a book, our first step is to make a systemic arrangement of the logical construct that gives unity and direction to the project.

## IN *READING*

The utility of the systemic use of language in the formative mode is not so apparent to the reader as to the writer, and yet nothing can be more important to understanding, to retention, and to learning.

Discovering the pattern of an article or a book is sometimes difficult, mainly because the contents are not well structured by the author. The difficulty is not that the author does not make sense but that he does not present his material as clearly as he might. In such a case the reader must ferret out the pattern if he would analyze and evaluate the document properly. To discover the pattern, he must ask himself the question *What is the author talking about?* When he has answered this question in one sentence or less, he has the working-title, which is made up of primary formators. Thereafter the task is simple: the secondary and tertiary formators must only be put where they logically belong.

If you discover the pattern of any important document, you will understand it. There will be no need to memorize anything. You will remember the author's idea because the pattern has become part of your structured thinking. And recall that "whatever else learning may be it is clearly *a disposition* to form structures,"[48] to form patterns.

## IN *LISTENING–SPEAKING*

Listening is akin to reading. The same process is involved. Yet finding the systemic use of language in the formative mode is easier in a printed document than in spoken language. The printed page will stay put; you can read the article over and over again, if need be. Not so, of course, in spoken language. Skill here is acquired only by consistent practice.

A young lawyer, a brilliant and successful man, attended my class in semantics for two consecutive years. I questioned him about his persistence in the course. He answered that he could sit at his desk and prepare a fine brief. The pattern was sharply economical, yet exhaustive, and well knit. More than that, he said, he could anticipate the pattern of his opponent's brief (and this, of course, was necessary preparation). He was primed, then, and ready for the courtroom. But, he said, every now and then, the unexpected happened and he was obliged to entertain some new situation that was totally unpredictable. In order to do this well he had to place the unexpected turn within a pattern, a logical construct, and evaluate it from the perspective of his purpose. And this he found difficult to do. He declared he would continue to attend class until he could handle any pattern that was tossed at him orally and under pressure. And he did.

Some time later the senior member of the law firm in which the young man worked came to the classroom. All he said was "I came to see what was going on here." He, too, stayed.

In a conference, intelligent participation depends entirely on the ability to penetrate to the logical construct presented by another. And sometimes upon the ability to do this without preparation of any kind.

In a conference, one logical construct is compared with others. What is likely to occur is the reconstruction of a means-to-end plan by collaborative thinking. Here economy of words is the very means of intelligent discussion. Patterns that are not stripped to the bone cannot be looked at critically. This is true of any situation in which there is discussion. A round table discussion usually centers on a common problem that requires analysis. Only after analysis can the discussion move toward a solution. Unless there is economy of statement, the discussion bogs down.

One important consequence of economy is that it prevents a topic from getting sidetracked. If we stay with essentials, the pattern will maintain direction.

WRITE IT! SAY IT! THINK IT! LIVE IT!

**Good listening-speaking means penetration to the logical construct, to the pattern. If we cannot do this, we cannot know what the other fellow is talking about. If we can do this, we can use PS/W.**

## IN *SPEAKING–LISTENING*

Recently, Professor S. I. Hayakawa sat with friends and talked informally. When Hayakawa talks, we listen. Hayakawa is the author of the classic *Language in Thought and Action*[104] and the founder and editor of the journal *Etc.: A Review of General Semantics.*

Hayakawa was talking about trouble spots in communication. He said that his experience was that the person in the middle, the in-between person, suffers from what he calls "the squeeze." Take a foreman, for instance. He is not a rank-and-file worker and yet he is not in management. He is neither here nor there. He represents the workers, he supervises the workers, and yet he is responsible to those above him for directions. He makes no decisions other than those on low-level routine questions.

I listened one morning to a supervisors' meeting of one of our great railroads. These men were *for supervisors;* they were indifferent to the workers and hostile to management. They were, emotionally, an isolated part of the organization.

When I was working with the nursing staff at Billings Hospital of the University of Chicago, this in-betweenness was again a problem. How far may a nurse go in interpreting what the doctor says to an anxious patient? The nurse looks in two directions and is sometimes immobilized between the two.

We all know that every organization has various levels of authority. Only the lowest and the highest levels do not suffer

238

acutely from in-betweenness, but even these levels are not immune. The top man is in between the organization and the directors and stockholders. The worker is in between the union and the plant.

Add to this that our industrial way of life is a kind of wheel of fortune. The organization pays workers to produce goods and services. The workers themselves are consumers of these goods and services. The workers pay money for these goods and services, and this money is used to produce even more. And add to this that industry is now run by paid managers, for the most part, and that workers, the country over, are owners of stock and, in this sense, have a voice in the making of policy.

Everyone is in between! The squeeze in some areas is tighter than in others, but the problem of in-betweenness is far more general than is supposed. Those in between must look upward and downward; they must interpret in two directions. This is very much like tearing the self apart. Let me quote again, and more fully, what Professor Karl W. Deutsch says in "Communication Theory and Social Science":

. . . all organizations are alike in certain fundamental characteristics, and every organization is held together by communication. . . . It is communication, that is, the ability to transmit messages and to react to them, which makes an organization.[105]

Deutsch puts it in a nutshell when he says that communication is the cement that *makes* an organization.[20]

I suggest that the systemic use of language in the formative mode, as set forth by Charles Morris, may facilitate communication between levels within an organization and relieve the squeeze-play on the person in the middle, the person in between.

239

**Remember, now, that the systemic use of language in the formative mode is the language of pattern designed to represent patterns in the world, actual, possible, or even plausible.**

Every organization is a patterned process, whether it is a local P.T.A. or the State Department. Every organization is a structured, organized *purposive* system.

**An organization is an organism that functions as a unit.**

Only to the extent that the separate elements of an organization become essential parts of a *purposive construct* can they function as a unit. The person in between, it seems, is not seeing the organization as a whole. He is not seeing the organization as a purposive construct unified by the communication process.

A *purposive construct* takes the form of a means-to-end pattern. The organization will not function smoothly unless all levels are involved in the means-to-end project. *What is the goal? Is it a common goal? In the industrial organization, is the goal money,* which is *not an end in itself* but rather a *means* toward the satisfaction of individual needs? For the industrialist, economic and social gains; for the worker, all the human gains that make life worth living for himself and his family.

Are the ultimate goals strong enough to compel *interdependent action?* In-betweenness that emphasizes isolation of parts within an organization can be circumvented only by concerted involvement in the means-to-end construct. Individual goals may be different, but money is the immediate end that becomes a means to those individual goals. There is no other way.

Wherever we are, we are related to others purposively. We

240

move from our family to our work to our fraternal order to our church to our political club, back to our family again, etc. We move from one organization to another—and sometimes they overlap. A man may, for example, be in business with his brother or his father; family interests and business interests may conflict. Each organization of which we are a part has a different purpose, and it is purpose that holds each organization together.

**Without communication an organization cannot exist. Each organization is a unity. Each situation is a multidimensional cyclic process.**

Systemic language in the formative mode is truly the cement that makes an organization. If every level within a structured organization—workers, foremen, supervisors, managers, officers, etc.—could see that organization as a unity that is possible only by communication, we might establish a cyclic relationship *between* the parts that is stabilized by a common purpose.

In a business organization there are two "ladders," one called "staff," which is consultatory and advisory, and the other called, frankly and significantly, "the line." Some bright personnel manager should invent a new word to replace "line." "Lines," upward and downward, are outmoded for the very reason that they emphasize and perpetuate in-betweenness.

## IN *SPEAKING*

I cannot suggest too strongly the need for desk work before you appear at the speakers' table, on the platform, or in a studio.

It is easy to speak when we are sitting down, but something seems to happen to us when we rise to our feet. Whether we speak sitting down or standing up, we must make sense. And to make sense means to make a verbal pattern.

You are already aware that the verbal pattern must be used in writing and reading, in speaking and listening. Communicator and reader or listener come together and understand each other only to the extent that they penetrate to the pattern. What you learn about any aspect of the communication process has a carry-over value for every other aspect of communication.

I must repeat, then, that your desk work is a necessary preliminary to speaking in conference, on a platform, or in a studio. Now you must ask yourself *What am I going to talk about?* When you have answered this question in one sentence or less, you have your working-title in the systemic use of language and in the formative mode.

The formators that make your working-title are the major parts of your pattern. Write them. Determine the nature of the relationship between them. *What kind of pattern are you dealing with? Time? Space? Cause to effect? Means to end? Sectional?* You must know the relationship, because the principle of organization gives the pattern its cohesiveness and progressiveness. You want a pattern that moves under its own steam.

Having established your working-title, which is made up of primary formators, the second step is to fill in the secondary formators that fall logically under the primary formators. These secondary formators are subordinate, in each case, to one primary formator. Secondary formators may be, and usually are, related according to a different principle of organization from that which unifies the primary formators.

242

Repeat this procedure if you need tertiary formators. These will, of course, fall logically under secondary formators. Etc.

Making a verbal pattern is not a simple task. Write the pattern. Study it. Work on it and change it until you are satisfied with it. By the time you are satisfied with the logical integrity of the pattern, you will know it. Knowing it is not accomplished by memorizing it. Knowing the pattern is the natural result of having made it yourself. When you have created it, you trust it. When you understand it completely, you cannot forget it. It is yours.

To know what you will talk about is to know your pattern; to know your pattern is to know what you will talk about.

When you are satisfied with the pattern, stand on your feet and try it out. Sitting down won't do. Mumbling to yourself won't do. Stand up and say it.

You will, of course, use no notes. The parts of your pattern are cohesive and progressive. They will hang together and move.

Your first attempts to extemporize around a pattern will be discouraging. You will begin sentences and throw them away. Words may not come easily. Stay with it. Try again and again—using different words, of course, with each try. The only invariable aspect of the speech is your pattern. Find your words as you go.

Time your effort and keep it within a specific time limit. At the Conference on Education in the Atomic Age, I was asked to talk on communication, and I was given fifteen minutes. I made my pattern and then tried it out on my feet. The first try ran forty minutes. I tried again and cut out some of the examples. This time it ran twenty-five minutes. I tried once more and cut out all examples and made the talk strictly informative, completely denuded of adjectives and adverbs. It ran fifteen minutes.

The point I make here is that the pattern remains the same, regardless of the time we take to develop it. If it is impossible to boil down the speech to the required time, it is necessary, then, to curtail the working-title. This will, of course, limit the scope of the pattern and therefore, the time required to deliver the speech.

I like to take all the time I need to make my verbal pattern. I cannot hurry. I will not hurry. I must write the pattern so that I can study it carefully. Then I must stand up on my feet to try it out. I have to be sure I can depend on my pattern. I want to know if the parts do indeed move. And, of course, I must time myself.

I do not write anything beyond the pattern, and I write that only for purposes of analysis and correction. Some students have protested that it is better to write the whole speech. I do not find it so. To write is to become enamoured of phrases, of words. I would prefer to struggle to find words that suitably express my ideas for a particular audience. I want to make my phrases fresh every time I talk about the same idea. There is a kind of joy in this. But you will have to experience it to know what I mean. We learn to write better by writing. We learn to speak better only by speaking.

When you practice on your feet, feel easy, but don't curl up. Don't sag at the knees. Pull yourself up. Don't rest on a hip. And don't lean on a table or a stand. A speaker must at least be able to stand up. Alone.

Begin to speak, as if before an audience. But do not coast along on your usual conversational volume. Your voice must get across. This will require a little more push, a little more force. Put enough power into your voice to hit the back wall, but keep your voice low. If you let the tone rise, it will be thin and hard and your voice will not carry across the room.

If you have never used this bigger, more forceful voice, you are due for some pleasant surprises. You will like the sound of it. If your voice sounds vibrant, confident, alive, you are likely to *feel* vibrant, confident, alive. Sound weak, and you are likely to pass out. Many persons with monotonous voices come to life merely with the use of more volume. A speaker must use a certain amount of force to reach a group. Reaching the group, he experiences a reaction—a favorable reaction. In practice, use the kind of voice you intend to use on the platform. *Give!*

Listen critically to the sounds you make. You are probably smooth and regular, holding the same rhythmic pattern. Subject, predicate, period. Subject, predicate, period. There are only a few ways in which to give life to the sound of your voice. Here they are:

Changes in volume

Changes in pitch

Changes in the quality of the voice

Changes in timing

Of these, timing is probably the most important. Timing clarifies thinking. We recognize the end of a sentence by a pause and the end of a part by a longer pause. But timing involves more than this. Changes in sentence structure and changes in sentence length are effective devices and should be used consciously to relieve monotony. Short sentences, long sentences, questions, imperatives, etc. *Change*.

Good timing is, of course, directly correlated with thought. Sometimes we speak slowly because we are covering ground that makes hasty movement perilous. We need to take our time. Then again we move quickly. The road is clear and straight before us.

Think-feel and let your voice go.

You will find that your whole body will enter into this job of expressing. Hands and feet are no problem to the speaker who knows how to stand still with his hands at his sides. Movement of any kind should, in the main, be involuntary. If you relax and let your ideas impel your movement, you are likely to be yourself, easy and natural. Your body will never fight with your ideas.

The hands can be very expressive. Do not hesitate to use them when you have the impulse. If your hands are resting loosely at your sides, they will respond automatically under deep thought and intense feeling. You do not need to "make" gestures; they are wrung from you.

When you are on your feet, it is true that you do not have to move. You *can* be alive and yet stand still. But you will find that you will want to move in the transitions and especially between the major parts of the pattern. At this point you are moving from one point to another, from one idea to another, and your body will want to collaborate in the effort. You will pause naturally in this transition. You will have to, because you are thinking. You're getting ready for the next part. *Let* yourself walk. You will stop when you are ready to speak.

Movement that is confined to the important transitions (from one major part of the pattern to the next) will help your listeners understand the structure of your verbal pattern. Movement in the right places is probably the best way to indicate structure. And it is a natural way.

## AND NOW YOU ARE ON THE PLATFORM!

When you appear before your audience, take a long look. And really see. You will never be so loved as you are at this moment. There they are, waiting and attentive. When you open your mouth, they may scatter, but this first, silent moment is yours.

You will begin, of course, with an introduction in which you tell what you are going to talk about and why. This is easy. This is feedforward. It is simply the short elaboration of your working-title. And then you will stop. You will pause —quite a long pause. You can't help yourself, because you are thinking. Every time you come to a transition in your pattern, you will pause. There is no other way. Take your pauses gratefully and keep them clean. (No "ahs.")

The rhythm of your pattern will transmit the rhythm of your thinking. Your listeners will stay with you and know where you are. If you stay with the pattern, your listeners will stay with the pattern—and with you.

You will be using informative, valuative, and perhaps even incitive language. When you inform, keep your structure cold and bare: use clean informative terms—no adjectives, no adverbs. But when you evaluate, infuse the structure with life: use feelingful language. If your interest is strong and honest, nothing will serve your purpose better than enthusiasm.

As you speak, you will find yourself pausing frequently to find a word. This is good. Nothing draws an audience closer to you than such a pause. Everyone is helping. Thinking. These are not moments of desperate clutching to find a word—any word. They are pauses to find the right word.

247

The best word for these particular listeners at this particular moment in your life. A true pause catches hold of listeners more effectively than any words can. You are never so close to listeners as when all of you are bound together in thought, in *silence*.

Don't do what so many beginners do. Don't try to think ahead. Thinking ahead is disastrous. For this you would need two heads. Stay where you are. Think. Find your words. When you are ready to move on, your pattern will take you.

And so you will move, from part to part, until you reach the last detail of the last part. But, of course, you have not yet reached the end. In order to wrap up the whole thing, you must get back to your working-title, which brings together everything you have said.

**We begin and we end with systemic language in the formative mode.**

And so you struggle through. You have stayed with the pattern and it has stayed with you. You have forgotten some details—but nobody knows and nobody cares. You have made your main points and you have come to your conclusion. Always the conclusion will bring you back to the beginning. Where ending meets beginning, the conclusion makes its goal.

Then it is over. But not quite over. Don't run off. Hold on. *Look*. Everything you have said has bound you to these listeners. Take your leave reluctantly, as reluctantly as from friends.

Struggle? Of course! Risks? Certainly!

We can be equal to the challenge only when we can combine the stability of the verbal pattern and the flexibility that derives from the free choice of words. Your verbal pattern is the only basis for stability and flexibility. Your verbal pattern is essential to feedforward and feedback.

**Without the systemic use of words in the formative mode, you are without direction. With the systemic use of words in the formative mode, you have the power to express an idea, newly made but firmly grounded.**

I talk about communication day after day. I am never bored with myself. I rely on my pattern, but, somehow, every experience is full of surprises for me. The people who listen are always different. Different groups, different interests, etc., and they stimulate me in new ways. I cannot tell you how, quite. I only know that when I *look* at them I find that I am energized by their inquiring attention. And because every situation is different, I, too, am different.

I find the question period following a talk to be most rewarding. The questions tell me what needs elaboration. The questions tell me that communication is a subject without boundaries. The questions tell me that, though I have struggled, my listeners have not been passive. And the interchange between us has been alive with excitement.

**So-called public speaking becomes an extension of conversation in PS/W.**

## IN *THINKING*

We have said that knowledge is the understanding of relationships. A verbal pattern that is isomorphic with an actual pattern is knowledge.

We have said that interpretation is the relating of a stimulus—words—to the pattern of experience of the perceiver.

We have said that information means, not an isolated

event, but a patterned relationship between events. The systemic use of words in the formative mode is the semantic formula by which to communicate patterned relationships; that is, information.

We have said that thinking, as defined by Einstein, is a relating function. Relationships are concerned with *what was, what is,* and *what will be.* To plan ahead on the basis of *what was* and *what is* is to create a means-to-end pattern which is our verbal speculative model designed to take us toward our goals. And this is thinking.

The brain physiologist Dr. W. Grey Walter tells us that the rhythms that sweep through the brain are a process of "goal-seeking and scanning."[106] And Walter defines "the process of scanning" as "searching for a pattern—which relaxes when a pattern is found."[107]

The electroencephalograph gives evidence that there is a physiological correlate with the conscious thinking process. And, Walter adds, "This scanning process is linked with the steering mechanism. . . ." The process "is a perfect example of self-regulation of negative feedback."[108]

To put this into the language of semantics: We are goal-seeking creatures. We are scanning, searching always for a pattern that will satisfy a need. The process stops when a pattern is "found," only to be reactivated by new search.

The rhythms that sweep the brain are correlated with the scanning, searching, process. As we think, as we speak, the rhythms that permeate our activity are expressive of the search for pattern. The punctuation—the timing—of our sounds marks out the pattern of our thinking. *And transmits the pattern of our thinking!* When we have found the pattern, when we have completed the pattern, there is pause and a waiting. Until a new search begins.

250

**Systemic language in the formative mode is the language of pattern. Patterns are linked with self-regulation by negative feedback. Patterns are central to Power-Steering With Words.**

If we could hear patterns instead of discrete words, if we could see patterns instead of isolated objects or events, we would be scanning for patterns on the *conscious* level in our daily lives. And such scanning would be linked with our steering mechanism—with our *words*.

## IN *SELF–MAKING*

Who would not wish to be creative and imaginative, capable of that swelling of the heart as well as of the mind that takes us into the new?

I think of creativity as an attribute of mankind. I do not believe that only the few are endowed with the creative gift of self-making. The differences between us are differences of degree and not differences of kind. To be alive is to be in the march of time that sets the pace for the march of humanity.

I am deeply attuned to the writings of the great biologist Edmund W. Sinnott, who speaks of life as creative by virtue of its innate tendency toward organization. At one point he says that life itself *is* the creative process. How can it be different? We are all patternmakers. If we have a spark of questing within us, that spark is struck from patterns already made but in the never-ending process of remaking.

We can, with conscious effort, attempt to reach to ever-higher levels of organization through thinking, through learning, through striving. There is more to it than that, I feel sure. There is more to it than the conscious will to become. There is something within us, built-in and essentially human, that is

251

creative—even as we give our selves over to the immediacy of the living life, even as we sleep!

Many psychologists believe that we are endowed with two approaches to creativity.

There is one approach in which we may participate actively. In it there is the necessity for conscious choice, for conscious search, for openness of the self to the world. Here the use of dynamic energy is the search for new relationships, for hitherto unknown relationships. Here is the use of dynamic energy to recreate the present state of affairs into preferred design. Here is the use of change in the interest of purpose. And all this by the conscious use of words thought and said.

There is another approach in which we simply permit our selves to live as human beings. In this approach there is a kind of receiving, a dividend, so to speak, from a life lived. And earned. Here the mysteries of human power defy conscious control. What happens is beyond knowing, except as we experience it. We know only that somehow the rearrangements, the interconnections, within the human brain create something akin to an emergent evolution. This is so staggering in its effects as to be allied with the creation of all life.

The creative process is both a giving and a receiving. A life cycle. The persistence of goal-seeking emerges, it seems, as much from hope, from promise, from faith, as it does from conscious search. Creativity is not only the will to live but also the will to believe.

Psychologists appear to agree that there is no separation between the two approaches. Everything hinges upon organization—and reorganization. Everything hinges, therefore, on the language of order, the language of structure. And this language is the systemic use of words in the formative mode.

252

The human being is a magnificent organization. When we *think* it, when we *feel* it, we are bound up with the *more,* such that we experience a relationship with everything that we can imagine. Beyond knowing and into what we strain to know.

**The whole concept of creativity, it seems, must be explained by organization, by dynamic pattern.**

There is that inner organization that is partly self-made and therefore man-made. But it is also, I believe, partly divine. What other word can describe that moment in time which dips back into the aeons and stretches forward into the Infinite More?[109] There is in man, as the psychologist Gardner Murphy suggests, the ability to establish a kind of greater organization. A superorganization. Murphy calls this cross organization[110] between the sentient living self and the moving, changing world around us. Thus cross organization means more than self-organization. Cross organization means a *relatedness* to our world—a giving and a receiving. Cyclic. The pattern now becomes a magnetic field, alive with human potential. And transcending *what is* as the now becomes *what may be.*

**The magic of words is so natural, so human, so powerful! Use the magic of words to cross over to others and with others. Use the magic of words to transform your self—and others.**

It is within the power of man to relate dynamically to the world, to become as one with the world, and yet to maintain his uniqueness, his individuality, and his ability to feel that stupendous, that magnificent, that all-encompassing sensation we call life.

For man, living means giving and receiving. For mankind

alone, words make living supremely possible. In words, with the passing of time, what we are today is held in trust for those who follow as we march into the future. Words make it possible for us to enjoy this sensation of becoming, not only as an individual experience, but also as a member of the race Mankind. For, as we relate, we become a dynamic part of the world in which we move, and this is a moment in time never lost.

Time "bulges," to use the apt phrase of H. G. Wells.[111] That instantaneous *Now* in which we live is as a growing branch, fed by the sap that may have been generations in the making. That instantaneous *Now* in which we live impinges upon the future with its own promise, with its own power.

We do not exist as a "flash" or a "series of flashes." This "bulging" is life, replete with memories and with hopes. Life is a swelling of the heart, an expansion of the self beyond knowing, beyond the power to tell.

I wish that I might be able to say something for you to keep. A kind of remembrance. A kind of farewell. Let me try.

I wish that you would feel, sweeping through your self, the rhythm of humanity that will extend your self beyond all knowing, beyond all feeling. Something wondrous. Wordless. But unspeakably alive!

To reach, to stretch, to search. That is our destiny. And the rhythms that sweep through the brain and the heart will not stop until the pattern is completed. But for this we need Eternity.

Salutation, friend!

# Glossary

The definitions given in this Glossary are relevant to the context of this book. Their usefulness in other contexts will depend upon your private extension of my meanings.

All definitions are circular. This Glossary would be useless if every word in it were not related to every other word in it. For these words belong together. And to think them together will increase your understanding of the separate words. If you will read this Glossary, and study it, to see what words are defined and how they are related, you will better understand the principles and the words that, together, make for Power-Steering with Words.

Many of these statements are skeletal. If you refer to the Index, you will find textual references that will amplify the meanings further.

**abstraction**   Every word is an abstraction, because a word takes away from the whole object, quality, or action that it signifies only such characteristics as are common to every instance of its use.

**analogy**   We reason by analogy when we compare two or more systems. When two or more things, events, etc., are analogous, they are similar in structure. A map of Illinois, for example, is analogous to the territory it represents.

   The worth of an analogy is measured by the degree to which similarity of *structure* holds. A poor map, for example, is worthless to the traveler, whereas a good map enables him to anticipate (predict) what is ahead.

**appraisor**   An appraisor is a word that puts a value on something (for or against, high or low, beautiful or ugly, important or worthless, etc.). Adjectives and adverbs are, in general, appraisors.

   Appraisors are in the appropriate mode to the valuative use of language, by which a communicator hopes to cause a listener to take a preferential attitude to something or someone.

**attitude**   An attitude is a disposition to *act* in one way rather than another. Our attitudes are intimately associated with our values.

**automation**   I use the word "automation" with respect to human behavior, and especially to the use of words, because, as with automated machinery, we can correct the deviation between the state of affairs and the programmed goal-state. Feedback is the control in both man and machine.

**cause-to-effect pattern**   There are two kinds of cause-to-effect verbal patterns: The bona fide cause-to-effect pattern is a verifiable *If this, then necessarily that* pattern; the imputed cause-to-effect pattern is an informed opinion.

The bona fide cause-to-effect pattern is isomorphic with a recurrent actual pattern in the world, and, as such, is both logical and true. The imputed cause-to-effect pattern is referable only to such evidence as is available; because all data are not in, and perhaps cannot be in, it is necessary to impute—to ascribe—causes on the basis of what data are in.

**character**   "Character" signifies the integration of the self. I use the word "character" to stand for the *organized* past experience of the human being. I use "character" to signify the whole self—knowledge and values—as a unified idea system.

Character is the backbone of personality. (I use "personality" to signify the relationship between the unified self, "character," and the social and physical environment.)

**communication**   Communication is a behavioral science that belongs with the social sciences. Communication is structured change that takes place in goal-seeking behavior. Two or more systems—persons, machines, etc.—are in communication if the state of one changes the state of the other. Communication is a patterned process that involves all participants.

**competition**   Within our selves, there is competition of impulses, competition of wants, competition of needs. One idea competes with another; one plan competes with another. Stimuli compete for our attention and interest.

Competition is inescapable. Competition is defined, not as emanating from an "ego drive," but as a fact of life in goal-directed behavior.

**concept** Einstein defines a concept as a series of related elements. He defines thinking as the process of relating elements, of connecting elements, that is of *forming* concepts.

When a recurrent element becomes an instrument of order, we have a concept. When a recurrent element connects or relates things that are not otherwise connected or related, we have a concept.

**concretize** To "concretize" a word is to exemplify an abstraction. Such words as "goodness," "cruelty," "mercy," "compassion," "justice," do not have reference to an actual, particular, instance of the quality they signify. They are concretized when an actual instance is cited, when, for example, a particular act of mercy is described.

**criticism** Think of criticism as an operation that makes it possible for us to appraise the consequences of our words with respect to a goal-state. Criticism is evaluation. The term may be used positively or negatively.

**cross organization** In the cyclic *trans*action that takes place between a communicator and his listeners, the communicator is organized and the environment (physical and social) is organized. The communicator and his listeners, together, enter into a patterned process. Gardner Murphy calls this "cross organization." In cross organization, when there is change in any aspect of the situation as a whole, there is change in every aspect of the situation as a whole. When the speaker changes, the listener changes; when the listener changes, the speaker changes.

**cybernetics**   "Cybernetics" derives from a Greek word that means "steersman." In a broad sense, it means the study of control and communication in both Man and the Machine. It may be used as a short cut for "self-correcting behavior by the use of words." The communicator uses the consequences of his words as new information by which to control his future output with respect to his goal. This is the exercise of feedback.

**cyclic**   I use "cyclic" to signify the moving, swirling relationship between a communicator and his listeners in cross organization. The relationship is one of indivisible on-going connectedness. The word "cyclic" signifies, in this book, *trans*action, cross organization, a circular binding relationship of communicator and listeners within an open system.

**decision(s)**   A decision is a choice. The choice may be made with respect to a goal that is calculated to satisfy a need or the choice may be made with respect to the best strategy to pursue in the attainment of that goal.

Life is a decision-making continuum. Some decisions are made on a habitual basis; others involve analysis and prediction. In the communication process we prescribe three stages in decision-making: (1) the analysis of the *status quo* (which takes the form of a cause-to-effect verbal pattern); (2) the consideration of competing means-to-end verbal patterns; (3) the propulsion of the whole self (conscious and unconscious) in the choice of the most promising means-to-end strategy.

259

**denote**  A designator denotes when there is something in the world to which it refers. Ogden and Richards call the thing to which a word refers the referent.

**designator**  A designator is a word that is used to cause a listener or a reader to act as if a certain object, person, event, etc., in the world has certain characteristics. When the designators do, indeed, refer to such objects, persons, events, etc., in the world, they are said to denote. Designators that denote are true.

The designative mode is appropriate to the informative use of language. Nouns and verbs are, in general, in the designative mode.

**developmental construct**  A developmental construct is a plan that is calculated to reach a desired goal. In this context we set up such a plan as a means-to-end verbal pattern.

**dynamic**  In this book the word "dynamic" refers to conditions of change in the communication process.

**dynamic relationship**  The relationship between communicator and listeners is binding. The relationship is energized. It is a dynamic structure—dynamic in all of its elements and in the situation as a whole.

**empathy**  Empathy is different from sympathy. Empathy is a *feeling with* someone else; sympathy is a *feeling for* someone else. Empathy between persons may be, and often is, on the silent (nonverbal) level, but empathic relationships may also be developed on the verbal level.

**fact**  Statements that are arrangements of designators that denote are statements of fact (at that date).

Relationships between controllable data and repeatable operations give us bona fide cause-to-effect verbal patterns. This is the language of fact.

260

A verbal pattern that is isomorphic with a recurrent actual pattern in the world is a statement of fact. Such a verbal pattern is true and logical.

**feedback**  When the communicator uses the consequences of his own words as new information by which to control his future output (with respect to his goal), he exercises feedback.

There are two kinds of feedback: positive and negative.[112] When the consequences of the words of a communicator are as desired, positive feedback continues according to strategy. The output of the communicator maintains the favorable present state. This is a continuance of feedforward.

When the communicator finds that his words are not having the desired effect, he will change his tactics. When the controls are altered (by the use of words) so as to reduce the difference between the undesirable present state and the goal-state, this is the exercise of negative feedback.

**feedforward**  Feedforward is the strategic semantic device. The communicator uses a verbal pattern to feed forward. Because the verbal pattern is both cohesive and progressive, when the communicator starts a verbal pattern, the listener or reader can anticipate what is to follow. He can, indeed, jump ahead of the communicator. When the listener or reader does anticipate what is to follow, the communicator has fed forward.

**field**  A field is a system whose parts are dynamically connected in such a way that a change in any one part results in a change in all other parts of the system.

In our conception of communication, each part of the field is conceived as in *trans*action with every other part. There is no separation between participants in face-to-

face communication; there is continuous change as a result of varying currents.

**force**   In this book "force" is the cause of change. The
properties of force are a point of application, a target,
strength, and direction. The point of application is the
integrated self. The strength of words lies within the integrated self, which projects verbal and nonverbal signs that
are intended to move the communicator in the direction
of his target—his goal.[113]

**formator**   Formators are related terms that are used to
make verbal patterns. They are the components of a verbal pattern. The only function of the formator is to systematize a communication process.

A formator, as I use the term, is a general word that
prescribes and delimits the scope of a communication.
It is sufficiently general to make a place for subsidiary
formators and all the details that support the major formators. But the formators should not be broader than the
area to be covered.

The formators must be joined by a principle of organization to make a verbal pattern. They may be related as
cause-to-effect, as means-to-end, as a time sequence, as a
space sequence, as sections, etc.

**frame of reference**   The frame of reference puts a circumference around a communication. It is necessary to cir-
cumscribe the formators by a frame of reference in order
to determine relevance, to keep out the irrelevant and to
include only the relevant. The frame of reference is the
only criterion for inclusion or exclusion of formators.

**function**   "Function" is what something does. Function is
related to structure. My hand has structure (shape and
form, physical characteristics), but it also has function
(movement, grasping).

We can think of the nervous system in terms of structure and in terms of function, but here we find it impossible actually to separate the two. Thus Korzybski invented the hyphenated word "neuro-linguistic" to bring the nervous system (structure) and the language system (function) together.

**general semantics**   "General Semantics" as expounded by Korzybski in *Science and Sanity* is the *science* of man (as understood by Korzybski[1933]) that prescribes human disciplines by which to achieve *sanity*. The disciplines are grounded in the conception of the individual as an organism-as-a-whole-in-an-environment (a conception not very different from Gardner Murphy's "personality in a field"). The basic assumptions from which Korzybski moved forward are process, uniqueness, relatedness, and order.

**generalization**   A generalization is the saying of something that applies more than once. We generalize on successively higher levels when we move from "this" to "a few" to "some" to "most" to "all." We reach the highest level of generalization when we say "all."

**goal-state**   A goal-state is an objective toward which we aim. When we plan to reach a goal-state, we set up a means-to-end verbal pattern.

**heirarchy**   A hierarchy is a structure that takes the form of a pyramid. At the bottom are the specifics, the particulars, and at the top the controlling agency.

The experience of a person is a hierarchy. At its peak is an idea-system that encompasses everything he knows and believes (whether on the conscious or the unconscious level). At the lowest level are the particular instances of his experience, including all kinds of awareness, of learning, of knowing, of thinking-feeling-doing.

**idea**   An idea is something signified, something symbolized, something put into words. It is a *thinking-of* verbalized.

**ideal** An ideal is something toward which we would strive. An ideal is an idea with a lure.

**idea-system** The word "idea-system" may be used synonymously with the word "philosophy." An idea-system is a bringing together of all the knowledge and beliefs of a human being (or a group of human beings), insofar as this can be accomplished.

The idea-system is verbalized in the highest generalizations of which the human being is capable and makes a place for experience on all lower levels of thinking-feeling-doing.

**incitive use** When the intention of the user of words is to incite a listener or a reader to a specific action response, he uses incitive language. Imperatives serve this purpose. *Do this! Don't do that!* Prescriptors are therefore in the appropriate mode of language for the incitive use.

**information** By "information" is meant, not symbolized bits of isolated data, but a series of *connected* elements. It is the *connection* of incoming information to a reservoir of experience that makes possible learning, thinking, interpretation, memory and an idea-system.

**informative use** When the intention of the user of words is to inform a listener or a reader, he will use words in the informative use that refer specifically and accurately to persons, objects, events, etc. Designators are in the appropriate mode of language for the informative use. In general, nouns and verbs are appropriate to the informative use. Adjectives and adverbs are not, in general, appropriate.

**input** In this context, the word "input" refers to anything that is perceived by participants in a communication proc-

ess. When a stimulus changes the behavior of the partici-
pant, he perceives; otherwise not.

**integrated self**   The word "integrated" refers to the degree
of connectedness, of organization, of the experience of a
human being. Conflicts within the self tend to disorganize
a person in ways that are likely to cause his conduct to be
indecisive and without direction.

**integration**   Integration of the self is order within the self.
Order is a concept that permits of predictability in varying degrees of probability. Integration of the self is, therefore, a factor in the image which we create in others. We
are "dependable," "unreliable," etc., to others to the degree
that we manifest integration of the self.

A well-integrated self is likely to be open (receptive and
responsive) to incoming stimuli, with the result that the
individual reaches increasingly higher levels of organization and moves consistently toward a unified idea-system.

**interest**   An interest is an activity that moves in the direction
of a goal that is calculated to satisfy a need. The meaning
of the word "interest" is, therefore, multidimensional in
that it has three facets—need, activity, and goal—and can
be discussed with emphasis on one or more of these facets.
When there is no activity, there is no interest.

**interpretation**   The interpretation of an incoming stimulus
—words, actions, a work of art, etc.—is effected by relating it to something in our past experience. If we cannot so
relate a stimulus, it is meaningless to us and without significance to us. Interpretation is, in this sense, always personal to a degree. Private and public interpretation should,
however, be differentiated.

**isomorphic**   When two things have identical structure, they
are said to be isomorphic. When the structure of a church

is identical with the pattern of the blueprint, building and blueprint are isomorphic, regardless of their differences.

**learning**   The word "learning," as used in this book, is defined as the disposition to form patterns or as the act of forming patterns.

**logic, logical**   In this context, the word "logic" is relevant to verbal patterns. When a verbal pattern is isomorphic with an actual pattern in the world, the verbal pattern is true and logical.

**logical construct**   A logical construct is a verbal pattern.

**means-to-end pattern**   Because the means-to-end verbal pattern looks to the future and involves operations by human beings, it is in the area of opinion. A means-to-end verbal pattern cannot be said to be "right" or "wrong." Such a pattern is "better" or "worse," depending on the inclusiveness, the relevance, and the quality of evidence that supports it.

**memory**   Memory is stored information, stored learning, stored knowledge. Memory is the reservoir of experience. Ideally, the reservoir of experience is a composite of related patterns. Remembering is the retrieval of information.

**modes of language**   The modes of language have relevance to the kind of words that are appropriate (suitable) to a purpose.

Designators are in the appropriate mode to the informative use.

Appraisors are in the appropriate mode to the valuative use.

Prescriptors are in the appropriate mode to the incitive use.

Formators are in the appropriate mode to the systemic use.

266

It is important to know the intention of a communicator. The mode that the communicator uses provides a clue to that intention. It alerts us to the reasons for the inclusion and possible omission of relevant information. The systemic use in the formative mode is probably the best clue to the intention of the communicator, for it systematizes the other three uses and shows their relative importance in the context as a whole.

**multidimensional**  A multidimensional word may have various connections, various facets, thus becoming an element in various patterns. It reaches out in different directions.

**open system**  A system is a patterned process. An open system, though a self-contained pattern, has input and output. The human being is an open system and, though self-contained, is a process in which input and output are in cyclic *trans*action. An open system is, though a self-contained pattern, a *process* in which there is constant *change*.

**opinion**  An opinion is a leap of the mind beyond the facts, because all the facts are not in, perhaps cannot be in. This is the case in matters that relate to human behavior (personal and social). Because an opinion cannot be said to be "right" or "wrong" (since it is not subject to verification), an opinion should be open-end and looked at critically in the light of new information.

**output**  In this context, our primary output is words. We associate output primarily with feedforward, with our use of verbal patterns that arouse expectations in listeners or readers of what is to follow. Negative feedback is corrective output.

**perception**  When a stimulus object or event changes the behavior of the communicator, he perceives; otherwise not. Perception is defined by the psychologist Floyd Allport as an "event-structure."[66] Perception is an *event* in that it occurs when a stimulus object changes the behavior of the communicator. Perception is a *structure* in that it cannot occur except where input fits into a pattern and somehow amplifies or reorganizes that pattern, thus to change future output in the interest of goal-seeking behavior.

**personality**  I use the word "personality" to describe the cyclic relationship of a human being to his social and physical environment. Personality is cross organization between self and environment, such that when there is change in any aspect of the field, forces will produce a change throughout the whole field. "Personality" is distinguished from "character," which is defined as the integrated self.

**policy**  Policy is the operational value-system. Policy puts the value-system to work. Policy is the value-system concretized. Policy determines what an individual will *do* on the basis of his value-system.

**power**  In this context, we speak of a power field as the sphere of influence of a person in a communication process. The communicator acts as a force to induce change in the interest of his goal.[113]

**preference system**  The preference system of the human being screens out everything that is irrelevant to his needs and his goals. It monitors what we shall say and what we shall do. It is a natural shield against unwanted intrusion. The preference system is therefore evaluatory. It is the mechanism that sets the controls in feedback, negative and positive.

**prescriptor**  When the intention of the user of words is to ask for a specific action response, he will use incitive language in the prescriptive mode. The appropriate mode in the incitive use of language is the prescriptor. Prescriptors are imperatives.

**purposive**  To say that we are purposive creatures is to say we are, by nature, goal-seekers. Self-actualization, self-realization, and self-fulfillment are inherent in man. The word "self-determination" sums up purposive activity. We may want many things in life, but fundamentally we strive to fulfill our selves. The human being *determines* consciously what he would become. The human being is *self*-directing, *self*-organizing, and *self*-corrective. He is an open-system moving from his self-image toward his ideal self-image.

**recurrence**  When recurrent patterns in nature (social and physical) are discovered, we gain knowledge. Prediction is possible only when we understand recurrent relationships, recurrent patterns.

**referent**  A referent is something (an object, a person, an event, etc.) out there in the world to which a word refers.

**relevance**  Incoming information has relevance to the degree that it updates our state of readiness to adapt purposively to a goal-state.

**retrieval**  In this book "retrieval" means remembering. Remembering is not a result of memorization. Past experience is stored in the memory as related elements. When we understand recurrent connected elements, we have a basis for remembering even a part of such a connected series.

**rhythm**  Rhythm is timing. In speech, the pattern of thinking is communicated primarily by rhythm—the rhythm of sentence structure, the rhythm of the voice, the rhythm of the interplay of voice and silence. In writing, the pattern of thinking is, of course, communicated by punctuation, by sentence structure, and by paragraphing, but most of all by the use of formators that indicate the structure of the entire communication. The very pulsation of life—thinking-feeling-doing—is communicated by rhythm.

**scan**   To scan means "to analyze into rhythmic components," "to search for patterns."

**sectional pattern**   The sectional verbal pattern is used to examine the *parts* of a *whole* in terms of their logical relations. There are four sectional patterns: this *and* that: this *or* that; this, *not* that; this *is* that. The *conjunctive* sectional pattern joins the parts of the pattern by the conjunction "and." If the parts, together, complete the frame of reference, the conjunctive sectional pattern is said to be *closed*; otherwise the pattern is *open*. The *disjunctive* sectional pattern joins the parts by the conjunction "or." The *negative* sectional pattern joins the parts by the negative "not." The *equivalence* sectional pattern joins the parts by the equals sign ($=$) or "is."

**self-actualization**   The word "self-actualization" refers to the process of *becoming* what we may be. Purposive activity is inherent in living organisms, and that inherent tendency is to actualize—to make actual, to make real—the promise of one's hereditary potential.

**signify**   To *signify* means "to make a sign." We make signs on both the verbal and nonverbal levels. Words are signs; so also is a yawn.

**silence**   Silence cannot be ignored. For us, silence is active nonverbal communication. Silence involves communication on the physical level—as the moment of silence between a speaker and his listeners, as gesture, as facial expression. Even the silence between words is communication.

**space pattern**   The parts of the space pattern are related in space. Arrangements of furniture fall into a space pattern; an itinerary of a travel expedition falls into a space pattern; astronomy can be taught as a space pattern.

**storage**  Storage implies a structured self. This means that incoming information, which is stored as verbal patterns, is arranged on successively higher levels of organization until the hierarchy of experience is brought together as an idea-system.

**strategy**  In the communication process, strategy is planned program. The word "strategy" is therefore synonymous with verbal pattern. When the communicator hopes to reach a goal, he feeds a verbal pattern forward. This is his strategy.

**structure**  The word "structure" is synonymous, in this book, with the word "pattern." So, also, are the words "form" and "logical construct."

**symbol, symbolize**  To *symbolize* is "to make a sign." A word is a sign. A word may therefore also be called a symbol.

Ogden and Richards use the word "symbol" to refer only to words that have referents; that is, to words that *refer to* some*thing* in the world—an object, a person, an event, etc.

We use the word "symbol" more broadly to refer to all words, whether they have referents in the world of people and things or not. Abstract words such as "love," "beauty," "mercy," etc., are, in our account, symbols.

Every time we use words—informative, appraisive, incitive, or systemic—we symbolize.

**system**  A system is a dynamic pattern. A system is an interacting set of distinct and individual elements (people, things, events, ideas). Every essential element in the system requires all the other essential elements to be what it is and to mean what it means. Human beings are *open* systems.

**systemic use**   The systemic use of words systematizes—organizes—the other three uses: informative, valuative, and incitive. Formators are in the appropriate mode to the systemic use of language. The only function of the systemic use of words in the formative mode is to organize the other three uses of language.

**tactics**   Tactics is the semantic device that corrects deviation between an unfavorable state of affairs and the goal-state. Whereas we associate the word "feedforward" with *strategy*, we associate the word "feedback" with *tactics*. When the responses to our own words are not favorable to the goal-state, we correct the deviation between the actual state of affairs and the desired goal-state. This corrective control is tactics.

**tension.**   Tension is a force that induces change. Without tension the communicator cannot effect desired change.

**thinking**   Thinking is the process of *connecting* recurrent elements, or *relating* recurrent elements, thus to make verbal patterns. And thus to form concepts, as defined by Einstein. Thinking results in knowledge.

**time pattern**   The parts of the verbal time pattern are related in time: past, present, future; before, during, after; eighteenth century, nineteenth century, twentieth century, etc. A calendar is a time pattern. A production line schedule is a time pattern.

**transaction**   In this word I emphasize, especially, the meaning of the prefix *trans-*, "on the other side of, to the other side of, over, across. . . ." Communication is an *action* that crosses over, as in cross organization. In conversation or in conference of any kind, the process is such that *trans-*

action gives participants a measure of control over the cyclic change by the exercise of feedforward and feedback.

**true, truth**   A statement of fact is true. This means that designators that denote are true. Such designators are subject to verification. A verbal pattern that accurately designates an actual pattern in the world is true. Such verbal patterns are subject to verification.

**uses of language**   There are four uses of languages: informative, valuative, incitive, and systemic. Uses refer to the *intention* of the communicator.

Informative language aims to inform. Designators are in the proper mode in the informative use.

Valuative language aims to cause a preferential attitude in the listener or reader. Appraisors are in the proper mode in the valuative use.

Incitive language aims to cause a specific action response. Prescriptors are in the proper mode in the incitive use.

Systemic language has only one function. When the intention of the communicator is to organize all the responses of his listeners or reader, formators are in the appropriate mode.

**valuative use**   The valuative use of language places a value on something with the hope that the percipient will place a like value on whatever is appraised. Valuative language is the language of persuasion, because it is unlikely that anyone will be activated unless he *wants* to be so activated. Appraisors are in the appropriate mode in the valuative use. Adjectives and adverbs are, in general, appraisors.

**valuatory mechanism**   The valuatory mechanism, about which we know little, screens out stimuli that have no relevance to the purpose at hand. In this sense, the valuatory mechanism stems from the preference system.

The valuatory mechanism tells us whether or not our strategy is advancing toward a goal and sets the controls to reduce the difference (if any) between the actual state of affairs and the goal-state by negative feedback. Where the difference reading is zero (or an acceptable approximation), positive feedback takes over to maintain the strategic advance.

**values**  Anything that has worth for us is a value. Value accrues to *anything* that contributes to self-actualization.

**verbal pattern**  A verbal pattern is a pattern of words written or said, thought or heard. A pattern is an arrangement that is characterized by the *order* of the elements of which it is made rather than by the intrinsic nature of the elements. This means that two patterns are identical if for each part of the one there is a corresponding part in the other, and for each relation of order between the parts of the one there is a corresponding relation of order between the parts of the other.

We may say then that when a verbal pattern accurately designates an actual pattern in the world, the verbal pattern and the actual pattern have all their logical characteristics in common. When a verbal pattern accurately designates an actual pattern in the world, the verbal pattern is true.

The following are the arrangements into which the formators of verbal patterns may fall: (1) the time pattern, (2) the space pattern, (3) the cause-to-effect pattern, (4) the means-to-end pattern, and (5) the sectional pattern.

Because the verbal pattern is made up of parts that are

related according to a principle of organization, the parts "hang together" and yet move. The verbal pattern is, therefore, both cohesive and progressive.

A verbal pattern, when started, enables a listener or a reader to anticipate what is to follow.

There are as many kinds of verbal patterns as there are patterns in nature, actual, possible, or even plausible.

**working-title** A working-title is precisely what it says—it is the title from which the speaker or author *works*. A working-title is, in other words, a verbal pattern that establishes the form of a communication.

A working-title is made up of the primary formators of a verbal pattern, and these formators are joined together according to a principle of organization: time, space, cause-to-effect, means-to-end, and sectional.

# Appendix

This appendix takes the form of annotated bibliographical footnotes that correspond serially to superior numbers in the text.

This form of appendix is used for two reasons: first, to support the opinions expressed in this book, and second, to provide the reader with a guide to source materials.

1. Charles Morris, *The Open Self* (New York, Prentice-Hall, 1948), p. 54.

2. Heinz von Foerster, "Perception of Form in Biological and Man-made Systems," an address delivered at the annual meeting of the Industrial Design Education Association, held at the University of Illinois, March 17, 1962.

   "We are finally in a position to formulate theories of perception and to check them by probing into different regions of the brain. . . . At first I would like to establish certain relationships between two concepts 'form' and 'perception.' Both these concepts deal with a process which is well understood and generally referred to as 'abstraction.' Take as an example this cubical box. . . . This box is not going to change. It stays the same box in my head, despite the fact that you see always something different. There is obviously something constant in all these gyrations. (Movements by von Foerster of the cube in his hand) The object's cubicality . . . does not vary. Mathematically, the entities which do not vary are called 'invariants.' Form does not vary, hence it is an invariant. We give invariable names, as e.g., 'cube' to these invariants. By naming it we have immediately defined the invariability of the form of the entity in my hand and call it a cube. Having formed the concept of an 'invariant,' let me now show you what is meant by an abstraction. The process of abstraction is nothing else but the computation of some invariants." (pp. 10–11)

3.  Alfred Korzybski, *Science and Sanity: An Introduction to Non-aristotelian Systems and General Semantics* (1st edition, 1933, 4th edition, 1958, International Non-aristotelian Library Publishing Company, Distributed by the Institute of General Semantics, Lakeville, Conn.). All references are to the 4th edition.

"If we consider that all we deal with represents constantly changing sub-microscopic, interrelated processes which are not, and cannot be 'identical with themselves,' the old dictum that 'everything is identical with itself' becomes in 1933 a principle invariably false to fact." (p. lxxxiv)

"In life we have, and deal with, *individuals*. . . . If we take a number of individuals, we have a number of them, yet they all remain individual." (p. 432)

"Without some higher abstractions we cannot be human at all. No science could exist with absolute individuals and no relations; so we pass to higher abstractions and build a language of say $X_i$, (i-1, 2, 3, . . . n). . . . From a structural point of view, such a vocabulary is similar to the world around us; it accounts for the individuality of the external objects, it also is similar to the structure of our nervous system, because it allows generalizations or higher order abstractions. The subscript emphasizes the differences; the letter X implies the similarities." (p. 262)

Henri Laborit, "The Need for Generalization in Biological Research: The Role of the Mathematical Theory of Ensembles," The Institute of General Semantics, *General Semantics Bulletin*, No. 30, 1963/64.

"We should now attempt to explain . . . what we mean by generalization. Using the terminology of the theory of ensembles [structures], we feel justified in saying that 'to generalize is to create new ensembles or relationships encompassing a certain number of ensembles whose basic characteristics have already been defined."

4. Shann Kreuger, private collection, unpublished.

5. F. S. C. Northrop, *The Logic of the Sciences and the Humanities* (New York, Macmillan, 1947).

"the moment one reports what one observes, at a meeting of historians or in a book written for sociologists, at that moment one has not pure facts but facts brought under concepts, and hence theory." (p. 317)

6. Erwin Schrödinger, *What Is Life?* (Cambridge, Cambridge University Press, 1944).

"Physical laws rest on atomic statistics and are therefore only approximate." (p. 8)

George H. Mead, *Movements of Thought in the Nineteenth Century* (Chicago, University of Chicago Press, 1936).

"In this generation we have had fundamental conceptions brought forward that entirely change the character of the physical universe. Take such experience as that represented in the quantum theory, a theory in accordance with which reality has had to be regarded as both continuous and discontinuous. You are brought up against something that in the nature of the case you cannot predict." (p. 117)

7. Thomas A. Cowan, "Decision Theory in Law, Science, and Technology," *Science*, Vol. 140 (June 7, 1963), pp. 1065–1075.

> "Not even a rudimentary scientific apparatus exists for studying any *individual* entity, whether person, event, state, or decision. The arts and the sciences are concerned with individuals, but no general scientific theory can handle them yet.
>
> "*Factor analysis*, which is the attempt to isolate behavioral traits and to bunch them by means of mathematical statistical techniques, has important clinical applications. *But it is not scientific investigation. . . .*" (p. 1072)

Dwight J. Ingle, "Testing Claims to Knowledge," *Perspectives in Biology and Medicine* (Autumn 1961), pp. 65–85.

> "The statistical view of quantum phenomena recognizes that the behavior of individual particles does not conform to the laws of classical mechanics but seems to be disorderly. The order of the whole system emerges as a statistical average out of the disorder of the particles, and some degree of uncertainty remains. . . . The error of the average relates to the number of its parts ($n$) according to the $\sqrt{n}$ law. This concept holds that there is a degree of uncertainty in all natural phenomena which has anything to do with the obvious limitations of the observer. . . ." (pp. 68–69)

> "Errors of Sampling. A basic principle is that a sample must be chosen in such a way that we are willing to argue from it to its population. Each sample is to some unknown degree not representative of its population, but approximate statistical design enables the experimenter to estimate the error of sampling. The risk in extrapolation depends in part upon how well the sample represents the population. Nowhere along the evolutionary scale can it be assumed that the difference between populations are unimportant. . . ." (p. 70)

8. Erwin Schrödinger, *What Is Life?* (Cambridge, Cambridge University Press, 1944).

279

". . . incredibly small groups of atoms, much too small to display exact statistical laws, do play a dominating role in the very orderly and lawful events within a living organism. They have control of the observable large-scale features which the organism acquires in the course of its development, they determine important characteristics of its functioning; and in all this very sharp and very strict biological laws are displayed. . . .

"Let me use the word 'pattern' of an organism in the sense in which the biologist calls it 'the four-dimensional pattern'. . . . Now this four-dimensional pattern is known to be determined by the structure of that one cell, the fertilized egg. . . .

"The chromosome structures are at the same time instrumental in bringing about the development they foreshadow. . . . They are law-code and executive power—or, to use another simile, they are architect's plan and builder's craft—in one." (pp. 19, 20, 21)

W. Grey Walter, *The Living Brain* (New York, Norton, 1953).

". . . where there is pattern there is significance." (p. 65)

"Consider the significance of pattern. So much of brain physiology rests on this conception that it must be thoroughly understood before going further." (p. 67)

"Pattern, then, may be defined as any sequence of events in time, or any set of objects in space, distinguishable from or comparable with another sequence or set. The first significant attribute of a pattern is that you can remember it and compare it with another pattern. This is what distinguishes it from random events or chaos." (p. 68)

Alicia Hills, Albert Rosenfeld, and others, "DNA's Code: Key to All Life," *Life* Magazine (October 4, 1963).

F. H. C. Crick, "On the Genetic Code," *Science*, Vol. 139 (February 8, 1963), pp. 461–464.

Richard V. Eck, "Genetic Code: Emergence of a Symmetrical Pattern," *Science*, Vol. 140 (May 3, 1963), pp. 477–481.

W. Grey Walter, *The Living Brain* (New York, Norton, 1953).

Floyd H. Allport, *Theories of Perception and the Concept of Structure* (New York, Wiley, 1955).

Gardner Murphy, *Personality, a Biological Approach to Origins and Structure* (New York, Harper, 1947).

9. Erwin Schrödinger, *What Is Life?* (Cambridge, Cambridge University Press, 1944).

> "First, a physical organization, to be in close correspondence with thought (as my brain is with my thought) must be a very well-ordered organization, and that means that the events that happen within it must obey strict physical laws, at least to a very high degree of accuracy. Secondly, the physical impressions made upon that physically well-organized system by other bodies from outside, obviously correspond to the perception and experience of the corresponding thought, forming its material. . . . Therefore, the physical interactions between our systems and others must, as a rule, themselves possess a certain degree of physical orderliness, that is to say, they too must obey strict physical laws to a certain degree of accuracy." (p. 8)

Lancelot Law Whyte, *Accent on Form* (New York, Harper, 1954).

Gardner Murphy, *Personality, A Biosocial Approach to Origins and Structure* (New York, Harper, 1947), pp. 6–9.

10. Thomas A. Cowan, "Decision Theory in Law, Science, and Technology," *Science,* Vol. 140 (June 5, 1963), pp. 1065–1075.

> "No general theory of social action exists that has received widespread acceptance even among social scientists. No one knows why groups . . . decide to act as they do.
> "No general theory of human motivation in the individual exists. No one knows why the individual decides to do what he does." (p. 1072)

11. Kenneth Burke, *Permanence and Change* (New York, New Republic, 1936).

> "We have advanced as follows: (a) there is a sense of relationships, developed by the contingencies of experience; (b) this sense of relationships is our orientation; (c) our orienta-

tion largely involves matters of expectancy, and affects our choice of means with reference to the future. . . ." (pp. 29–30)

Kenneth E. Boulding, *The Image* (Ann Arbor, The University of Michigan Press, 1956), p. 169.

12. Alfred Korzybski, *Science and Sanity: An Introduction to Non-aristotelian Systems and General Semantics* (1st edition, 1933, 4th edition, 1958, International Non-aristotelian Library Publishing Company, Distributed by the Institute of General Semantics, Lakeville, Conn.).

"It should be noticed that in a four-dimensional world dating is only a particular temporal index by which we can deal effectively with space-time." (p. xlviii)

13. Charles Morris, *The Open Self* (New York, Prentice-Hall, 1948), pp. 144–148, 168.

14. Kenneth Burke, *Permanence and Change* (New York, New Republic, 1936).

"The problems of existence do not have one fixed unchanging character, like the label on a bottle. They are open to many interpretations—and these interpretations in turn influence our selection of means [by which to accomplish predetermined goals?]. Hence the place of 'trained incapacity' in the matter of means-selecting. One adopts measures in keeping with his past training—and the very soundness of this training may lead him to adopt the wrong measures. People may be unfitted by being fit in an unfit fitness. . . . Their training has become an incapacity." (p. 18)

15. W. Grey Walter, *The Living Brain* (New York, Norton, 1953), Ch. VIII.

". . . when two people display unreasonable and irreconcilable differences of approach to a question, before concluding that this is due to innate antagonism or incompatibility of purpose, a discrepancy in their ways of thinking may be worth looking into. Communication between them might be easier through an intermediary type—who on occasion can use both ways of thinking." (pp. 219–222)

"For the time being we must be satisfied to summarize the material intimations of personality found in the electrical activities of the living brain. . . . They have at least the merit of being not opinion or elements of a theory but facts recorded in experiments which can be repeated." (p. 231)

16. Karl W. Deutsch, "Communication Theory and Social Science," *Selected Papers on Psychotherapy, Purpose and Communication* (New York, American Orthopsychiatric Association, 1952), pp. 469–483.

"Actually, the meaning of the term *analogy* is often poorly understood. Analogy means limited structural correspondence. All mathematics is based on analogies, and so is a large part of every science. . . . The test by which we discriminate between a false analogy and a good analogy consists in the extent of actual structural correspondence between the two systems between which the analogy is drawn. . . . It is suggested that cybernetics [the analogy between 'the animal and the machine' of Norbert Wiener and others] is currently proving itself a good analogy. . . ." (p. 471)

17. Norman Cousins, "The Default of the Educated Man," *Saturday Review* (June 29, 1963), p. 18.

18. Rabbi Max Kadushin, *The Rabbinic Mind* (New York, Jewish Theological Seminary of America, 1952).

Rabbi Max Kadushin, *Organic Thinking* (New York, Jewish Theological Seminary of America, 1938).

19. Eliott Jaques, M.D., *The Changing Culture of a Factory* (London, Tavistock Publications, 1951), p. 289.

20. Karl W. Deutsch, "Communication Theory and Social Science," *Selected Papers on Psychotherapy, Purpose and Communication* (New York, American Orthopsychiatric Association, 1952), p. 470.

21. "How to Undercut the Personnel Department, Ways to Sabotage the Personnel Department," *Brevities from Employers' Association of Greater Chicago* (January 1961).

Paul Pigors and Charles A. Myers, *Personnel Administration* (New York, McGraw-Hill, 1956).

Malcolm P. McNair, "Thinking Ahead: What Price Human Relations?" *Harvard Business Review*, Vol. 35, No. 2 (March-April 1957), pp. 15–16, 20ff.

22. Norbert Wiener, *Cybernetics, or Control and Communication in the Animal and the Machine* (New York, Wiley, 1948).

23. Bionics Symposium, March 19–21, 1963, Air Force Systems Command, United States Air Force, Wright-Patterson Air Force Base, Ohio.

24. Norbert Wiener, *Cybernetics, or Control and Communication in the Animal and the Machine* (New York, Wiley, 1948).

"We have decided to call the entire field of control and communication theory, whether in the machine or in the animal, by the name of Cybernetics, which we form from the Greek *kybernētikē*; or steersman." (p. 19)

25. Norbert Wiener, *The Human Use of Human Beings, Cybernetics and Society* (Boston, Houghton Mifflin; Cambridge, The Riverside Press, 1950).

Claude Shannon and Warren Weaver, *The Mathematical Theory of Communication* (Urbana, The University of Illinois Press, 1949).

D. M. MacKay, "Operational Aspects of Some Fundamental Concepts of Human Communication," *The Journal of Communication,* Symposium on Foundations of Communication Theory, Bess Sondel, Symposium Ed., Vol. XI, No. 4 (December 1961), pp. 183–189, 219.

Colin Cherry, *On Human Communication,* (Cambridge, Technology Press; New York, Wiley, 1957).

26. Robert S. Scott, "Communication—a Binding Energy," unpublished paper read at the Institute of Radio Engineers (September 14–15), 1961, Philadelphia, Pa.).

27. Floyd H. Allport, *Theories of Perception and the Concept of Structure* (New York, Wiley, 1955).

". . . the events or encounters in the cycle or between cycles can be regarded not only as geometric features, having a role of format-connection, but as units or increments of energy. For events, as happenings in the physical world, always involve energies. The ongoings of the cycles provide the 'formats' in which these units of energy occur. A concept of 'structural-dynamics' is thus interlaid within the 'structural-kinematic' framework. Energy, even in its smallest units, always implies structure." (p. 646)

28. Kurt Goldstein, "The So-called Drives," *The Self, Explorations in Personal Growth*, Clark E. Moustakas, ed. (New York, Harper, 1956), p. 23.

29. *Ibid.*, p. 17.

Gordon W. Allport, *Becoming, Basic Considerations for a Psychology of Personality* (New Haven, Yale University Press, 1955).

"While we learn dependable modes of reducing tension we also abandon old habits and take risks in searching out new courses of conduct. It is only through risk-taking and variation that growth can occur. But risk-taking and variation are fraught with new and often unavoidable tensions, which however we scorn to avoid. . . .

"Propriate striving confers unity upon personality, but it is never the unity of fulfillment, of repose, or of reduced tension. . . ." (pp. 66, 67)

30. I. A. Richards, "Communication Between Men: Meaning and Language," *Cybernetics, Transactions of the Eighth Conference* (March 15–16, 1951), Heinz von Foerster, ed. (New York, John Macy, Jr., Foundation, 1952).

31. *Ibid.*

"You have no doubt fed forward enough to see that what I am going to talk about from now on is feedforward. I am going to try to suggest its importance in describing how language works, and, above all, in determining how language must be learned. . . ." (p. 54)

"I am trying to draw attention to what is the distinctive mark of what I am calling feedforward. . . . It is 'taping' plus resort to a memory store. . . . (p. 55)

I understand the word "taping"—now used in connection with computer "memory" as stored in magnetic tape—to be synonymous with the word "engram" as used by Ogden and Richards some forty years ago in *The Meaning of Meaning*. Engram is defined by them (page 53) as a "gestalt" or "configuration"—a pattern of past experience that is stored in the memory. Further, these authors say, a stimulus that is a *part* of an engram sets up expectations of recurrence of the engram as *a whole*. (pp. 55-57)

I wrote, in "Communication in the Teaching-Learning Experience," published in *The Journal of Communication*, Vol. IX, No. 4 (December 1959):

*"Feed part of a verbal pattern forward and the whole pattern is likely to be anticipated."* (p. 156)

"I am tempted to call attention, parenthetically, to a statement of Warren Weaver in 'Some Recent Contributions,' contained in Claude Shannon and Warren Weaver, *The Mathematical Theory of Communication* (Urbana, University of Illinois Press, 1949), p. 102: 'A system which produces a sequence of symbols . . . according to certain probabilities is called a stochastic process and a special case of a stochastic process in which the probabilities depend on the previous events is called a *Markoff process* or a Markoff chain.' " (p. 156 fn.)

And now comes "Markovian Model of Time Patterns of Speech," by J. Jaffe, L. Cassotta, and S. Feldman, *Science*, Vol. 144 (May 15, 1964), that tells us "The time pattern of speech is describable as a first-order Markov process." This means that there is now verifiable evidence of a "sequential dependency" in the simple vocal time pattern of speech—"in the durations of sound bursts and the intervening durations of silence." (pp. 884–886) and this means that when *part* of a vocal time pattern is fed forward, the *whole* vocal time pattern is likely to be anticipated.

32. *Ibid*.

"Perhaps this thing on which I want to put the spotlight [feedforward] will be considered to be included in some ingenious way under the word 'feedback.' " (p. 54)

As far as I know, the word "feedback" had never been linked operationally with "feedforward" in semantics until 1958, when *The Humanity of Words* was published.

Bess Sondel, *The Humanity of Words* (New York, World Publishing, 1958), pp. 204, 206–208, 222, 223.

33. Norbert Wiener, *The Human Use of Human Beings, Cybernetics and Society* (Boston, Houghton Mifflin; Cambridge, The Riverside Press, 1950).

34. Alfred Korzybski, *Science and Sanity: An Introduction to Non-aristotelian Systems and General Semantics* (1st edition, 1933, 4th edition, 1958, International Non-aristotelian Library Publishing Company, Distributed by the Institute of General Semantics, Lakeville, Conn.).

"It would seem that the overwhelming importance *for mankind* of systems based on 'relations,' 'order,' 'structure,' etc., depends on the fact that such terms allow of an exact and 'logical' treatment, as two relations of similar structure have all their logical characteristics in common." (p. 60)

". . . the only possible link between the objective world and the linguistic world is found in *structure, and structure alone.* The only usefulness of a map or a language depends on the *similarity of structure* between the empirical world and the map-language. (p. 61)

H. Laborit, "The Need for Generalization in Biological Research: The Role of the Mathematical Theory of Ensembles," The Intitute of General Semantics, *General Semantics Bulletin,* No. 30, 1963/64.

"The word 'structure' calls for a definition. We offer a very general definition of *structure* as *the sum of relationships existing among the elements of an ensemble.* Thus, in the living organism, structures will consist of the relationships of the elements among themselves, and of the relationships between sub-ensembles of their component parts. Structures will therefore be characteristic of all *levels of organization.* . . . our essential aim is to 'relate the static to the dynamic, i.e., *the morphology to the function.*'

"We cannot conceive of the preservation of the structure

of a living organism in a surrounding medium unless there exists a continuous interchange of matter, i.e., energy, between them. . . . We believe that the *cybernetic* approach is indispensable for gaining an understanding of these regulatory mechanisms.

"The maintenance of living structures is essentially the consequence of the flow of a *current of energy* through them and through the open systems that they form." (pp. 1–3)

C. K. Ogden and I. A. Richards, *The Meaning of Meaning*, 5th ed. (New York, Harcourt, 1938).

"True reference is reference to a set of referents [things in the world] as they hang together. False reference is reference to them as being in some other arrangement than that in which they actually hang together. The advance in knowledge is the increase in our power of referring to referents as they actually hang together. This is all we can do." (p. 82)

"Logic . . . may be regarded as the science of the systematization of symbols. . . ." (p. 87)

". . . 'meaning' in the sense of reference becomes, according to this theory a matter open to experimental methods." (p. 73)

35. Charles Morris, *Signs, Language and Behavior* (New York, Braziller, 1955), pp. 86–88, 153–86, 268.

36. *Ibid*.

". . . formators . . . are especially economical and trustworthy signs for the systemic use." (p. 104)

James G. March, Herbert A. Simon, with collaboration of Harold Gustzkow, *Organizations* (New York, Wiley, 1958).

"A . . . method for increasing the organization's tolerance for interdependence is to increase the efficiency of communication by making it possible to communicate large amounts of information with relatively few symbols. An obvious example is the blueprint . . . accounting systems. . . .

"Prominent in these technical languages are categories for classifying situations and events. . . ." (p. 162)

37. Thomas A. Cowan, "Decision Theory in Law, Science, and Technology," *Science*, Vol. 140 (June 7, 1963), pp. 1065–1075.

> ". . . the computer is a logic machine. It performs very elementary and very fundamental operations of logic. It performs the operation of *disjunction*, the operation of choosing this *or* that. It knows *conjunction* (this *and* that); *inference* (if this, then that); *negation* (not this). . . . The computer can perform the operation of *comparison*. (Is this the same as that? If so, *do* x; if not, *do* y.)" (p. 1070)

38. John Dewey, *Logic: The Theory of Inquiry* (New York, Holt, 1938).

> "The difference between social and physical inquiry does not reside in the presence or absence of an end-in-view, formulated in terms of possible consequences. It consists in the respective *subject-matters* of the purposes." (p. 50)

> "Social phenomena are so interwoven with one another that it is impossible to assign special consequences . . . to any given body of facts unless the special consequences are . . . *differentially* determined. . . ." (p. 511)

Garrett Hardin, "The Cybernetics of Competition," *Perspectives in Biology and Medicine*, Vol. VII, No. 1 (Autumn 1963), pp. 58–84.

> "In the development of social theory we must follow the path that has proven successful in the natural sciences: we must be critical but not too critical. We must be willing to *entertain* partial theories while we see whether they are capable of fruitful enlargement. . . . Some of the principles worked out in one field should be at least part of the theoretical structure of the other. Particularly relevant are the principles of *cybernetics*, the science of communication and control within organized systems." (pp. 60-61)

39. Harold D. Lasswell, "The Policy Orientation," *The Policy Sciences*, Daniel Lerner and Harold D. Lasswell, eds. (Stanford, Calif., Stanford University Press, 1951).

> "Speculative models of the principle social changes in our epoch can be called 'developmental constructs.' They specify

289

the institutional pattern *from* which we are moving and the pattern *toward* which we are going. Strictly speaking, developmental constructs are not scientific hypotheses, since they do not formulate propositions about interdependence of factors. A developmental construct refers only to the succession of events, future as well as past. It should be noted that many hypotheses about the future purport to have scientific validity. . . . But no claim of 'inevitability' can be accepted. Events in the future are not knowable with absolute certainty in advance: they are partly probable and partly chance. Developmental constructs are aids in the total task of clarifying goals, noting trends, and estimating future possibilities." (p. 11)

Garrett Hardin, "The Cybernetics of Competition," *Perspectives in Biology and Medicine*, Vol. VII, No. 1 (Autumn 1963), pp. 58–84.

"Only a total complex of theory ('model') can be tested against a factual complex. If the elements of a theoretical construct are tested against a complex world, they will, one by one, be disproved.' " (p. 59)

40. John Dewey, *Human Nature and Conduct* (New York, Holt, 1922).

"To attain a remote end means to treat the end as a series of means. To say that an end is remote . . . is equivalent to saying that obstacles intervene between us and it. If, however, it becomes a distant end, it becomes a *mere* end, that is a dream. We must change *what* is to be done into *how*. . . . The end thus reappears as a series of 'what nexts,' and the next of chief importance is the one nearest the present state of the one acting." (p. 36)

41. Donald M. MacKay, "Operational Aspects of Some Fundamental Concepts of Human Communication," *Synthese*, Vol. IX, Issue 3, Nos. 3–5 (Netherlands, F. G. Kroonder Bussum, n.d.).

"In the organism there should be one or more *evaluatory mechanisms* embodying criteria of success or failure: mechanisms, that is, emitting signals indicating the difference between the present state of the organism and some equilibrium condition or goal-state.

"Then (the crucial feature) these signals must be allowed to alter the controls that govern activity, (including the choice of subsidiary goals if necessary) in such a way as to reduce (at least statistically) the difference between the present state and the goal-state. Evidently the controls can come to rest only if the goal-state is attained and the difference signal reads 'zero.' Unless this is so they should always be found actively opposing any changes in the state of affairs which would tend to increase the difference-reading. An adaptive or matching response is one which is goal-directed in this way toward minimizing the degree of mismatch as indicated by the evaluatory mechanisms. We might define it as 'activity under the correction of evaluatory signals.' " (p. 191)

Garrett Hardin, "The Cybernetics of Competition," *Perspectives in Biology and Medicine*, Vol. VII, No. 1 (Autumn 1963), pp. 58–84.

"If a system that includes positive feedback is to possess stability, it must also include 'negative feedback.' The meaning of this term can be made clear by an example from engineering. . . .

"The temperature of the room will fluctuate about the 'set point' of the thermostat—and this is what we mean when we say 'the temperature is held constant.' The variations do not exceed certain limits. . . . Negative feedback produces stability about a 'set point.' " (pp. 63, 65)

Floyd H. Allport, *Theories of Perception and the Concept of Structure* (New York, Wiley, 1955).

"We thus identify our self-closing structures as an open-system, having, in terms of system theory, its energic 'input' and 'output.' In the receipt and passing on by the structure of energies from and to the outside the 'steady state' characteristic of open-systems aggregates is maintained; or, by progressive displacement of energy within the structure, it can be said that the structure itself 'comes to its own equilibrium.' In so doing, however, *it retains, in either case, its cyclical character*. These relationships of a structure to other (outside) structures are called 'out-structural tangencies.' " (p. 646)

"In the energetic balance of the organism's structural manifold it can be said to represent the 'homeostatic' level of structure." (p. 652)

Homeostasis, or "steady-state" in the physical organism, is comparable with Operation Feedback in verbal behavior.

42. Quoted by Marshall W. Fishwick, "Everything Nailed Down Is Coming Loose," *Saturday Review* (June 29, 1963).

"Robert Oppenheimer . . . attempts to tell us in which sense the new world, in which the unity of knowledge, the nature of human communities, the order of society, the order of ideas, the very notions of society and culture have changed, and will not return to what they have been in the past." (p. 11)

43. Alfred Korzybski, *Science and Sanity: An Introduction to Non-aristotelian Systems and General Semantics* (1st edition, 1933, 4th edition, 1958, International Non-aristotelian Library Publishing Company, Distributed by the Institute of General Semantics, Lakeville, Conn.).

". . . the structure of nervous systems consists of *ordered* chains produced by the impact of external and internal stimuli in a four-dimensional space-time manifold, which have a spatial and also a temporal *order*." (p. 184)

"It should be noticed that the 'is' of predication also expresses a sort of *partial identity*. . . . Once this is realized, we see clearly that all statements about the objective level, which is made up of absolute individuals, are only *probable* in different degrees and can never be certain." (p. 202)

"We live in a four-dimensional space-time manifold, which . . . consists of absolutely individual events, objects, situations, abstractions, etc., and we must conclude that structurally we live in an *indefinitely many-valued* or infinite valued world. . . ." (p. 462)

44. Edmund W. Sinnott, "The Biology of Purpose," *Selected Papers on Psychotherapy, Purpose and Communication* (New York, American Orthopsychiatric Association, 1952), pp. 457–468.

45. I. A. Richards, *Practical Criticism* (New York, Harcourt, 1939), p. 364.

46. Charles Morris, *The Open Self* (New York, Prentice-Hall, 1948), pp. 63–64.

47. Alfred Korzybski, *Science and Sanity: An Introduction to Non-aristotelian Systems and General Semantics* (1st edition, 1933, 4th edition, 1958, International Non-aristotelian Library Publishing Company, Distributed by the Institute of General Semantics, Lakeville, Conn.), p. 61.

> "Two important characteristics of maps should be noticed. A map *is not* the territory it represents, but, if correct, it has a *similar structure* to the territory, which accounts for its usefulness. If the map could be ideally correct, it would include, in a reduced scale, the map of the map; the map of the map, of the map; and so on, endlessly. . . ." (p. 58)

48. Gordon W. Allport, *Becoming, Basic Considerations for a Psychology of Personality* (New Haven, Yale University Press, 1955), p. 27.

49. Lancelot Law Whyte, *Accent on Form* (New York, Harper, 1954).

> "Even when human ignorance was still absolute there was present in organic nature a formative process, a surplus vitality, a creative, exploratory, or inventive instinct which, when the time came, would shape in human brains and minds ideas that would bring enlightenment. This organic faculty . . . is the one unchallengeably favorable fact about man." (p. 8)

*General Systems*, Yearbook of the Society for General Systems Research, Ludwig von Bartalanffy and Anatol Rapoport, eds. (Ann Arbor, Mich.)

50. *The Humanist Frame*, Sir Julian Huxley, ed. (New York, Harper, 1961). See especially pages 13–48.

51. I. A. Richards, *Speculative Instruments* (Chicago, University of Chicago Press, 1955).

> "The most resourceful words in a language are the indispensable words, those which give structure to thoughts and connect them in larger structures . . . they are the unavoid-

> able tools . . . and the key terms of all understanding." (p. 75)

> "It is this which makes insight into the *patterns of resource* able to knit different studies together." (p. 77)

> ". . . language . . . is an organ—the supreme organ of the mind's self-ordering growth . . . language is an instrument for controlling our becoming." (p. 9)

> "An instrument is a tool, an agency, a means, a stage in a process, a circumstance, something in which or with which or through which or by which some outcome may be forwarded. . . . All meanings are means, are instruments. . . . To sum up . . . words [are instruments] free to experiment with one another as to which meanings they may jointly support . . . giving things structure." (pp. 152–54)

52. C. K. Ogden and I. A. Richards, *The Meaning of Meaning*, 5th ed. (New York, Harcourt, 1938), p. 82.

53. *Ibid.*, p. 73.

54. Alfred Korzybski, *Science and Sanity: An Introduction to Non-aristotelian Systems and General Semantics* (1st edition, 1933, 4th edition, 1958, International Non-aristotelian Library Publishing Company, Distributed by the Institute of General Semantics, Lakeville, Conn.), p. 61.

55. *Ibid.*, p. 60.

56. Albert Einstein, "Autobiographical Notes," *Albert Einstein: Philosopher-Scientist*, trans. Paul Arthur Schilpp, The Library of Living Philosophers, VII, Paul Arthur Schilpp, ed. (LaSalle, Ill., Open Court Publishing Company, 1949).

> "What precisely is 'thinking'? When, at the reception of sense-impressions, memory-pictures emerge, this is not yet 'thinking.' And when such pictures form series, each member of which calls forth another, this too is not yet 'thinking.' When, however, a certain picture turns up in many series, then—precisely through such return—it becomes an ordering element for such series, in that it connects series which in themselves are unconnected. Such an element becomes an instrument, a concept. I think that the transition from free

association or 'dreaming' to thinking is characterized by the more or less dominating role which the 'concept' plays in it." (p. 7)

Two criteria should be noted here: (a) recurrence and (b) connectivity.

57. I. A. Richards, "Communication Between Men: Meaning and Language," *Cybernetics, Transactions of the Eighth Conference* (March 15–16, 1951), Heinz von Foerster, ed. (New York, John Macy, Jr., Foundation, 1952).

58. C. K. Ogden and I. A. Richards, *The Meaning of Meaning*, 5th ed. (New York, Harcourt, 1938), pp. 55–58, 244.

59. *Ibid.*

"Interpretation . . . is only possible thanks to these recurrent contexts, a statement which is very generally admitted but which if examined will be found to be far more fundamental than has been supposed. To say, indeed, that anything is an interpretation is to say that it is a member of a psychological context of a certain kind. An interpretation is itself a recurrence." (p. 55–56)

Concerning the word "context," Ogden and Richards indicate clearly the way in which it should be understood:

"Throughout the present volume the term 'context' is used in a strictly technical sense . . . which differs from the ordinary use. A literary context is a group of words, incidents, ideas, etc., which on a given occasion accompanies or surrounds whatever is said to have the context; whereas a determinative context is a group of this kind which both recurs and is such that one at least of its members is determined, given the others." (p. 58, footnote)

In this sense a psychological context that is isomorphic with a physical context is said by Ogden and Richards to be true and logical.

"all learning by experience will illustrate the point that to be an act of interpretation is merely to be a peculiar member of a psychological context of a certain kind; a psychological context being a recurrent set of mental events peculiarly related to one another so as to recur, as regards their main features. . . .

"Behind all interpretation we have the fact that when part of an external context recurs in experience this part is, through its linkage with a member of some psychological context (i.e., of a causally connected group of mental events often widely separated in time) *sometimes* a sign of the rest of the external context." (p. 57) [My italics.]

This passage links interpretation with prediction in goal-seeking behavior. Every step we take is an *If this, then that* hypothesis. When we leap into the future, our only basis for prediction is our knowledge of recurrent "clumps of experience." But we must operate in a world of people and things in which prediction is far from absolute. More often than not, we are obliged to take a calculated risk. Notice that Ogden and Richards say that part of an external context is *sometimes* (not always, mind you) a sign of the rest of the external context. When it is not, "we are said to have been mistaken."

60. I. A. Richards, *Speculative Instruments* (Chicago, University of Chicago Press, 1955).

"The entire activity . . . seems to consist of choices. Initial choices would be free; but when choice has been made, the subsequent choices are bound thereby while the choice is held." (p. 19)

". . . to a much greater extent than we profess we communicate through offerings of *choices*, not through presentations of *fact*." (p. 139)

"The most important choices—and it is these which generate the strongest values—are . . . choices as to how we will in future choose. These join the major purposings and they may be organized in an immense variety of ways." (p. 140)

61. I. A. Richards, *Principles of Literary Criticism* (New York, Harcourt, n.d.)

". . . priorities mentioned must be taken only as illustrations. We do not know enough yet about the precedences, the hierarchies, the modes of systematization, actual and possible, in that unimaginable organization, the mind, to say what order in any case actually exists, or between what the order holds. We only know that a growing order is a principle of the mind, that its function is to co-ordinate. . . . That organization which is the least wasteful of human possibilities is, in short, the best . . . [exemplified by] those fortunate people who have achieved an ordered life, whose systems have developed clearing-houses by which the varying claims of different impulses are adjusted." (pp. 50, 52, 53)

62. Alfred Korzybski, *Science and Sanity: An Introduction to Non-aristotelian Systems and General Semantics* (1st edition, 1933, 4th edition, 1958, International Non-aristotelian Library Publishing Company, Distributed by the Institute of General Semantics, Lakeville, Conn.), p. 61.

63. Theodore C. Sorensen, "How the President Makes a Decision," *Saturday Review* (July 27, 1963).

Albert Einstein, *Out of My Later Years* (New York, Philosophical Library, 1950). The following quotation from this work suggests the inseparability of "desire and fact" in the "valley of decision."

"What is it that brings about such an intimate connection between language and thinking? Is there no thinking without the use of language, namely in concepts and concept-combinations for which words need not necessarily come to mind? Has not everyone of us struggled for words although the connection between 'things' was already clear?" (p. 112)

This statement, it seems to me, is corroborative of the deep psycho-physio-logical oneness of human experience. If there is a wordless understanding, does it not spring from that deep reservoir of experience which might be termed "the linguistic unconscious"? Einstein continues:

"We might be inclined to attribute to the act of thinking complete independence from language if the individual formed or were able to form his concepts without the verbal guidance of the environment. Yet most likely the mental shape of the individual, growing up under such conditions, would be very poor. Thus we may conclude that the mental development of the individual and his way of forming concepts depend to a high degree upon language. This makes us realize to what extent the same language means the same mentality. In this sense thinking and language are linked together." (p. 112)

64. I. A. Richards, *Principles of Literary Criticism* (New York, Harcourt, n.d.), p. 61.

65. Alfred Korzybski, Preface to the Third Edition, *Science and Sanity: An Introduction to Non-aristotelian Systems and General Semantics* (1st edition, 1933, 4th edition, 1958, International Non-aristotelian Library Publishing Company, Distributed by the Institute of General Semantics, Lakeville, Conn.).

"*General* Semantics turned out to be an empirical natural science of non-elementalistic evaluation, which takes into account the living individual, not divorcing him from his reactions altogether, nor from his neuro-linguistic and neuro-semantic environments, but allocating him in a *plenum* of some values, no matter what." (p. xxii)

66. Floyd H. Allport, *Theories of Perception and the Concept of Structure* (New York, Wiley, 1955).

"Surely, some kind of event-structuring goes on in the organism, or in the cortex, when an act of perception takes place. This structuring, moreover, is not a human artifact, but a part of the very constitution of the organism, and, as such, is not particularistic, but *highly lawful and general*." (p. 630)

67. Richard P. Blackmur, "The Language of Silence," *Language: An Enquiry into Its Meaning and Function*, planned and edited by Ruth Nanda Anshen (New York, Harper, 1957), pp. 134–152.

"If there were no gaps between words—in which silence speaks, and in which we recollect ourselves . . . we should never find our thoughts or recognize the thoughts of others: the rhythm would not transpire. . . . Rhythm is how we feel and how we translate action in the soul. The action may not be our action, though it is what moves us, but we move in through silence into words and when it is there the words remain alive . . . speech is heightened with silence. Meaning is what silence does when it gets into words." (p. 152)

What is Blackmur saying here? We know that we *live* on the silent unspeakable level. Perhaps Blackmur is saying that when this *immediate* experience of the living life gets into words, this and only this constitutes meaning.

Andre Malraux, *The Voices of Silence* (Garden City, N.Y., Doubleday, 1953).

68. W. Grey Walter, *The Living Brain* (New York, Norton, 1953), pp. 57–58. This entire book is relevant to personality theory as evidenced by the EEG.

69. Erich Fromm, "Selfishness, Self-Love, and Self-Interest," *The Self, Explorations in Personal Growth,* Clark E. Moustakas, ed. (New York, Harper, 1956), pp. 58–69.

70. Gardner Murphy, *Personality, A Biosocial Approach to Origins and Structure* (New York, Harper, 1947), p. 251. Chapters 2 and 27 are especially relevant.

A. H. Maslow, *Motivation and Personality* (New York, Harper, 1952).

Maslow makes a distinction between what he calls "pure" expressiveness and expressiveness in purposive (goal-directed) behavior. He associates this "pure" expressiveness with "non-communicative artistic activity," with "pure self-actualization, etc."

I would be inclined to reject "pure self-actualization," or, indeed, "purity" in any aspect of human behavior whether conscious or unconscious, verbal or nonverbal. But Maslow does acknowledge an expressive component in "most acts of behavior" and says, in fact:

"Thus at the highest levels of human development, the distinction between coping and expression, like so many other psychological dichotomies, is resolved and becomes useless." (pp. 179, 183)

Gordon W. Allport, in "The Trend in Motivational Theory," —printed in *The Self, Explorations in Personal Growth*, Clark E. Moustakas, ed. (New York, Harper, 1956)—holds this opinion regarding expressiveness:

"A test of normality . . . may lie in the harmony of expressive behavior (facial expression, gestures, handwriting) with the individual's fundamental motivational structure. There is evidence that discoordination between conscious motives and expressive movements is an ominous sign." (p. 39)

71. John Dewey, "Theory of Valuation," *International Encyclopedia of Unified Science*, Vol. II, No. 4: Foundations of the Unity of Science (Chicago, University of Chicago Press, July, 1939), pp. 17–66.

72. Charles Morris, *The Open Self* (New York, Prentice-Hall, 1948).

"An idea is something signified. An ideal is something that when signified is found so attractive that one is lured to its attainment. . . ." (p. 12)

"Ideals differ from ideas precisely in the fact that we now prefer what is signified. This increment of preference stems from the urgencies of the self as it is at the moment." (p. 14)

73. Gardner Murphy, *Personality, A Biosocial Approach to Origins and Structure* (New York, Harper, 1947).

"At least three levels of complexity must be considered when confronting personality problems. Personality may be conceived, first as an object . . . in a larger context. . . .
"At a second level of complexity, personality may be likened to a chrysalis. It is again identifiable and strictly bounded, but it has internal structure . . . it is organized.
"At the third level of analysis . . . the organism exists because outer changes and inner adjustments are nicely attuned . . . the organism [is] literally a node in a physical field, defined, limited, governed by the field relations. Such a view may be called a field view . . . world and self flow into one another. The boundary is often vague and non-existent, but the flow is always directed to some extent by the relations between the outer and inner structures.
"All three conceptions of personality . . . will need to be used." (pp. 3–5)

74. Gardner Murphy, "Toward a Field Theory of Communication." *The Journal of Communication*, Symposium on Foundations of

Communication Theory, Bess Sondel, Symposium Editor, Vol. XI, No. 4 (December 1961), pp. 196–204.

75. Gardner Murphy, *Personality, A Biosocial Approach to Origins and Structure* (New York, Harper, 1947), p. 5.

76. Edmund W. Sinnott, "The Biology of Purpose," *Selected Papers on Psychotherapy, Purpose and Communication* (New York, American Orthopsychiatric Association, 1952), p. 462.

77. Edmund W. Sinnott, "The Biological Basis of Communication," *The Journal of Communication*, Symposium on Foundations of Communications Theory, Bess Sondel, Symposium Editor, Vol. XI, No. 4 (December 1961), p. 191.

78. Jeremy Bernstein, "Profiles, The Analytical Engine," *The New Yorker* (October 19 and 26, 1963). The reference is to page 108 of the October 26 issue.

   David L. Johnson and Arthur L. Kobler, "The Man-Computer Relationship," *Science* (November 23, 1962), pp. 873–879.

   Ulric Neisser, "The Imitation of Man by Machine," *Science* (January 18, 1963), pp. 193–197.

79. P. W. Bridgman, *The Intelligent Individual and Society* (New York, Macmillan, 1938), p. 75.

80. Rudolph Carnap, *Meaning and Necessity* (Chicago, University of Chicago Press, 1947).

   "Should we require complete specificity with respect to all properties of the given thing or things involved, and also with respect to all relations between the given things and all other things? It seems somewhat arbitrary to draw a line at any of these points. If we do not stop at some point but go the whole way, then we arrive at the strongest F-true proposition, which is the conjunction of all true propositions and hence implies every true proposition. If we require of a fact this maximum degree of completeness, then there is only one fact, the totality of the actual world, past, present and future." (pp. 28–29)

   Kurt Lewin, *Principles of Topological Psychology* (New York, McGraw-Hill, 1936).

"In psychology also there is a more or less close dynamic connection between all the facts which belong to the same psychological space. . . . So therefore, as in physics, a change is the result of conditions or events within the same space." (p. 69)

"From the point of view of dynamics the life space of each single individual is a totality which is equivalent to the totality of the whole physical world." (p. 68)

H. Laborit, "The Need for Generalization in Biological Research: The Role of the Mathematical Theory of Ensembles," The Institute of General Semantics, *General Semantics Bulletin,* No. 30, 1963/64.

*"What remains is not facts but structures.* When serious investigators state that they believe only in observed facts . . . they commit a very serious mistake in semantics. They mean to say that they believe only in structures, in stable, permanent, relationships between facts which are evanescent, changing, uncertain, 'sensory.' Facts are valuable only because they lead us to structures, to what scientists call 'laws.' We can be *sure* of the existence of these structures since in spite of the variability of the factors which condition the multiplicity of these never identical facts, the structures remain." (p. 5)

81. C. K. Ogden and I. A. Richards, *The Meaning of Meaning,* 5th ed. (New York, Harcourt, 1938), p. 11.

82. *Ibid.,* p. 82.

83. Charles Morris, *Signs, Language and Behavior* (New York, Braziller, 1955), p. 97.

84. *Ibid.,* p. 66.

85. *Ibid.,* p. 96.

86. *Ibid.,* p. 107. *See also* "T-ascriptor," *ibid.,* p. 355.

87. *Ibid.,* p. 23.

88. Einstein settled this for the atomic age. A book that addresses itself to relativity in the behavioral situation is:

John Dewey and Arthur F. Bentley, *Knowing and the Known* (Boston, Beacon Press, 1949).

89. Alfred Korzybski, *Science and Sanity: An Introduction to Non-aristotelian Systems and General Semantics* (1st edition, 1933, 4th edition, 1958, International Non-aristotelian Library Publishing Company, Distributed by the Institute of General Semantics, Lakeville, Conn.).

"Here we introduce a most important technical term which describes a fundamental characteristic of a correct attitude toward language; namely, that most terms are '$\frac{\text{over}}{\text{under}}$ defined.' They are over-defined (over-limited) by intension, or verbal definition, because of our *belief* in the definition; and are hopelessly under-defined by extension or facts, when generalizations become merely hypothetical." (p. lii)

90. Charles Morris, *Signs, Language and Behavior* (New York, Braziller, 1955), pp. 96, 99–101.

91. Susanne Langer, *Philosophy in a New Key* (Cambridge, Mass., Harvard University Press, 1951).

"What music expresses is eternal, infinite and ideal; it does not express the passion, love, or longing of such-and-such an individual on such-and-such an occasion, but passion, love, or longing itself. . . ." (pp. 221–222)

A. H. Maslow, *Motivation and Personality* (New York, Harper, 1952).

"Much overlapping with conative and cognitive needs makes it impossible to separate them sharply. The needs for order, for symmetry, for closure, for completion of the act, for system, and for structure may be indiscriminately assigned to *either* cognitive, conative, or aesthetic . . . needs" (p.97)

Is Maslow saying here that conative or aesthetic needs seek order, system, structure? If so, his position is analogous to Langer's.

92. Kenneth Burke, *Permanence and Change* (New York, New Republic, 1936).

". . . It is 'perspective by incongruity' since it is established by violating the 'properties' of the word in its previous linkages. The device . . . establishes . . . perspectives by a constant juxtaposing of incongruous words, attaching to some name a qualifying epithet which had heretofore gone with a different order of names. . . .

"It appeals by exemplifying relationships between objects which our customary rational vocabulary has ignored." (p. 119)

93. Bertrand Russell, *Human Knowledge, Its Scope and Limits* (New York, Simon and Schuster, 1948), p. 182.

94. Charles Morris, *Signs, Language and Behavior* (New York, Braziller, 1955), pp. 26, 106, 121.

95. *Ibid.*, pp. 83–86, 102–104.

96. D. M. MacKay, "Operational Aspects of Some Fundamental Concepts of Human Communications," *Synthese*, Vol. IX, Issue 3, Nos. 3–5 (Netherlands, F. G. Kroonder Bussum, n.d.), pp. 196–197.

97. Harold D. Lasswell, "The Policy Orientation," *The Policy Sciences*, Daniel Lerner and Harold D. Lasswell, eds. (Stanford, Calif., Stanford University Press, 1951), p. 5.

98. *Ibid.*, pp. 9–10.

99. Carl R. Rogers, *On Becoming a Person* (Boston, Houghton Mifflin, 1961), pp. 64–65.

100. Charles Morris, *Signs, Language and Behavior* (New York, Braziller, 1955), p. 98.

101. *Ibid.*, p. 96.

102. *Ibid.*, p. 104.

103. John G. Bennett, "General Systematics," *Systematics, the Journal of the Institute for the Comparative Study of History, Philosophy and the Sciences* (Kingston-upon-Thames, England, Coombe Springs Press, June 1963).

". . . the study of all the possible forms of connectedness can . . . be called *systematics*. The word system is commonly used for every kind of group or collection of interacting things or ideas. The meaning common to nearly all uses of the word is that of an inner connectedness that distinguishes what forms part of a system from all that is 'outside' it. I want to define the word system in another more precise way as a set of *distinct but mutually relevant terms*. . . . By 'terms' I mean any part of experience that can be identified by some persistent token or recurrent property. A term may be a thing, an idea, a relationship or a complex system of things, ideas and relationships—provided only that we can recognize it. . . . Finally, there is the condition that the terms must be mutually relevant. This means that each of the terms of the system requires all the others in order to be what it is and mean what it means." (p. 6)

As I use the term "working-title," the formators are mutually relevant. This means that each of the terms of the working-title requires all the others in order to be what it is and mean what it means.

As I use the term "working-title," the formators are related according to a principle of organization (time, space, cause to effect, means to end, sectional, etc.) such that the working-title has an inner connectedness which I have called both cohesive and progressive.

104. S. I. Hayakawa, *Language in Thought and Action* (New York, Harcourt, 1941).

Burleigh B. Gardner and William F. Whyte, "The Man in the Middle: Position and Problems of the Foreman." *Applied Anthropology, Problems of Human Organization* (Spring 1945).

105. Karl W. Deutsch, "Communication Theory and Social Science," *Selected Papers on Psychotherapy, Purpose and Communication* (New York, American Orthopsychiatric Association, 1952), pp. 470–471.

106. W. Grey Walter, *The Living Brain* (New York, Norton, 1953), p. 125.

107. *Ibid.,* p. 109.

108. *Ibid.,* p. 127.

109. H. Laborit, "The Need for Generalization in Biological Research: The Role of the Mathematical Theory of Ensembles," The Institute of General Semantics, *General Semantics Bulletin,* No. 30, 1963/64.

When I look to the future in self-actualization, my mind turns to the "Infinite More" of William James. Laborit takes a backward look before he moves ahead. This is what he says about research and researchers:

"The elaboration of a working hypothesis often calls on what is generally called *Intuition.* This is not a mythical figure related to the Muses or a special gift similar to a 'knack.' It is not quite an inborn gift. However, as it can be accepted that 99% of our past experience has become subconscious, although always present in our nervous system, in our opinion, intuition is the confidence granted to this now subconscious acquired experience. Whoever accepts only clear ideas, a working hypothesis based on conscious, logical . . . reasoning, deprives himself of the enormous mass of information he has accumulated since childhood and that populates his subconscious. His experiments will explore only a limited number of possible solutions—those connected with his present state of consciousness—with his consciously available information. Thus we believe it behooves the researcher to let his 'sixth sense' guide him, with the knowledge that this guidance is probably no more than an integrated expression of the information that he has been able to acquire, and that constitutes the experimental capital acquired by his nervous system.

"The consequences of such a concept is that one of the essential duties of a researcher is the search for and the storage of information." (pp. 9–10)

*Creativity and Its Cultivation,* Harold A. Anderson, ed. (New York, Harper, 1959).

Russell F. W. Smith, "The Deliberate Induction of New Ideas," *Essays on Creativity in the Sciences,* Myron A. Coler, ed. (New York, New York University Press, 1963), pp. 207–220.

110. Gardner Murphy, *Personality, A Biosocial Approach to Origins and Structure* (New York, Harper, 1947).

"A personality is a structured organism-environment field, each aspect of which stands in dynamic relation to each other aspect. There is organization within the environment, but it is the cross organization of the two that is investigated in personality research. . . .

"We shall, in this way, attempt for personality study a point of view that has long been commonplace in the biological sciences, a view which emphasizes the full reciprocity of inner and outer events. This inner-outer reciprocity means that the *life process* is itself a matter of world as much as organism. The organism is structurally definable for some purposes in terms of a spatially localized capsule, but its *life functions* are organized in terms of an adaptation polarity which gives the environment pole the same relation of absolute necessity to the process, the field, as that held by the organism pole." (pp. 8, 9)

111. H. G. Wells, *The Way the World Is Going* (Garden City, N.Y., Doubleday, 1929), p. 232.

112. Garrett Hardin, "The Cybernetics of Competition," *Perspectives in Biology and Medicine,* Vol. VII, No. 1 (Autumn 1963), pp. 58–84.

"If a system that includes positive feedback is to possess stability, it must also include 'negative feedback'. . . ." (p. 63)

"Recognition of the dangers of this positive feedback must surely be almost universal among practical men and produces the most diverse stratagems, many of which would seem quite paradoxical to one who was ignorant of the positive feedback of power. . . ." (p. 75)

113. Kurt Lewin, *Principles of Topological Psychology* (New York, McGraw-Hill, 1936).

"FORCE: Cause of change; a basic concept of vector psychology. Properties of force are: strength, direction, and point of application. Strength and direction can be represented by a vector." (p. 218)

A vector is a bearer—a carrier—drawn from its point of origin to its final position.

# Index

Bess Sondel received her university education after her marriage and while she was rearing her daughter, Shirley Ann. It is characteristic of this dynamic woman that she could be wife and mother and still find time to become a recognized authority in the communications field.

She was elected to Phi Beta Kappa and received her Ph.B. from the University of Chicago in 1931, her Ph.D. from the same institution in 1938. She taught at the University College of the University of Chicago until 1961. She was consultant in Communications to the Industrial Relations Center from 1945 to 1950 and to the faculty of the Graduate School of Business from 1957 to 1959, both at the same university.

She has written a newspaper column for the *Chicago Tribune* and is also the author of the books *Speak Up!, Are You Telling Them?, Everyday Speech, Humanity of Words,* and *Communication, A Field Theory.*

Her present interest lies in the great analogy of our time—that of man and the machine. In connection with this she has often appeared before, and written for, electrical and electronic engineers, "trading" information about the human nervous system and the computer systems. *Power-Steering with Words* is in a sense a summation of her years of teaching and learning about communication as an essential art in everyday living.

ABIGAIL E. WEEKS MEMORIAL LIBRARY
UNION COLLEGE
BARBOURVILLE, KENTUCKY